ARGENTINE PERSPECTIVES ON THE FALKLANDS WAR

The Recovery and Loss of Las Malvinas

NICK VAN DER BIJL

CASEMATE

Philadelphia & Oxford

Published in the United States of America and Great Britain in 2023 by
CASEMATE PUBLISHERS
1950 Lawrence Road, Havertown, PA 19083, USA
and
The Old Music Hall, 106–108 Cowley Road, Oxford OX4 1JE, UK

Hardback Edition: ISBN 978-1-63624-164-7
Digital Edition: ISBN 978-1-63624-165-4

A CIP record for this book is available from the British Library

Printed and bound in the United Kingdom by CPI Group (UK) Ltd, Croydon, CR0 4YY

For a complete list of Casemate titles, please contact:

CASEMATE PUBLISHERS (US)
Telephone (610) 853-9131
Fax (610) 853-9146
Email: casemate@casematepublishers.com
www.casematepublishers.com

CASEMATE PUBLISHERS (UK)
Telephone (01865) 241249
Email: casemate-uk@casematepublishers.co.uk
www.casematepublishers.co.uk

Contents

Foreword

Forty years ago, in the early hours of Friday 2 April, I woke up to go to my Philosophy of Law class at the Law School. The radio-clock sounded, but the usual music that woke me up every morning had that day been replaced by military marches. I was quickly wide awake since, despite my young age (20 years), I knew that military music was the usual sign in Argentine history that a military coup had taken place. However, this time it was not a coup. A martial voice announced that the Argentine Armed Forces had recovered the Malvinas Islands. This surprise was repeated in every home in the country, even for the great majority of the Argentine military, including those of high rank, who heard the news that same morning over the radio.

Surprise, joy, disbelief and celebration for a country that had not suffered an international war for more than a century. The memory of the war against terrorism was still very close, whose annihilation was ordered by a democratic government in 1975 but resurrected by the Military Junta after the March 1976 coup. The population felt relieved by the pacification, but little was known at the time about the methodology used against subversion.

In April 1982, after the recovery of the Malvinas, the Military Junta was betting on a peaceful solution, limited to diplomatic protests from Great Britain. But it was not to be, with Prime Minister Margaret Thatcher announcing to the UK Parliament that she had ordered a task force to set sail.

Argentina had resorted to the use of force to resolve a territorial dispute, an action that was not accepted by the international community, but which left open the dispute over sovereignty, and in many cases,

Argentine rights over the islands. In November 1982, this implied the defeat of Great Britain in the United Nations General Assembly, which resolved to urge the parties to continue negotiating. The Argentine military defeat in the islands in June was followed months later by a diplomatic victory, to the fury of Margaret Thatcher and her Foreign Office Secretary, Francis Pym.

The Argentine population was anxious to know about the events in the South Atlantic, but the Military Junta established guidelines to control the dissemination of news that could compromise military action. However, the euphoria of the media led to exaggeration and distortion in the reporting of events.

From the other side of the Andes Mountains, Chile was also carefully following Argentina and Britain's movements, and carried out its own preventative actions; for instance, they allowed the British to carry out exploration flights from San Félix Island, in the Pacific Ocean, and provided a radar to install in Balmaceda. This radar, together with another one in Punta Arenas and the positioning of British submarines off the coast, provided the early detection of combat aircraft take-offs from Argentine bases in Patagonia, information that reached the British fleet, enabling it to prepare for the attacks.

We Argentines followed the conflict very closely, through newspapers, magazines and via the television. The communities of foreign populations residing in Argentina carried out ceremonies in support of Argentine sovereignty over the Malvinas, and the politicians 'dusted off' their ban and went on tour to spread Argentine rights abroad.

Finally, and to the surprise of many in Argentina, after the short visit of Pope John Paul II during which the population prayed for peace, an 'un-agreed ceasefire' was announced on the afternoon of 14 June. In the cold winds and wet peat of the islands, the fighting was not what the news described in Buenos Aires. Until reality finally broke the deception.

Disillusionment and disappointment flooded the population. The Military Junta's propaganda machine had gone too far this time. The damaged aircraft carrier HMS *Hermes* heading under tow to the Caribbean for repairs in Curaçao, the *Canberra* sunk in San Carlos, countless planes and helicopters shot down, more ships sunk and hundreds of British casualties formed the basis of the news frequently heard on the radio and TV.

People had been deceived by the communication of the events in the Malvinas, which hurtled from 'We are Winning' to the sudden 'un-agreed ceasefire' – used because the media could not use the word 'surrender' in the news.

Faced with this state of scepticism and disappointment, people did not want to hear more about the Malvinas War, and sympathised with the soldiers, considering them victims of the military, and for a long time were uninterested in reviewing and analysing what had truly happened.

The accusations began between the services in the armed forces, with stories of the '*Chicos de la Guerra*' suffering hunger and hardship, requests from courts of honour, many military personnel saying, 'I did not surrender!' Defeat is said to be an orphan. In Argentina, everyone desperately sought to find someone to blame.

Nevertheless, the Army was – unfairly – hit the hardest in its image by the war. One must remember Division General Osvaldo Jorge García asking Menéndez to take out the troops, to attack the British in San Carlos, because the Air Force and the Navy 'had already contributed their quota of blood', to which was added the first British chronicles praising the performance of the Argentine pilots and the Marine Corps.

Even before the end of the war, at the beginning of June, General Leopoldo Fortunato Galtieri had appointed a Commission in the Argentine Army to determine whether the conduct of the personnel could be framed in any infraction or to be the object of an honorary recognition. On 17 July, another order was issued for the study and exploitation of experiences related to the Malvinas Conflict, which would consist of 'the gathering, selection, compatibility and study of the most important experiences obtained, by area of conduction and at all levels of Army command, up to and including the tactical unit'. Thus, the Argentine Army began a silent task of collecting and analysing what had happened.

To fulfil this task, an Investigation Commission was appointed, chaired by Division General Edgardo Néstor Calvi, and made up of four members. This Commission limited itself to analysing around 5,000 reports from personnel who were in the Malvinas Islands, and some 600 special reports that were requested from people who were there. Based on this, with very few calls, an executive decision was made on each one of the cadre personnel that intervened in the Malvinas Islands. In addition, even due to the Army's own professional interest, to save the historical fact, all the operations were reconstructed, or everything that was possible, since the reports that were made confirmed to the commission the problems that arose.

I had the honour of personally meeting General Calvi, a great connoisseur and lover of ancient military history. In conversations with me, when discussing Hannibal's campaigns against Rome, he would occasionally break off the dialogue, to wonder – with some frustration and pain – about the fate of all his work in the commission collecting documentation and accounts of the experiences and lessons that could be drawn from the war, and if one day all this would become material for new historians.

The decision was made that the commission's report, in relation to the account of the actions of the Argentine Army, be made public. It was the first official report of one of the Argentine Armed Forces involved in the conflict and was published only a year and a half after it ended.

In parallel, the commission chaired by General Benjamín Rattenbach was already working with the aim of evaluating the responsibilities of the members of the Military Junta and of the strategic high command. When the Military Junta received the report, it was decided that it should be kept secret. President General Reynaldo Bignone sanctioned a decree in which the character of 'Political and Military Secret' was established, 'until such time the full exercise of sovereignty over the Malvinas Islands, the South Georgia Islands and the South Sandwich Islands is achieved'.

The leak to the press of some alleged copies of the Rattenbach report had a great impact on the population, especially the alleged request for the execution of the members of the Military Junta and the degradation and imprisonment of high-ranking officers. It seemed to satisfy the need to punish the architects of military defeat.

However, in the midst of so much scandal, an editorial in the national newspaper *La Nación* on 2 December 1983, criticised the secrecy imposed on the report, while pointing out the need to access the information properly, not through leaks, about what happened in Malvinas:

> ... But the way in which this document has reached public opinion indicates the persistence of a fundamental error committed by the authorities that have succeeded those who are primarily responsible for the episode.
>
> That error consists in having considered – and continuing to consider – as a secret a text that should have been made known in its entirety and immediately...
>
> The authorities should have remembered that once the war episode ended as it did, nothing would have helped the country more than a complete, rapid and immediate investigation made available to all citizens.
>
> Always, in social life, concealment or half-truths only serve to increase confusion, bitterness, and problems...
>
> Argentina lived for many years... within political regimes that took pleasure in hiding the truth, or distorting it, or presenting it to the people in a partial and incomplete way.
>
> After all, experience shows – it has been shown on countless occasions – that the pure truth, at the right time, gives better results for everyone.

In those early days of December 1983, the Argentine Army published and presented its Official Report, prepared on the basis of the 'Calvi Report'. General Edgardo Calvi himself made the presentation to the press, accompanied by Colonel Francisco Cervo, Intelligence Officer of the General Staff in Malvinas, but the Rattenbach leak scandal made it go unnoticed and quickly forgotten. On 10 December 1983, Dr Raúl Alfonsín assumed the presidency of the nation, and Argentina returned to democratic life.

Since then, and slowly over 40 years, a large number of books have been published in Argentina using testimonials from veterans, mainly focusing on the performance and acts of courage of the Argentine military. However, published only in Spanish, they were not widely read outside Argentina.

In May 1983, while the Calvi and Rattenbach Commissions were still working on their reports, General José Teófilo Goyret – General Galtieri's defender before the Supreme Council of the Armed Forces, and president of the Institute of Argentine Military History – on the occasion of the publication of an article on the Argentine Army in Malvinas, expressed the need to know about ground operations, and that this should be a continuous process. Goyret said:

> Little or nothing is known about the land operations carried out in the Malvinas from April 2 to June 14, 1982, in which the Argentine Army was the main agent of historical events, which is absolutely necessary to do know, because of the importance that this knowledge will have in the national and institutional future... aware that this work does not constitute a complete and indisputable exposition of the events in which the Army troops were the main protagonists in the military confrontation with the United Kingdom forces. That ideal or aspiration will be satisfied by other studies that will surely follow this one, carried out on the basis of more extensive documentation and with a greater availability of time and space.

Surprisingly, this aspiration of Goyret's was also initially fulfilled by the author of this book, Nick van der Bijl. In the intelligence cell of the 3 Brigade Commando, Nick managed to unravel the Argentine order of battle in the islands, and with the seizure of documentation in Puerto Argentino (Port Stanley) after the Argentine surrender, it led him to learn from within the Argentine defence planning and actions in the islands through the documents found at the Argentine command post.

All this information and knowledge about the Argentines in the Malvinas led him to write several books about the 1982 conflict, in which the Argentine story is interspersed with the British, with *Nine Battles to Stanley* being the first book to recount the complete land campaign, with stories and information from both sides giving a more complete approach. For many years, land actions have been overshadowed by the publication of books with more glamorous histories of planes and ships.

The book was translated and published in Argentina, receiving a good reception from the public. Many Argentine veterans found in this book answers to their questions about the result or consequences of their own actions, and learnt what units and names they had faced. An important conclusion of *Nine Battles to Stanley* was, 'Compared to other twentieth century wars, it had been a relatively gentlemanly affair – no atrocities, no great long-lasting hatred for the Argentines, mercifully short and certainly not as voracious as other wars at the same time'.

For this book, Nick van der Bijl has worked with Argentine documentary and testimonial sources, and analysed the Calvi Report, with the aim of unravelling the Argentine perspective of the operations in the Malvinas. A great challenge but one that will allow the reader to understand the origin and motivation of many strategic decisions in South America and at the tactical level on the islands.

Malvinas has always been a feeling for the Argentine people, beyond the result of the war in 1982. It was the disappointment of what happened then that led to the approval in 1984, in a referendum, of the papal proposal on the dispute with Chile in the Beagle Channel. The conviction that territorial disputes must be resolved through peaceful negotiations, and the vocation for peace, led to the insertion of a transitory provision in the National Constitution in 1994. The Constitution declares:

> Its [Argentina's] legitimate and imprescriptible sovereignty over the islands Malvinas, South Georgia and the South Sandwich and the corresponding maritime and insular spaces, as an integral part of the national territory.
>
> The recovery of said territories and the full exercise of sovereignty, respecting the way of life of its inhabitants, and in accordance with the principles of international law, they constitute a permanent and inalienable objective of the Argentine people.

Despite the harshness of the Rattenbach Report on the conduct of the Military Junta and higher commands, in its conclusions it leaves the performance of the military on the islands safe.
The Report expressed:

> There are numerous acts of extraordinary valour produced in all the Armed Forces and Security Forces in the Theatre of War by those who, serving their duty, accredited the validity of our best military traditions. We should be proud of the courtesy with which the country's arms proceeded, which, at no time, violated the rules of war by incurring in actions at odds with the ethics of the fighting troops, such as attacking non-combatants, or ships and aircraft affected to rescue tasks. Beyond the result of the war, our Armed Forces can be satisfied with their performance during the conflict, since they faced a world power of the first magnitude, politically and logistically supported by the United States.

2022 marked the 40th anniversary of the Malvinas/Falklands War. The Argentine government began the year with the issuance of Decree 17/2022 of 13 January, which declared the year 2022 to be 'a tribute by the Argentine people to those who fell in the 1982 conflict, as well as to their families and to veterans of Malvinas'. The decree also stated that during 2022 all official documentation of the government offices must bear the legend: 'The Malvinas are Argentine'.

This new book by Nick van der Bijl is an important step to analyse – with its rights and wrongs – the Argentine perspective and achieve a better understanding of what happened 'on the other side of the hill', and the feeling of the Argentine military and population for their 'Malvinas'.

Alejandro Amendolara
Buenos Aires, February 2022

Introduction

In 1982, I had been serving in the Intelligence Corps for twelve years, after three years on tanks. Our skills base included knowledge of the Soviet Army Forces and Spanish-speaking Guatemalan Armed Forces, but not the Argentine Armed Forces – that was a Royal Marines problem – until I joined 3 Commando Brigade in 1981 and experienced a very steep learning curve in 1982, concentrating our effort on the Argentines. My experiences 'down south' included analysing documents and convincing members of the Argentine Armed Forces to share information. The more of these men I met, the more I wanted to understand why an Army, Navy and Air Force had chosen to go to war against the very experienced and highly trained British Armed Forces.

Since 1982, there have been interesting accounts of the war published in the United Kingdom by individuals, as well as histories, such as the *Official History of the Falklands Campaign* by Sir Lawrence Freedman. However, there have been very few, if any, accounts published that describe the Argentine point of view. I played my part, writing several books and articles, but the dearth of information about the Argentines was disappointing as I wanted to know more – not only why they went to war, but what happened on the battlefield and why?

This book evolved from conversations that I had with Señor Alejandro Jose Amendolara Bourdette, a Buenos Aires lawyer, who has become an expert on the Falklands in Argentina. Over several years, we have met and exchanged views and information about the Falklands War. During one conversation, Señor Amendolara mentioned the Calvi Report, a formal post-combat Staff Report assembled by Major-General Edgardo Néstor Calvi, a senior Argentine officer.

Calvi had reproached President Fortunato Galtieri for not consulting his generals on political decision making during the war and urged him to resign as president of the Argentine nation and Commander-in-Chief of the Army. Calvi chaired a commission of generals that analysed the Argentine Army's performance and produced a report – the Calvi Report – in 1983. However, the Junta was still in power and so, for political reasons, the report was shelved. An alternative report by another general was released, but it was far less hard-hitting than the Calvi Report – indeed it included little examination of why Argentina had been so decisively defeated in a short time.

While in May 1983, the Calvi and Rattenbach Commissions were reviewing the performance of the Armed Argentine Armed, General José Teófilo Goyret, who had defended General Galtieri during appearance before the Supreme Council of the Armed Forces, wrote:

> Little or nothing is known about the land operations carried out in the Malvinas from April 2 to June 14, 1982, in which the Argentine Army was the main agent of historical events, which is absolutely necessary to do know, because of the importance that this knowledge will have in the national and institutional future. ... aware that this work does not constitute a complete and indisputable exposition of the events in which the Army troops were the main protagonists in the military confrontation with the United Kingdom forces. That ideal or aspiration will be satisfied by other studies that will surely follow this one, carried out on the basis of more extensive documentation and with a greater availability of time and space.

When I wrote *Nine Battles to Stanley*, it was the first book to describe the land campaign, with accounts and information from both sides. The actions have been overshadowed by the publication of books with more glamorous histories of planes and ships. After the Argentine surrender, I collected information from command posts in Puerto Argentino [Stanley] and used it to expand my knowledge about the Argentines and I have subsequently written several books about the 1982 conflict. *Nine Battles* was translated into Spanish by Señor Amendolara in 2016 and received a good reception by the public. Many Argentine veterans found answers to their questions about the result or consequences of their own actions and to know what units and names they had faced. An important conclusion of *Nine Battles to Stanley* was "Compared to other twentieth century wars, it had been a relatively gentlemanly affair – no atrocities, no great longlasting hatred for the Argentines, mercifully short and certainly not as voracious as other wars at the same time".

For this book, I have worked with Argentine documentary and testimonial sources and analysed the Calvi Report with the aim of unravelling the Argentine perspective of the operations in the Malvinas. It was a great challenge but it will allow the reader, throughout the book's chapters, an approach to understanding the origin and motivation of many strategic decisions on the continent and at the tactical level on the islands.

Finally, I must thank several people. My wife, Penny, is an invaluable and supportive critic. I am most grateful to Señor Amendolara for his support, for checking the content and facts and also for writing the Prologue. I must thank Ruth Sheppard, Felicity Goldsack and the staff of Casemate for their confidence in me and the editing and production.

Nick van der Bijl
6 March 2022

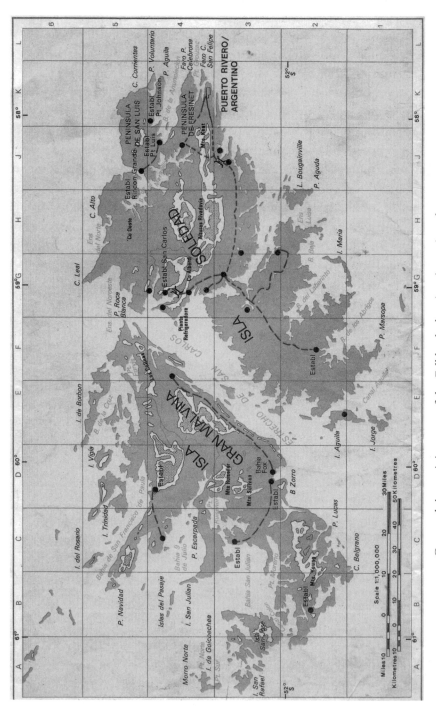

Captured Argentinian map of the Falklands showing Argentine place names

CHAPTER I

Planning the Recovery

The British presence in the Falklands can be traced to 1690 when Captain John Strong made the first recorded landing. When France established a colony, a year later, a British captain claimed the islands for Britain. The Spanish name for the archipelago, *Islas Malvinas*, is derived from the French *Îles Malouines*, the name given by the French explorer Louis-Antoine de Bougainville when he landed in 1764. In early 1770, a Spanish force attack against the British garrison at Port Egmont, which became an important port-of-call for British ships sailing around Cape Horn, almost led to war. Economic pressures stemming from the American War of Independence led to the British withdrawing from the garrison in 1776, leaving behind a lead plaque asserting Britain's continuing sovereignty over the islands. In 1780, the Spanish authorities ordered that the British colony be destroyed.

After a force commanded by Brigadier-General William Beresford had seized the Cape of Good Hope in 1806, he was then informally encouraged to raid the Spanish enclave of Buenos Aires. At the time, France and Spain were allies and although Beresford captured the town in April, local forces compelled him to surrender. The raid was known as the 'English Invasion'. Six months later, he escaped and returned to Europe where he commanded Portuguese forces during the Napoleonic Wars. Spain administered the town of Buenos Aires from Montevideo, but when Spain deserted Napoleon Bonaparte during the Peninsular War in 1811 and switched to the allies, the United Province of Rio de la Plata was one of several Spanish colonies that declared independence, including the Falkland Islands. The departing Spanish also left a plaque proclaiming sovereignty over the islands.

The new state of Argentina survived until 1831 but when Governor Luis Vernet arrested two American schooners poaching seals, the emerging United States retaliated by destroying the Argentine settlement on East Falkland and declared the islands to be free of government; this did not sit well with Argentina or, indeed, with Great Britain, seeing her strategic relationship with the Cape of Good Hope being threatened. On 2 January 1833, Captain James Onslow, commander of the sloop HMS *Clio*, restored order, raised the Union Jack and three years later expelled the few Argentine officials. Twelve years later, the Falklands was declared to be a British colony. As the Falklands historian W. F. Boyson wrote, 'The young republic was ablaze with indignation at the insult of her dignity and the resentment lasted for long.' That resentment is largely based on the fact that Argentina had succeeded in the Spanish territories formerly ruled from Buenos Aires; Spain had purchased the islands from France; Great Britain had abandoned its claims to the islands in 1771, which is incorrect; and Great Britain abandoned West Falklands in 1774, leaving behind a lead plaque.

The seizure of the Cape of Good Hope at the southern tip of South Africa and the Falkland Islands off South America had given Great Britain considerable strategic influence into the Pacific and Atlantic oceans. The Falklands government had governed the polar Falkland Islands Dependencies since 1908. When in 1914 the German East Asia Squadron, based in China, was returning to Germany and using the shortest route via Cape Horn, it clashed with a British squadron at the battle of Coronel off Chile in November and sank two cruisers with a heavy loss of life. The German squadron then attacked the Falklands in early December but was ambushed at the battle of the Falklands and also suffered a very long casualty list. In December 1939, a Royal Navy squadron centred around HMS *Exeter* forced the German surface raider, *Graf Spee*, to be scuttled at Montevideo.

Notwithstanding the legal and diplomatic arguments, the Argentine claim was based on anti-British principles developed by Alfredo Palacios who in 1934 first published *Las Islas Malvinas, un archipelago Argentino* (*The*

Falkland Islands, an Argentine Archipelago). German subversion had led to the 'Committee for the Recovery of the Malvinas' in October 1939, formed specifically to take advantage of the outbreak of war as a diversion from domestic issues, a tactic with which the Falklands have since become familiar. On 26 September 1941, Captain Ernesto Villanueva, an Argentine Navy officer presented a 34-page paper at the Naval War School titled 'Army and Navy Co-operation. Occupation of the Malvinas Islands' a detailed plan to develop an archipelago that belongs to Argentina, and which in its strategic situation is of vital significance for the maritime defense of the nation. Villanueva 'believed that Great Britain was too occupied in other world theatres as to address the luck of a few small colonial islands', namely the Second World War. His plan was to land Marines in Berkeley Sound and establish a beachhead at Port Louis and then land at Port Stanley (Puerto Argentino during the1982 Argentine occupation) at dawn with vessels and aircraft destroying the defence batteries with air-naval forces operating from Puerto Deseado.

British fears of Japanese ambitions led in 1942 to Operation *Tabarin* and the deployment of 1,500 troops to defend British regional interests of approaches from the Pacific. It was also a secret operation conducted by the Admiralty on behalf of the Colonial Office to strengthen British claims to sovereignty of the British territory of the Falkland Islands Dependencies against territorial claims from Argentina and Chile.

'Rich as an Argentine' was once a common phrase when the nation was one of the wealthiest in the world and had consistent growth of about five per cent each year. The country possessed endless supplies of raw materials and natural resources such as water, gas and oil and made a fortune exporting meat, grain and leather to war-torn Europe. The country was barely affected by the First and Second World Wars, indeed immigrants left the wreckage of Europe to rebuild their lives in a climate of prosperity and opportunity. During the Second World War, General Juan Domingo Perón, who was elected president in 1946, had favoured the Axis and Argentina had profited during the war. But his policy of treading the path between capitalism and socialism and desire for Argentina to be self-sufficient did not materialise, as his policy of high wages and social benefits and buying and promoting state companies in the

'Argentina first' undermined wealth and induced a weak industrial base. When, in December 1947, Perón extended Argentine South Atlantic and Antarctica territorial claims to include South Georgia and the Falklands, the British were alarmed enough to send warships to Antarctica. Perón rejected offers of negotiation in 1948, saying that Argentine territory was not a discussion for arbitration. Foreign Secretary Ernest Bevin warned Argentina that the Royal Navy had recent extensive experience and attacking the Falklands was an attack on Great Britain and offered to take the dispute to the International Court of Justice in 1947, 1948 and 1955. But Argentina declined each offer. Matters intensified in 1960 when the United Nations General Assembly passed a resolution to 'bring to an end everywhere colonialism in all its forms' and suggested that both countries find a solution. When the United Nations called on both governments to negotiate an agreement five years later 'bearing in mind the provisions and objectives of the Charter of the United Nations and of General Assembly Resolution 1514 (XV) and the interests of the population of the Falkland Islands (Malvinas)', Great Britain suggested such a decision must be democratically decided by the Islanders, a concept not openly recognised by Argentina. Talks rumbled on with discussions on economic and transport links, but not sovereignty.

For decades, Argentine children had been taught that *Las Malvinas es Argentina* (The Falklands is Argentina) and the Islanders were largely shepherds loyal to a country 8,000 miles to the north. Central to British diplomacy was that sovereignty would be transferred when and if the Islanders demanded it. At present, they wished to remain under British rule. Argentine nationalists lauded themselves as agents of civilisation, like the British had during their colonial adventures, and in 1966, 20 armed *El Condor* Argentine revolutionaries hijacked an Aerolineas Argentinas DC-4 aircraft and forced the pilot to land on Stanley Racecourse where four Islanders were taken hostage and the Argentine flag was run up. It was the first hijacking of a civilian aircraft. The reservist Falkland Islands Defence Force (FIDF) and the small Royal Marines Naval Party 8901 garrison deprived the hijackers of food, water and sleep and when they surrendered, handed them to the Argentine authorities. When a British Embassy lawyer advised the Falkland Islands Company to lobby for the Islands, by

1968 the Falkland Islands Emergency Committee undermined successive transfer proposals in spite of determined Foreign Office opposition. In November 1968, the passengers of a light aircraft that landed on Eliza Cove Road turned out to be inquisitive Argentine journalists.

London and Buenos Aires strengthened economic ties with the 1971 Communications Agreement by establishing an air route using a Grumman HU-16b Albatross amphibious seaplane from Air Force Base Comodoro Rivadavia to Stanley Harbour operated by the Lineas Aereas del Estado (LADE; State Airline). Although managed by an Air Force officer acting as Consul, LADE was a front for intelligence collection. When the Foreign Office failed to secure adequate funds for an airstrip, Argentina built one for twice weekly Fokker-27 flights. Language promotes identity and when an agreement was reached in 1974 for regular flights, the flight attendants gave the safety instructions in Spanish. While fuel and engineering support by Argentine Air Force personnel was welcome, the Foreign Office considered Argentine military presence on British territory still a step too far but failed to fund a permanent runway until 1978 when Yacimientos Petroliferos Fiscales (YPF), the Argentine national oil and gas company who regularly supplied the island, built one.

Perón's political principle of profligacy had led to reckless extravagance and wastefulness and had created inflation, widespread debt and corruption and the tripling of state expenditure. Perón purchased the railway built by the British, but it had fallen into disrepair and inefficiency and was a significant loss. His politics led Argentina into its first deep economic crisis, and in 1955 he was exiled by a weak government and then a military government. In 1973, Perón returned from exile and died in July 1974 and was replaced as president by his third wife, Isabel. Adored by the poor in a nation whose economy collapsed within 20 years and whose future was unclear, she was generally despised because her principle of charity was not financially compensated and corruption permeated society. Amid increasing political violence, in particular from Marxist guerrillas operating in the mountains, and right-wing kidnappings and assassinations in urban areas, social unrest, corruption and hyper-inflation and her inability to control *machismo* Army officers, in March 1976, General Jorge Videla deposed Isabel and appointed a Military Junta of the three commanders-in-chief of the armed services to develop the National Reorganisation Process (Spanish: *Proceso de Reorganización Nacional*, often simply *el Proceso*, 'the Process') to restore law and order. Videla used Operation *Condor*, which had been formed by the US in 1968 in Central America to undermine political oppression and gather intelligence. In 20 years, Argentina had been converted from a vibrant and lively country with a bright future to a police state in which about 30,000 left-wingers and idealist students were abducted and murdered in 'the Process', which also became known as the War on Terrorism or the 'Dirty War' (1975–83). Harry Milner, who was the Falkland Islands Company General Manager during the 1982 occupation, told an Argentine journalist in 1976 that the Falklands preferred to maintain its links with the United Kingdom because at least the monarchy represented stability.

While the Soviet Union had been grateful to Argentina for supplying grain during the American embargo by the Carter administration, the US supported the Argentine stand against the spread of Marxism in Latin America and encouraged healthy economies, a softer touch by the police, broadened press freedom and increased union and political activity. However, these principles were met with a public battered by political unrest and subversive suspicion. With its commitments in Northern Ireland and NATO and Allied commitments, Argentina had plenty of reasons to doubt the ability of Great Britain to resolve the defence of the Falklands. The British government had not reacted to the November 1976 Argentine military occupation on Southern Thule when 50 'scientists', mainly Argentine Air Force, occupied one of the South Sandwich Islands, which were part of the Falkland Islands Dependency, and then built a small military base named Corbeta Uruguay complete with barracks, concrete helicopter landing pad, weather station, radio station and flew an Argentine flag. When Argentina became aware of the British despatch of Operation *Journeyman*, a task force of the nuclear-powered submarine HMS *Dreadnought*, two frigates and two fleet auxiliaries to intervene, the 'scientists' were instructed to remain. Prime Minister James Callaghan softened his approach and ordered a 50-mile protected zone around Thule. Argentine confidence grew that the UK would not oppose the Recovery of the Falklands.

When Lord Shackleton was instructed by Prime Minister Callaghan to assess the economic viability of the Falklands, he concluded that the economy was in decline and recommended strengthening ties between Argentina and the Falklands, and that the sovereignty issue be discussed. There was further Argentine antagonism in 1977 after the Argentine Navy cut off the fuel supply to Port Stanley Airport and insisted its merchant ships would not fly the courtesy Red Ensign in Falklands waters.

After Margaret Thatcher was elected prime minister in May 1979, her foreign minister Nicholas Ridley followed the familiarisation tours to Buenos Aires and Port Stanley in July and learnt that Argentina had developed invasion plans in 1976 and the British government decision not to despatch a naval task force in the South Atlantic did not unduly concern the Islanders. Ridley promoted a leaseback settlement that saw Argentina gain possession of the Falklands and the Islanders preserving their lifestyle for future generations; in December 1980, Parliament objected, he warned, 'If we don't do something, they will invade. And there is nothing we could do.' The Falklands Legislative Council discontinued all negotiations on the transfer of sovereignty due to the strength of the pro-Falklands lobby from both the Houses of Parliament and Islanders, reminding politicians and officials that self-determination was paramount.

After President General Jorge Rafael Videla resigned in March 1981, the Military Junta veered towards civilian rule by selecting retired Army General Roberto Viola. However, he was undermined in December by Army General Leopoldo Fortunato Galtieri, Navy Admiral Isaac Anaya and Air Force Brigadier-General Arturo Dozo, who were all determined Malvinists. The Spanish name for the Falklands is Las Malvinas.

Internally, the improved economy, softer social measures, relaxation of the grip of the police, broadened press freedom and increased union and political activity were again met by public suspicion. The Argentine presence on Southern Thule was still tolerated in the UK; the 1978 squabble with Chile over the jurisdiction of three islands in the Beagle Channel nearly brought both countries to war.

When the UK announced defence cuts in 1981 that included the Ice Patrol Ship HMS *Endurance*, the two amphibious assault ships and two fixed-wing aircraft carriers and reduced commitments in Northern

Ireland and NATO, Cyprus, Hong Kong, Gibraltar and Belize, Argentina saw an opportunity for the Recovery of 'Las Malvinas'. The Argentine newspaper *La Plensa* reported in January 1981 that Galtieri had pledged to recover the Islands no later than 3 January 1983, the 150th anniversary of Britain's occupation. A fortnight later, he claimed the Recovery would be welcomed with international approval, and if Britain failed to accept Argentine demands for sovereignty the United States would support Argentina because the nation was seen as a Latin American bastion against the spread of Marxism in the region. A high-level meeting held in London in June 1981 attended by Foreign Secretary Ridley, Falklands Governor Rex Hunt and the British Ambassador to Argentina, Anthony Williams, concluded that since a negotiated settlement seemed most unlikely and Argentine military action likely, the intelligence threats suggested that there would potentially be denouncement of Britain at the United Nations, an air and fuel embargo of the Falklands, action against British economic interests in Argentina, a landing on South Georgia or an invasion.

In February 1982, Argentina won a promise of neutrality from Uruguay and then in early March, the Junta formally implied that after 15 years of negotiation they had achieved very little progress, so Argentina reserved the 'right' to end British rule and recover sovereignty of a territory illegally occupied by Great Britain and retained since 1833. The top table Planning Committee consisted of three senior military figures: Major-General Osvaldo Jorge Garcia, born in 1927, former Director of the Infantry, commander of the National Guard and Commander, Fifth Army Corps at Bahía Blanca. His area of responsibility included the Atlantic Littoral coast and Las Malvinas (the Falklands); Vice-Admiral Juan Lombardo, also born in 1927. He was head of Naval Operations and the Higher School of Mechanics of the Navy (Escuela Superior de Mecánica de la Armada (ESMA)), an infamous interrogation and detention centre, was under his command; and Brigadier-General Siegfried Martin Pless, born in 1928. He was Chief of Operations when Argentina formed the Canberra Bomber Task Force in 1969 and had served as Air Attaché in France, the Netherlands and Belgium between 1976 to 1979 and was Air Force Chief-of-Staff.

The Military Junta approved the Schematic Strategic Campaign for the Recovery, occupation and defence of the Las Malvinas, the Georgias (South Georgia) and South Sandwich Islands in a three-stage operation of preliminary and strategic military operations to capture objectives, secure the defence and establish a Military Government. Political and military surprise was crucial. Intelligence on the nature and size of a British military reaction was not known, which therefore affected assessing the size and nature of a response. It was assumed that the main operation would be directed against Stanley. Once Las Malvinas had been captured, its defence would be absorbed into the Argentine strategic order of battle as the Malvinas Theatre of Operations and its military commander would follow strategic direction. Four principles were regarded as important to attract international and national support: the population should be respected; military operations should be conducted without bloodshed; there should be minimal damage to private installations and public services; and the number of British casualties should be minimised and thereby defuse British propaganda highlighting the 'often and alleged' poor human rights image of Argentina.

In commendable secrecy, the Recovery was named Operation *Rosario* – in English, 'rosary'. A Working Committee updated several National Strategic Directive Military Strategies. DEMIL 1/82 (Military Strategic Directive) detailed the requirements of the Armed Forces to capture, consolidate and defend a military objective. The operational concept was an amphibious and airmobile landing followed by an offensive to converge on Port Stanley. Airmobile operations can be defined as those in which combat forces are moved about the battlefield in helicopters, as opposed to airborne which involves parachute troops.

DENAC 1/82 (Malvinas) Phase 4 (Maintenance of the Military Objective and Government) was 'Achieving the Administration of Malvinas, Georgia's and South Sandwich Islands under a military governor appointed by the Military Committee to exercise the executive, legislative and judicial authority'. Stage one had already been achieved with the seizure of Thule. It concluded that,

> The Argentine Republic must resolve a military problem and also the handling
> of a population which even if not being of Argentine origin nor considering

itself as such, live in a territory that we consider as Argentine and that is going to be returned to the national sovereignty. Therefore, such population must in no way be considered as hostile with total correctness and flexibility in order to gain its good disposition.

DENAC 2/82, the strategy for invasion day, detailed the actions to be taken by the differing areas of resources of Argentina to contribute to achieving the ultimate political objective.

Navy and Marines
Capture Royal Marines Barracks at Moody Brook, the capital of Port Stanley, St. Philip Lighthouse and Stanley Airfield.
Amphibious and port operations.

Army
East Falklands. Airmobile insertion of two infantry platoons to block the road between the Royal Marines Barracks Moody Brook and Port Stanley.
A reinforced platoon to occupy Goose Green and seize the airstrip.
Two airborne companies and combat and logistic support to drop onto Port Stanley Airfield and relieve naval forces that had landed.

Air Force
Seize Stanley Airfield.
Support occupation forces.
Control air space.

After D-Day
Defend the Falklands.
Support the Military Government.
West Falklands. A reinforced infantry company to occupy Fox Bay.

Following the Recovery, the Falkland Theatre of Operations would be disbanded, and command and control would be transferred to a military commander able to follow strategic direction beyond the capabilities of the Joint Staff. Surprise was crucial, as was supporting the Military

Junta. 15 May was proposed as the Recovery date with 15 days' notice provided for recalling the Class 1982 conscripts. A date after 15 May would be at risk from the prevailing atmospheric conditions of South Atlantic weather.

A major administrative and training issue throughout the armed forces was the annual conscription. Argentina first introduced conscription (*servicio militar obligatorio*) into the Army in 1896 when men aged 20 years were drafted during a period of tension with Chile. Military service for males aged 18 years was introduced in 1901. Every year, a lottery assigned a number between 1 and 1,000 to the last numbers of every male's lottery number and those numbers corresponded to the lottery number, and those who passed a medical were conscripted for 12 months with the option of transferring as regulars. Conscripts were inducted in March and joined one of three annual training cycles that closed in October. Recruits were progressively released in November, January and March. Therefore, some conscripts served eight months. The constant changeover meant the armed forces were inadequately prepared for war, with the lowest number of conscripts between January and March. The Navy and Marines organised five recruitment rotations, which helped to maintain a core of experienced conscripts during the full year; the Marines served a fixed time of 14 months.

In April 1982, 50 per cent of Class 1962 had been discharged and the Class 1963 conscripts were undergoing basic training. This meant that in March 1982, a reasonable percentage of soldiers were inexperienced and untrained. Such was the strength of opinion to correct a national wrong, young men responded to the demand for volunteers by post, telephone calls and personal visits from friends, particularly in cities and towns. To that extent, Army conscription was a cultural weakness.

In 1982, Army Class 1963 was in the process of basic training with Class 1962 having been discharged – with a liability to be recalled. For instance, in a 10th Brigade unit, 134 of Class 1963 conscripts replaced those from Class 1962 who had not reported. But, only about half of Class 1962 had done any military training since their discharge final exercise in November. Only 3rd Regiment failed to reach the Class 1962 quota with gaps filled from Class 1963. Many of the discharged Class

1962 conscripts were indignant not to be called up because they had learnt from an early age that *Malvinas es Argentina* should be defended and they were already trained. Some officers and other ranks of men were allocated to garrison duties while others were on leave. Class 1963 were not tasked with providing guards at bases; regimental Rear Parties, Administration Services Platoons on garrison duties and Duty Operational Platoons were mobilised in the event of internal unrest. Generally, the seconds-in-command remained at unit HQ in Argentina to support the administration and moves. This meant that in March 1982, a reasonable percentage of soldiers were new and inexperienced conscripts, and a programme was initiated to recall trained soldiers to fill in the gaps, something not everyone was enthusiastic about after having been so recently discharged.

Once the Military Committee had drafted the Schematic Plan, the three commanders-in-chief made recommendations to the Military Junta, including recommendations if Great Britain adopted a military response. One recommendation was that the Falklands Theatre of Operations should be replaced with a committee covering a regional military function. General Garcia sent task force commanders principles that would apply to Recovery and occupation. In early March, General Galtieri appointed Brigadier-General Menéndez as Governor of Las Malvinas after the Recovery who was to form a committee to compile a rapid study of the Islands and list any recommendations.

Brigadier-General Mario Benjamin Menéndez was born on 3 April 1930. Members of his family had been governors of Las Malvinas between 1820 and 1831. He had attended the National Military College and by July 1975 was a colonel in the 5th Infantry Brigade on counter-insurgency operations against the People's Revolutionary Army in Tucuman Province, and also commanded the 6th Mountain Infantry Brigade in Neuquén Province. He was a member of the Military Committee that briefed the Argentine president weekly on a range of issues that included foreign diplomacy, military matters and the military budget. Others assembled included Air Force Commodore Carlos Bloomer-Reeve, recalled from his appointment as the Air Attaché in Bonn, West Germany, who had managed the LADE operation and had been posted to the Falklands between 1975 and 1976 during which he was known for driving a Citroen CV; Army Lieutenant-Colonel Francisco Machinandiarena who was recalled from his post as an assistant military attaché in the USA; and Navy Captain Barry Hussey who had been the naval attaché in 1973 in West Germany and was known as *El Inglis* in the Argentine Navy. Fluent in English, he had humane principles.

The Committee, retitled the Falklands Military Government, had an Executive and a Legislative Council that over the next month agreed several principles:

- Falklanders with strong colonial links or anti-Argentine views would not be permitted to sit on either body.
- Harmonise the existing administration of justice through Justices of Peace, Commissions for Oaths and the General Registry with the practices in Argentina.
- Ensure fair administration and delivery of goods and services.
- Bring the Falklands and British pound sterling into line with the Argentine peso as the only currency.
- Schools ranged from boarding to day schools. Ninety-five per cent of the children were of British nationality, three per cent were local and two per cent were US citizens. Teachers needed to be retained. Most were on contract. One subject to be enhanced was knowledge about the geography, culture, history and language of Argentina.
- Ensure the provision of essential public services such as water, electricity, garbage collection, maintenance of roads, port installations and air services and maintain postal services, telephone exchanges, telegraph and radio-telephone communications.
- Ensure that healthcare reached all population centres.
- Encourage trading companies and undermine the monopoly of the Falkland Islands Company with competitive business for the benefit of the Falklanders.
- Residents would have the option of applying for Argentine citizenship. Arrangements would be made to facilitate those who wished to leave.

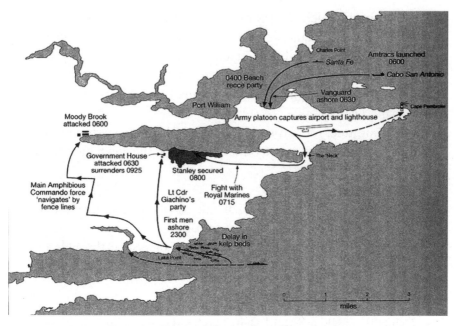

Operation *Rosario* - the capture of Port Stanley

- Improve pastures by linking farming and agriculture with the National Institute of Agricultural Technology.
- Some children boarded in Stanley. Locally employed teachers set up classes in houses in the town and in rural areas alongside Falkland Islanders who had continued teaching.

CHAPTER 2

Operation *Rosario*:
Recovery of Las Malvinas

Navy Rear-Admiral Juan Jose Lombardo, Head of Naval Operations and who had masterminded Operation *Rosario*, was on holiday in Uruguay when he learned of the proposed landing at Leith in South Georgia from newspapers and immediately returned to Buenos Aires to challenge Admiral Anaya's double-cross of not advising him of the decision to recover Las Malvinas. The Military Junta had agreed to order Operation *Rosario* at once by using any troops and ships that were available and achieve the Recovery before the United Kingdom and the world realised. The Argentine Embassy in London kept Buenos Aires informed on how the crisis was developing in Parliament and the media in Great Britain. Anaya warned that if British submarines appeared, the Navy would return to port. It is a measure of Lombardo's organisational skills that within a week he had assembled an invasion task force.

On 25 March, HQ 9th Brigade, commanded by Brigadier-General Americo Daher, placed 8th Mechanised Infantry Regiment (Lieutenant-Colonel Ernesto Repossi), 25th Regiment and 9th Engineer Company on immediate notice to deploy. The next day, the brigade Chief-of-Staff, Colonel Ernesto Alais, briefed Lieutenant-Colonel Mohamed Ali Seineidin of 25th Infantry Regiment about Operation *Rosario*. The regiment had been formed in 1943 as part of the Patagonia Group and was based in the town of Capitán Sarmiento, Chubut. The regiment had deployed to Tucuman in the late 1970s and fought left-wing guerrillas/

radicals. Morale was high and equipment and weapons were described as 'adequate'. Seineidin briefed his officers about Operation *Rosario* and the role that was to be played by his regiment.

The intelligence assessment was that the enemy was weak. The Falklands garrison consisted of 68 Royal Marines due to the annual spring rotation in March of Naval Party 8901/81 handing over to 8901/82. Twenty-two had embarked on *Endurance* to support the British Antarctic Survey on South Georgia. The ship usually had a naval party of 12 Royal Marines. The Falklands Islands Defence Force was a part-time Army volunteer force maintained by the governor that had several former servicemen.

By 26 March, the Military Committee had been informed that a Royal Navy nuclear submarine had departed from Gibraltar and a destroyer from Belize was en route to the South Atlantic. Recovery was set for 1 April and orders were issued. Defenders were to be persuaded that resistance was pointless. The Amphibious Commando Grouping was to seize Moody Brook Barracks and prevent Naval Party 8901 from entering Stanley or withdrawing inland. 25th Regiment was to seize Government House, capture the governor and secure the airport for follow-up forces. The 2nd Marines was to land at Yorke Bay and capture Stanley; once Stanley Airport was secure, the Air Force would fly in the garrison supplied by 25th Regiment and other resources.

The Argentine invasion force consisted of:

- Type-42 Destroyer ARA *Santissima Trinidad* (sold to the Argentine Navy by UK) as flagship. On board:
  - Commander Falklands Theatre of Operations Major-General Garcia.
  - Commander Air (Commander 9 Air Brigade) Brigadier Castallanos.
- Task Force 40. Amphibious Task Group Landing Force.
- Commanded by Rear-Admiral Jorge Allara; recently naval attaché in London and appointed Chief of Fleet Operations.
- Task Force 20. Outer Naval and Air Screen.
- Aircraft-Carrier ARA *Veinticinco de Mayo*. Captain Sarcona flying his pennant 'commanding air operation'.
- Naval Icebreaker ARA *Almirante Irizar.*

Marine Landing Force

- Eight hundred and seventy four-strong Battalion Landing Team commanded by Marine Commander Alfredo Raul Weinstabl, consisting of A Company, 1st Marine Infantry Battalion and D and E Companies, 2nd Marine Infantry Battalion. The latter had recently exercised with the US Marine Corps. He issued Plan *Llamada* for the landing force to embark, ostensibly for another exercise.
- Commander Land Forces (Commander 9th Infantry Brigade) Brigadier Daher.
- 1st Platoon, C Company, 25th Regiment.
- Landing Craft Tank ARA *Cabo San Antonio.*
- 25th Regiment Transport Platoon.
- Special Forces Platoon.
- Amphibious Echelon.
- Special Task Force: 'Guppy 2' Balao Class submarine ARA *Santa Fe.*
- Detachment 14 Navy Tactical Divers (*Buzos Tácticos*).

Follow Up Forces

- 1st Amphibious Vehicle Company of 19 tracked LTVP-7 amtracs and 5 LARC-5 wheeled amphibians.
- Marine 105mm rocket battery and anti-aircraft battery and amphibious engineers.

After Major-General Garcia and Marine Rear-Admiral Carlos Busser had approved of the landing plan on 27 March, as the invasion force weighed anchor and Task Force 40 assembled in the Bahía Blanca de la Plata estuary and Air Transport Command made its final preparations, Foreign Minister Costa Mendez ratcheted the tension on the 28th by insisting that the persistent failure of Great Britain to recognise Argentine sovereignty over the Falklands, South Georgia and the South Sandwich Islands would remain so long as the dispute remained unresolved. This led to Great Britain despatching a nuclear submarine and Royal Fleet Auxiliary ships to the South Atlantic and placing the First Flotilla on notice to deploy.

29 March was a day of rough seas and poor weather. The galleys, particularly on the transports, struggled to provide enough food. Garcia was

unable to meet with his commanders and in spite of the risk of interception, he issued orders and instructions by radio. The *Almirante Irizar* reported that the 601 Combat Aviation Company Puma helicopter on board, tasked to land a 25th Regiment platoon and ordered to insert a roadblock between Royal Marines Barracks, Moody Brook and Stanley so as to capture the British governor, had been damaged beyond repair in the rough seas. The plan was changed to the Amphibious Commandos inserting the roadblock while the 25th Regiment was to seize Stanley Airport and clear the runway of obstacles. Argentine media announced that Navy leave had been cancelled and that several warships had sailed for 'operational reasons.'

At 6.30pm on 1 April 1982, in spite of the risk of interception, Garcia signalled the commanders of the Amphibious Task Force of the behaviour expected during and after the Recovery. It had been drafted by his Civil Affairs and Military Government Trials Unit.

No. 1. The mission must be complied with on our OWN TERRITORY, so it must be bloodless as permitted by the situation, so as to gain support among the population and worldwide approval.

No. 2. Respect for private property.

- Which comprises not to cause damage than the minimum required to comply with the mission.
- Not to conduct operations at places where they are not justified.
- The seizure of any elements must be avoided and, if indispensable, it must be controlled by each Task Force.
- Troops may not move around individually, but only in groups with a commander in charge.
- Firm treatment, but with all due respect deserved by a citizen who is not an enemy, but a person born in place usurped by a state nearly a century and a half ago.
- Special care in the treatment of women.
- Acceptance of the freedom of religion, for which reason all churches must be respected. Bear in mind that the Roman Catholic religion is professed by a minority.
- The administration of justice to the population will be exclusively exercised by the Military Government. Any infringement must be reported through hierarchical channels, and the military personnel must refrain from acting, unless in compliance with a concrete mission which encounters some difficulty.

No 3. Any English symbols exhibited at public places must be replaced by their Argentine equivalents with the usual formalities. The flag on the Town Hall shall be replaced in a ceremony presided over by the Commander Task Force in the presence of his three commanders.

No 4. Any noncompliance with this order will be subject to the penalties to that effect by the Laws and Regulations.

No 5. The success of the operation, apart from taking as bloodless as possible of the target, will be obtained if we can tilt the opinion of the population and the world in our favour, an outcome that will depend on each of the members of this Task Force. A wrong move, cunningly exploited by the propaganda, may bring about a serious problem at international level for the Nation whose greatness we are trying these days to enhance, both territorial and spiritually.

Marine Rear-Admiral Busser addressed the Marines:

In the islands we are going to meet a population that we must treat deferentially... They are inhabitants of Argentine territory and, therefore, they have to be treated the same as those who live in Argentina. You will respect personal property and integrity; you will not enter any private residence unless it is necessary for combat reasons. You will respect women, children, elders and men. Be tough to the enemy but also be courteous, respectful and kind to the population of our territory which we have to protect. If anyone engages in rape, robbery, or looting, I will immediately apply the maximum penalty.[1]

The submarine ARA *Santa Fe* had been lurking off Cape Pembroke collecting intelligence since 31 March. On board were the *Buzos Tácticos.* At about 10pm, a trawler was seen off Port Stanley and then at about 1.40am, the submarine surfaced off Kidney Island in Port William and launched 10 Tactical Divers in three Zodiacs. They landed on Red Beach east of Yorke Point at 4.30am and checked for enemy positions, erected navigation beacons and then captured St Phillips lighthouse at Cape Pembroke. A small patrol covered the eastern approaches of Port Stanley to watch for activity in the harbour.

Garcia reviewed the latest intelligence and was briefed of a poor weather forecast, then issued orders that D-Day was to be 2 April and H-Hour was to be 6am. During the day, the landing force assembled at its offshore concentration area. Garcia extended H-Hour to 6.30am.

At midnight, 25th Infantry Regiment and the remainder of 9th Engineer Company assembled at Air Force Base Comodoro Rivadavia.

At about 1.30am, the *Santíssima Trinidad* hove-to about 500 metres south off Mullet Creek in a light swell on a calm night with a full moon peeping out from scudding clouds. The coast itself was dark. The deck watch lowered 21 Zodiac inflatables for the 92 1st Amphibious Commandos commanded by Lieutenant-Commander Guillermo Sánchez-Sabarots and a small 1st Marine Infantry Battalion detachment commanded by Lieutenant-Commander Pedro Giachino, the battalion second-in-command; he had volunteered to capture Government House. Meanwhile, Rear-Admiral Allara on the *Santissima Trinidad* radioed Governor Hunt and asked him to consider a peaceful surrender.

The Amphibious Commando objective was the Royal Marines Barracks at Moody Brook, the site of a former wireless station, about 6 miles north of Mullet Creek over rough terrain. Lieutenant Bernardo Schweitzer and a small advance guard landed at Mullet Creek, but the main party were nudged by tide and current until the outboard engines spluttered to a halt as propellers became tangled in long entrails of unforgiving kelp, forcing them west to Lake Point. The single Royal Marine on the Sapper Hill observation post reported outboard engines to the command post at Government House. Picking up a fence line passing to the west of Sapper Hill, the commandos then split up, with Sánchez-Sabarots and the main body of 76 heading to Moody Brook Barracks. One Argentine commando officer later wrote:

> It was very hard going with our heavy loads; it was hot work. We eventually became split up into three groups. We only had one night sight; the lead man, Lieutenant Arias, had it. One group became separated when a vehicle came along the track we had to cross. We thought it was a military patrol. Another group lost contact, and the third separation was caused by someone going too fast. This caused my second-in-command, Lieutenant Bardi (lead scout), to fall and suffer a hairline fracture of his ankle; he was left behind with a man to help him. We arrived at Moody Brook by 5.30am, just on the limits of the time planned, but with no time for the one hour planned reconnaissance.[2]

The main party of Argentine Marines assumed the barracks was occupied. Although no sentries were seen, a light was seen in the office of the Royal Marine commander.

It was still completely dark. We were going to use tear-gas to force the British out of the buildings and capture them. Our orders were not to cause casualties if possible. That was the most difficult mission of my career. All our training as commandos was to fight aggressively and inflict maximum casualties on the enemy. We surrounded the barracks with machine-gun teams, leaving only one escape route along the peninsula north of Stanley Harbour. Anyone who did get away would not be able to reach the town and reinforce the British there. Then we threw the gas grenades into each building. There was no reaction; the barracks were empty. Most Falklanders were woken by the gunfire.[3]

Meanwhile, the *Cabo San Antonio* and its close escort of the destroyer *Hercules* and corvette *Drummond* hove-to in Port William about a mile north-east of Yorke Bay. Reveille for the landing force had been at 4.00am and after breakfast, the tannoy called the troops to the tank deck and within the hour the Marines and soldiers were sat inside 18 LVTP-7 amtracs and several LARC-5 wheeled amphibians. Commanders checked their weapons and drivers warmed the engines.

At 6.30am, 20 LVTP-7s of 1st Amphibious Vehicles Battalion commanded by Lieutenant-Commander Guillermo Cazzaniga and several LARC-5 stores-carrying vehicles landed at Yorke Bay. Five carrying the 25th Regiment platoon tasked to secure the airport landed without encountering any enemy and then deployed to defend it.

The main body of 14 LVTPs carrying D and E Companies commanded by the battalion second-in-command Lieutenant-Commander Hugo Santillán, bringing up the rear with a recovery Amtrac and the LARCs, waited. The noise was so great in the confines of the tank deck that messages could only be passed by the inter-vehicle radio net. At 6.37am, as the bow doors opened and released a cloud of blue exhaust, the LVTP-7 company commander was guided by a naval officer indicating when the ramp was clear. First-Lieutenant Forbice experienced a surge of patriotism as Argentina set off to recover territory he believed belonged to his nation and ordered the driver to, 'Move now'. Guided by a red lamp to hold vehicles and then a green lamp, the leading wave of four LVTP-7s, carrying Lieutenant-Commander Santillán's advance guard, a platoon of First-Lieutenant Carlos Arruani's E Company and Second-Lieutenant Roberto Reyes' 25th Regiment platoon, flopped into the sea and approached Red Beach. Santillán picked out the red navigation beacon planted by the

Tactical Divers and ordered the advance guard into an assault formation. The amtrac tracks gripped the sandy shallows and as the drivers switched from water propulsion to drive, the amtracs hauled themselves out of the sea and lumbered across the beach. Santillán radioed to Weinstabl that there was no sign of the enemy and allowed the upper hatches to be opened. Fully expecting to be ambushed, the amtracs negotiated a narrow exit gully and then reaching a track, turned west to Stanley Airport. Three took up fire positions to cover Reyes' infantry, who had disembarked from their LVTP-7 and were fanning out across the runway expecting enemy fire, but there was none. The Marines dismantled several obstacles while Reyes pushed on to capture the Cape Pembroke lighthouse.

The second wave of 14 amtracs carrying First-Lieutenant Francisco di Paola's D Company, the remainder of E Company and several command LVTPs, including Rear-Admiral Busser's and Lieutenant-Colonel Weinstabl's amtracs, launched, but the wave deflector plate of Busser's amtrac controlling the flow of water failed to engage and it turned in circles until the driver found a solution – engaging reverse. Thus Busser, planner of the landings, approached the beaches in Argentina's most high-profile campaign in ignominious reverse. Bringing up the rear was a LVTR-7 recovery amtrac and LARC-5s loaded with ammunition, medical supplies and other essential stores.

Meanwhile, D Company joined E Company on the road to Stanley. At about 7.15am, the column trundled past Hookers Point and the old airfield still expecting an ambush, and then near the Ionospheric Research Station encountered a roadblock of several obstacles on the road, including a yellow road repair machine. Lieutenant Bill Trollope's sections were defending in nearby houses:

> Six Armoured Personnel Carriers began advancing at speed down the Airport Road. The first APC was engaged at a range of about 200 to 250 metres with the three anti-tank infantry missiles. The Royal Marines thought the first three missiles, two 84mm and a 66mm, missed, however they later learnt that one 66mm hit the passenger compartment and an 84mm projectile had hit the front. Both rounds exploded and no fire was received from that vehicle. The remaining five APCs which were about 600 to 700 metres away deployed their troops and opened fire. We engaged them with GPMG, SLR and sniper rifle for about a minute before we threw a white phosphorus smoke grenade and leap-frogged back to the cover of gardens. Incoming fire at that stage was fairly heavy, but mostly inaccurate.[4]

In his post-combat report, Lieutenant-Commander Hugo Santillán wrote:

> We were on the last stretch of the road into Stanley. A machine-gun fired from one of the three white houses about 500 metres away and hit the right-hand Amtrac. The fire was very accurate. Then there were some explosions from a rocket launcher, but they were inaccurate, falling a long way from us. We followed our standard operating procedure and took evasive action. The Amtrac on the right returned fire and took cover in a little depression. Once he was out of danger, I told all three vehicles to disembark their men. I ordered the crew with the 105mm Recoilless Rifle to fire one round of hollow charge at the ridge of the roof of the house where the machine-gun was, to cause a bang but not an explosion. We were still following our orders not to inflict casualties. The first round was about 100 metres short, but the second hit the roof. The British troops then threw a purple smoke grenade; I thought it was their signal to withdraw. They had stopped firing, so Commander Weinstabl ordered the two companies to surround the position. Some riflemen in one of the houses started firing then; that was quite uncomfortable. I couldn't pinpoint their location, but one of my other Amtracs could and asked permission to open up with a mortar which he had. I authorised this, but only with three rounds and only at the roofs of the houses. Two rounds fell short, but the third hit right in the centre of the roof; that was incredible. The British ceased firing then.[5]

The Amtrac on the right manoeuvred off the road into a small depression and its Marines debussed, which encouraged the Royal Marines to believe they had scored a direct hit on the passenger compartment of the APC. Weinstabl ordered Santillán that the recoilless rifles and mortars form a firebase to support an assault by D Company, however the Royal Marines recognised the intent and withdrew to Stanley. According to Santillán, the amtrac was hit by 97 rounds and another lost its tracks. The 2nd Marines then fought running battles with the Royal Marines who then went to ground firing up the road when it became evident that they were cut off from Government House. A machine-gunner laced one amtrac, and when no-one was seen to debus it was assumed that everyone inside had either been killed or wounded. At about 6.45am, the first C-130s delivering the 25th Regiment landed and captured the airport.

The shocked people saw Argentine troops and Santillán's advance guard passing through Stanley heading for Moody Brook Barracks to meet Sánchez-Sabarots and his commando detachment plodding along the road to Government House. Six hours later as the 2nd Marines withdrew, 25th Regiment began an internal security operation to allocate areas of responsibility and requisition weapons. The Amphibious Force re-embarked.

Governor Hunt admitted in about 1983 that in 1981 he had given a set of plans of Government House to an Argentine visitor claiming to be an architect interested in its history and layout. Lieutenant-Commander Giachino had been tasked to capture Government House and, after landing, he and his section of 16 commandos skirted around Sapper Hill and reached a hillock overlooking the house from where his men took up positions to cover the east, south and west of the building. Using night vision aids, they noted several vehicles parked in the drive. But his men did not have radios.

Giachino planned to enter using a back door, however it does seem that he had either not seen the plans or, if he did, he misread the layout. As Lieutenant Gustavo Adolfo Lugo and his men gave covering fire, Giachino led four Marines to an entrance at the rear of the house. When this turned out to be the servants' annex, they then moved to the front of the house and came under fire. While Giachino and Lieutenant Diego Garcia Quiroga both dived for cover over a wall into the front garden, the remaining three retreated to the servants' annex. Giachino had been wounded but refused treatment from the defending Royal Marines and a stalemate developed with the defenders not understanding Spanish and the Argentines not understanding English, and both sides exchanged shots. Medical Corporal Ernesto Ubina then arrived to treat Giachino, but when he was wounded in an exchange of fire Giachino pulled the pin from a hand grenade and refused every attempt by the Royal Marines to persuade him to get rid of it or replace the pin so that he could be given medical treatment.

Busser was anxious. Nothing had been heard from the Amphibious Commandos, except for heavy firing in the western outskirts near Government House. At 7.30am he ordered Lieutenant-Commander Barro to send the white anti-submarine warfare Sea Kings from the *Almirante Irizar* with orders to land A Company, 1st Marine Infantry Battalion and Lieutenant Perez's 105mm rocket launchers. Meanwhile, two Royal Marines sections attempting to reach the sanctuary of Government House came under fire from three directions – the Argentines from behind and in front and the defenders in the house. Using the cover of trees on the ridge to the south and hoping to take the Argentines by surprise, they charged through their positions and ran down the slope toward Government House, but were forced into cover by heavy fire. They then planned to cross the football pitch and use a hedgerow but were discouraged by friendly fire from the gardens. Others made it to sanctuary via the kitchen door and were suspected to be an Argentine 'snatch' squad. An Argentine corvette chased another section of Royal Marines in a small boat, with orders to form a contact point for future operations, into the shadows of an anchored Polish trawler.

In the Falkland Islands Broadcasting Service studios, Patrick Watts, the lead announcer, had placed *James Last and his Orchestra* on the turntable and was eating a cheese-and-pickle sandwich when six Argentine Marines entered shouting in Spanish. Discretely activating the microphone so that the commotion could be broadcast, his audience heard him suggest, 'Take the gun out of my back'.

By about 8.30am, the Argentines had control of Stanley and Moody Brook, but Government House was still resisting, so an Argentine officer then instructed Watts to patch a message in English to Governor Hunt:

> This is a call to the Colonial British Government on the Islas Malvinas. In order to fulfil orders from the Argentine Government, we are here with a numerous task force remaining faithful to our Western and Christian beliefs for the purpose of avoiding bloodshed and property damage to the population. We hope that you will act prudently. Our concern is for the welfare and safety of the people of the Malvinas.[6]

Hunt and Major Mike Norman both pretended that distortion meant the message was unintelligible and agreed 'technical' issues were preventing transmission, namely bullets. Major Norman, who commanded NP 8901/1982, had just arrived on the Falklands. Chief Secretary Richard Baker identified the caller to be a diplomat and former officer who had been instrumental in developing the 'Malvinas' initiative in the 1970s. When reports at 9am suggested that shells were hitting houses, all false, Hunt telephoned the LADE (Lineas Aereas del Estado), the Argentine internal airline, and asked to discuss the matter with Air Force Vice-Commodore Hector Gilobert. He was a former representative in Stanley and had returned ostensibly to resolve some financial problems at the office, but was widely believed to be an intelligence officer and the main source of information about the Naval Party 8901 deployment. Carrying a white flag, Gilobert walked to Government House and told several Argentines shooting at him to note the colour of the flag that he was carrying. Inside, after an unsuccessful attempt to contact the Argentines using a Royal Marines radio, Baker and Gilobert fashioned a flag of white net curtain stretched across an umbrella and walked to the police station on Ross St. Gilobert and asked Patrick Watts to broadcast a message asking the 'commander of the forces' to meet a British representative in front of the Catholic church. Meanwhile, the HMS *Endurance* naval detachment began to shred official documents.

On board the *Santissima Trinidad*, Major-General Garcia was delighted and passing ceasefire proposals to Marine Vice-Admiral Busser in Stanley, suggested that he meet the British delegation in front of St Mary's church. However, the white flag ordered to be taken had not been packed and several plastic waste disposal bags were used instead. At the Argentine tactical command post in the Secretariat, a ceasefire was agreed; it was occasionally breached by small arms fire. Meanwhile at Government House, Major Gary Noott, who commanded NP 8901/1981, and Sergeant Gill, checking the Government House defences, were in the servants' annex when they heard low voices coming from the ceiling. Major Noott fired his Sterling sub-machine-gun but his selection lever was on single shot. A burst from Gill convinced three Argentines to surrender, the first prisoners of the war. Lieutenant-Commander Cufré, who commanded the Tactical Divers, then at Stanley Airport, later claimed that the three had been with Giachino until the end of the hostilities.

Sánchez-Sabarots had previously ordered the release of Argentine nationals that Vice-Comodoro Gilobert had reported being held at the Town Hall. Commander Weinstabl and his adjutant, Lieutenant Juan Carlos Martinelli, and several Marines had secured the town hall and Stanley Police. According to Weinstabl,

> The town was silent. Arriving at the place [Town Hall] we had chosen as the Battalion Command Post, we found abandoned weapons and packs. I ordered Lieutenant Martinelli to recce the building and within a short while he returned with about thirty men and women who came out of it smiling. They were Argentines who had been locked in that place the night before. Almost opposite was the Police Station. Inside were six or seven policemen with their Chief and a

group of sailors from an oceanographic research ship. I ordered the Police Chief to send the constables home and to tell them not to come out until they were told.[7]

Gilobert used a telephone at the police station, and then asked Patrick Watts to broadcast a message in Spanish asking to meet with the Argentine commander at the town hall. A few minutes later the Argentine commander replied that he would meet. About 20 minutes later, Vice-Admiral Busser and an escort of six Amphibious Commandos arrived and, still under occasional 'blue on blue' fire from Argentines, were taken to Government House by Gilobert. The Royal Marines defenders were less than impressed. Nevertheless, Busser was escorted to the governor's office. Governor Hunt, who had changed into a pinstriped suit and tie and had combed his hair, opened with, 'This is British territory. You are not invited here. You are the intruder. We don't want you here. I want you to go, and to take all your men with you now.' Busser retorted that 800 men had landed to recover Las Malvinas and he had 2,000 reinforcements. Busser acknowledged that the defence was unexpected, suggesting that defenders could lay down their arms with their military honour intact. After two visits to Government House from Busser, Hunt realised his options were limited, at about 9.20am:

> With a heavy heart, I turned to Mike [Major Norman] and told him to give the order to lay down arms. I could not bring myself to use the word 'Surrender'. Mike's face was a mixture of relief and anguish: it was not part of his training to surrender, but his good sense told him that there was no real alternative. As Gary accompanied Busser to tend the wounded round Government House, Mike told his radio operator to instruct all sections to down arms and wait to be collected.[8]

Weinstabl reached Government House as the defenders were surrendering. An immediate concern was the wounded. Giachino was alive but weak from blood loss and was first placed in one of the two NP 8901 Land Rovers to take him to Stanley Hospital, but both had been disabled by gunfire, so he was transferred to an amtrac, but he died soon afterwards. A eulogy written about him by a lady in Argentina was found on many prisoners during the campaign. Meanwhile, the defenders had been disarmed, searched and corralled on the Government House lawn. The Argentines seized equipment from the Falkland Islands Defence Force and, declaring it to be illegal, disbanded it and told the soldiers to go home. Several members were later arrested and sent to Fox Bay for the duration of the war.

When an Argentine Army officer asked Naval Party 8901 that everyone be accounted for, a headcount established that six were missing. Corporal Lou Armour and his section had reached the house and had fought on the second floor:

> There were three [Argentine] casualties lying in the garden of Government House. You think – What sort of mood are they going to be in when their 'oppos' are shot up? When we were actually lying down. I felt a bit humiliated but I also felt apprehensive about what was going to happen next. One of the Argentine officers came along and actually struck one of the guards and told us to stand up. We stood up and he shook my hand and a few other guys' hands and said that we shouldn't lie down, that we should be proud of what we'd done.[9]

Several Amphibious Commandos then escorted the Royal Marines section under Corporal Gerald Cheek and a member of the Falklands Islands Defence Force and ordered them to lie face-down in front of a LARC-5 amphibian. The Argentine photographer Rafael Wollman took a photograph. An officer then arrived and after apologising, the prisoners were escorted to the Government House lawn to join several other prisoners; one was photographed displaying his resistance with a one-fingered salute. If the images were a publicity stunt, they jointly galvanised British opinion and increased public opposition to the invasion. The Royal Marines were then escorted to Moody Brook Barracks at about 10am and given about 10 minutes to pack their personal belongings from the wreckage of their accommodation.

Major Patricio Dowling then appeared at Government House. Of Argentine-Irish parentage and holding strong Irish republican views, he was an experienced counter-intelligence officer detached from the First Corps Intelligence Department in Bahía Blanca. Under his command was 181 Military Police Company and the Falklands Joint Intelligence Centre. He quickly proved his disrespect and broke diplomatic protocol by frequently insisting that Hunt meet Argentine negotiators at the town hall. However, Hunt was not going to be hurried and the more he procrastinated, the more agitated Dowling became, until at about midday when Gilobert persuaded him to meet with negotiators or risk arrest by Dowling.

Shortly after midday, Governor Hunt and Gilobert walked to the Secretariat and after formally signing the surrender, at 12.30pm, the Argentines began replacing the Union Jack at Government House and other buildings and with it, 149 years of British governance was passed to an uncertain future. When the Argentine flag was raised, the hoist of the flag broke and fell down on the ground amid the halyards, Lieutenant Colonel Mohammed Ali Seineldín, the 25th Infantry Regiment commanding officer, ordered Second Lieutenant Reyes, one of his platoon commanders, to climb the flagpole pole and mend the hoist. The flag was about to be raised when Air Commodore Colonel Esteban Solis, the Argentine Air Line representative in Stanley, instructed that that the 'fallen flag' should be replaced with another one that he had. Solis kept the 'fallen flag' for several years and when he donated it to the Argentine Army, it was placed in a carved wooden box in the entrance hall at the Ministry of Defence under the War Memorial listing the names of the Argentine fallen of the conflict.

That evening Governor and Mrs Hunt emerged to leave in an Argentine aircraft and in an act of defiance, he was in his ceremonial uniform, complete with ostrich plumes and sword, and was driven in the governor's staff car, a London taxi, by Don Bonner to the airport. Hunt's tearful wife, Mavis, later told the British journalist Kenneth Clarke from the *Daily Telegraph*, 'We feel as though we are deserting everyone, but what can we do?' Major Dowling again breached diplomatic protocol by removing the governor's pennant from the car and conducting a detailed search of Hunt's luggage.

Later in the day, the Royal Marines and Royal Navy and relatives were flown to Comodoro Rivadavia in an Argentine Air Force C-130 Hercules and confined in the airport before being repatriated to Carrasco Airport in Montevideo, Uruguay, that same night, and then flown in a RAF VC-10, arriving on the 5th at RAF Brize Norton. In his final report from Port Stanley published on 5 April, Kenneth Clarke confirmed the tribute that the Argentine Marine Corps commander had paid to the Royal Marines defenders and denied that he and the other British journalists had been subjected to intimidation.

ORGANIGRAMA DE LA CA CDO

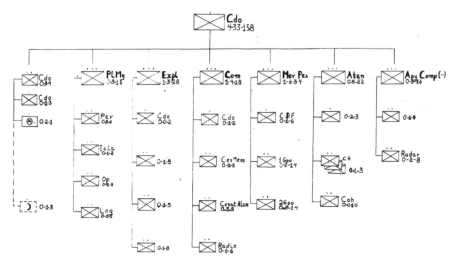

Map found at San Carlos on 21 May 1982, the day 3rd Commando Brigade landed, showing the order of battle of an Argentine infantry company.

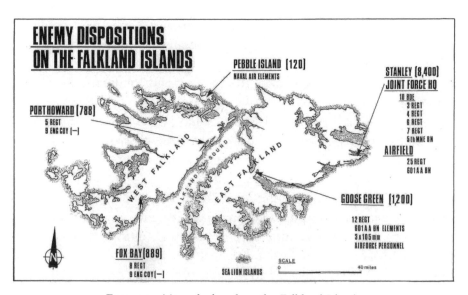

Enemy positions deployed on the Falkland Islands

CHAPTER 3

The Seizure of South Georgia

The British government had established a scientific laboratory at Grytviken on South Georgia in 1924 and later built Discovery House and equipped it with a laboratory, accommodation and a workshop. When the Falkland Islands Dependency took over stewardship of the British Overseas Territory (South Georgia) in 1950, the newly formed British Antarctic Survey developed a base. In 1904, a British–Norwegian, a US national and a Swedish banker had formed a whaling company in Grytviken and were given a lease granted by the British. The Compañía Argentina de Pesca (the Argentine Fishing Company) was granted whaling rights at the British Legation in Buenos Aires in 1906. The company ceased operation in 1960 and sold the whaling station to a Falklands Island company.

A year after the Argentines occupied Thule in 1977, and noting the lack of a British response, the Argentine Navy waited for opportunities to increase its influence in the region. An opportunity emerged a year later when the Argentine businessman Constantino Davidoff struck a deal worth $270,000 (£180,000) with Christian Salvesen to dispose of the largest whaling station on South Georgia that had operated between 1909 and 1965. In February 1982, Adrian Marchessi, claiming to be a commercial rival of Davidoff, made an unannounced visit to Leith in his yacht registered in Panama and spent three weeks apparently conducting an audit.

After sending the notifications to the British Embassy in Buenos Aires and the Falkland Islands Government, Davidoff landed at Leith on 19 December 1981 for the day from the Argentine naval ice-breaker ARA *Almirante Irízar* with a small group of contractors in order to conduct an inventory of the work, but did not complete immigration protocols. While he may not have understood the requirement, the Argentine commander was aware of the protocols. The British Embassy was alerted by Rex Hunt of his 'illegal landing' and summoned Davidoff for an explanation, after which he promised to fulfil the immigration rules for his next visit to South Georgia.

Meanwhile, Junta member Admiral Anaya had been provoking a crisis, seemingly because he objected to HMS *Endurance*, the Royal Navy Ice Patrol Ship, docking at Stanley on 20 March to begin a tour supporting British Antarctic Survey operations and claimed it had a military force on board. Most Royal Navy ships on operations embarked a Ship's Detachment of Royal Marines, in this instance Acting-Lieutenant Keith Mills, an NCO and 10 Royal Marines and also eight Royal Marines from the Falklands garrison slipped on board to reinforce the Naval Party to 22 all ranks. Fleet HQ at Northwood ordered *Endurance* to remain on station. When Davidoff's scrap workers arrived at Leith on 16 March in the naval transport ARA *Bahía Buen Suceso*, they raised the Argentine flag on territory they considered to be Argentine and sang the national anthem. Trefor Edwards, the British Antarctic Survey manager at Leith, reported the matter to Steve Martin, his manager and magistrate at Grytviken, who advised Rex Hunt, the Falkland Islanders governor. After, Edwards handed Captain Osvaldo Niella, the *Bahía Buen Suceso* commanding officer, a letter from the Foreign Office in London demanding that the flag be lowered; the next day, Mr Martin reminded the Argentines with a formal note from Governor Hunt ordering the flag to be lowered because it breached diplomatic protocols and because visitors were expected to follow the accepted immigration procedures at Grytviken. The flag was immediately lowered. When Argentina claimed to be applying the 1971 Communications Treaty, Hunt reminded them the act was British legislation and therefore applied only to those under Falklands jurisdiction.

When the *Bahia Buen Suceso* departed from Leith on 22 March and British Antarctic Survey observers noted that workmen remained ashore, the Foreign Office ordered HMS *Endurance* to intercept and remove any Argentine personnel. As *Endurance* left Port Stanley, the Argentines deployed two A-69 Corvettes ARA *Drummond* and *Granville* to patrol the seas between the Falklands and South Georgia and intercept the ship. *Endurance* docked at Grytviken on the 23rd.

As the crisis deepened, Foreign and Commonwealth Secretary-of-State Lord Carrington proposed to his counterpart Nicanor Costa Mendez that the contractors at Leith should be issued with temporary permits, but Mendez was ambivalent. No action was taken against the contractors. Steve Martin remained the diplomatic point of contact at Grytviken, unless Argentina violated British territory, in which case the most senior service officer would take command. The ARA *Bahia Paraíso*, a modern Navy polar transport, arrived at Leith on 25 March unannounced. On board was an Army 601 Combat Aviation Battalion Puma helicopter fitted with snow skis and a Naval Aviation Alouette, and 14 *Buzos Tácticos*, landed apparently to protect the civilian workers. The unit was commanded by Lieutenant-Commander Alfredo Ignacio Astiz. Born in November 1951, he was the subject of an international arrest warrant as he was suspected of the murders of two French nuns and a young woman of Swedish nationality. He was a covert operations specialist who had worked at Task Unit GT.33 counter-intelligence at the Naval Mechanical School in Buenos Aires established during the Dirty War.

Aware that southern right whales migrate to Golfo Nuevo to breed between May and December, the Argentine Navy and Marines had conducted an exercise on the 26th from the Port Madryn Naval Base on the coast of Patagonia. Argentina and Uruguay conducted a joint exercise in the River Plate Estuary. Meanwhile, the *Bahía Paraíso* and *Endurance* were playing cat-and-mouse among the icebergs around South Georgia until, on 31 March, they both lost track of each other, which gave *Endurance* the opportunity to land her Ship's Detachment at Grytviken.

During the morning of 2 April, Astiz briefed the Argentines in Leith that Malvinas had been recovered and he now intended to capture Grytviken (and, by association, South Georgia). Captain Cesar Trombetta, the Senior Officer, Argentine Antarctic Squadron, circulated an instruction that the Argentine naval force in the South Georgia region was to be known as Grupo de Tareas 60.1 (Task Group 60.1). The A-69 Corvette ARA *Guerrico*, which was commanded by Captain Carlos Alfonso, had expected to join the task force on the 1st but it had been delayed by very poor weather. The ship had very recently been in dry dock at Naval Base Puerto Belgrano and Alfonso had considerable reservations about the combat readiness of his ship and exposing his ship in the confined waters of King Edward Point. On board were 40 1st Marines commanded by Lieutenant Guillermo Luna.

By dawn on 3 April, the weather had improved. The absence of HMS *Endurance* led to Trombetta believing that he was dealing only with the BAS party and at 10.30am, he implied in a radio message that the previous day Governor Hunt had surrendered the Falklands and its dependencies, which was not correct, and demanded the surrender of Grytviken. In order to buy time, Mills replied on a high-frequency radio in the hope that *Endurance* would respond. His rules of engagement authorised Mills to 'fire in self-defence, after warning' and 'not to resist beyond the point where lives might be lost to no avail'. Civilians were encouraged to take refuge in the church. Meanwhile, the Royal Marines had fortified the beach at King Edward Point with wire and landmines and prepared defences around BAS buildings. *Endurance* provided communication with London. Lieutenant Mills then walked to the jetty expecting to meet negotiators.

The Argentine rules of engagement authorised the corvette to fire their weapons only at the request of the landing parties. The landing plan was for the Alouette to recce the inlet and the Puma on *Bahia Paraíso* to land the Marines in three waves. Astiz's men were held in reserve on board. At about 11am, Lieutenant Remo Busson, his co-pilot Sub-Lieutenant Guillermo Guerra and the loadmaster Petty Officer Julio Gatti reconnoitred Grytviken and King Edward Cove in the Alouette. The Puma then collected about 15 Marines, however Busson was not happy about the proposed landing site and guided the helicopter to a beach at Hope Point, but considered this also unsuitable. He was about to abort when he saw the Marines were jumping into the shallow water and wading ashore; he then collected the second 'stick' and as it was about to lift, Lieutenant Luna needed his 60mm mortar section and asked Busson to relay his request to *Guerrico*. The Puma returned to the landing site and as it prepared to land, the Royal Marines opened fire and bullets ripped into the hydraulic and engine systems and the troop compartment causing casualties. First-Lieutenant Juan Villagra, the pilot, and First-Lieutenant Eduardo Leguizamón coaxed the crippled helicopter across the bay where it crashed onto a small plateau and rolled onto its side, with two Marines killed and several wounded. The Alouette had also been hit and when it landed near the Puma, the Argentines salvaged a machine-gun and opened fire on the Royal Marines.

Meanwhile, Busson was flying a shuttle service from the *Bahia Paraíso*, delivering reinforcements two Marines at a time, and evacuating casualties when the *Guerrico* entered the bay to protect and cover the Marines landing. The warship was a big target and the Royal Marines ashore could hardly miss with rifle and machine-gun fire and a Carl Gustav projectile. A sailor was killed and several wounded. The Marines then advanced around the cove, past Grytviken Harbour and cornered the defenders and 13 civilians in Grytviken. Judging that the defence of British sovereignty had been sufficiently compelling for 'the Argentine troops to use military force', at 12.48pm, Lieutenant Mills ordered his Royal Marines to cease fire and waving a white Arctic warfare jacket, approached the Argentine positions to negotiate surrender and the guarantee of fair treatment, in particular for Corporal Nigel Peters who had been wounded.

Endurance arrived too late to influence the battle. Nevertheless, her Wasp pilot established that the Argentines had captured Grytviken. The ship remained on station for two days and then early on Monday 5 April Captain Barker set a course heading north and met the leading elements of the task force heading south. The *Guerrico* and the *Bahia Paraíso* headed for Argentina. Such was the damage to the corvette that it returned to Puerto Belgrano Naval Base and spent three more days in dry dock.

CHAPTER 4

Malvinas Theatre of Operations

As part of the public strategy to embrace Las Malvinas into the Republic of Argentina, the Military Government deployed a strategy of 'must obey' edicts and 'information' communiques, given first in Spanish by an authoritarian voice and then in English with an Argentine accent by a man who seemed slightly embarrassed. Immediately after the Recovery, an Argentine announcer read that:

> From here after, April 2, 1982, begins its transmissions LRA Islas Malvinas Broadcasting Station for the whole of the Argentine Republic. We shall now listen [to] the Argentine National Republic for the first time.

Communique Number 1.

The Commander of the Malvinas Theatre of Operations, in compliance with the mission entrusted by the Argentine Government, hereby materialises the historical continuity of the Argentine sovereignty on the Malvinas Islands.

At this moment, so significant for all of us, it is an honour for me to greet the population of Malvinas and invite them to cooperate with the new authorities by complying with the instructions to be issued through oral and written communiques, for the purpose of facilitating the normal life of the population.

Signed by: Osvaldo Jorge Garcia, Lieutenant-General, Commander of the Malvinas Theatre of Operations.

Communique Number 2. Change of Authorities.

As of now, the British Government's colonial and military authorities are effectively removed from their positions and will be sent back to their country together with their families and personal effects.

Communique Number 3. Instructions to the Population.

As a consequence of the actions carried out and in order to ensure the security of the population, all persons shall remain in their homes until further notice. The population must take into account in order to ensure compliance with these instructions that the military troops will arrest any persons found outside of their homes. In order to avoid any problems or personal inconvenience, all must comply with the following:

First: If a serious problem arises and a person wishes to report it to the authorities, such a person must place a piece of white cloth on the street door. The military patrol will be sent to the house, establish the problem and provide a solution.

Second: All schools, business concerns, groceries, banks, pubs and clubs will remain closed until further notice.

Third: Any additional instructions will be announced to the population through the local radio station which will remain permanently in operation.

Communique No 4.

The Governor of Las Malvinas, South Georgias and South Sandwich Islands notifies the population that in full compliance with the principles established in the National Constitution, and according to the traditions and uses of the Argentine people, it hereby guarantees:

The continuity of the way of life of the local population; freedom of religion; respect for private property; freedom to work; freedom to leave or remain on the islands; improvements of the population's living standards; normal supply, medical attention, normal operation of public services.

The population is also invited to continue with their normal activities with the support of the Argentine government, in an environment of peace and harmony.

The tone and emphasis changed for several militaristic edicts:

Edict No 1. The Commander of the Malvinas Theatre of Operations hereby orders the following:

- Anyone who disturbs the normal course of the operation and provision of a public service will be punished with up to 60 days imprisonment.
- Anyone who disobeys the order to remain at his domicile whenever so indicated will be sanctioned with up to 15 days imprisonment.
- Anyone who, being under the effects of alcohol, causes any alteration of the public order or harasses the military authorities will be sanctioned with 7 day's imprisonment.
- Anyone who makes inconsiderate actions or gestures against the military forces will be punished with 30 days imprisonment.
- Anyone showing irreverent behaviour in front of the national symbols will be punished with 60 days imprisonment.

- Anyone who assumes attitudes which disturb normal co-existence or the public order will be punished with up to 180 days imprisonment.
- Anyone who without a justifiable reason provides inaccurate information about events or attitudes attributable to military personnel, which damage their image or causes undue alarm to any third parties will be sanctioned with 60 days imprisonment.

Those military authorities which verify the commission of the above-mentioned acts will proceed to detain any person or persons responsible therefore, and will send to the respective police station together with a detailed report by command. The undersigned will determine the sanctions to be imposed and will issue the relevant communications.

In case of recurrence of the infringements detailed therein, the sanctions will be duplicated. If the offenders are under 18 years of age, the appearance of their parents will be required for them to be conveniently admonished, after which they will be released from detention. Anyone who commits acts or whose behaviour is contemplated by the Argentine Criminal Code, will be subject to the relevant provisions contained therein.

At the United Nations on 3 April, Security Council Resolution 502 was passed:

Recalling the statement made by the President of the Security Council at the 2345th meeting of the Council on 1 April 1982 calling on the Governments of Argentina and the United Kingdom of Great Britain and Northern Ireland to refrain from the use or threat of force in the region of the Falkland Islands (Islas Malvinas),

Deeply disturbed at reports of an invasion on 2 April 1982 by armed force of Argentina,

Determining that there exists a breach of the peace in the region of the Falkland Islands (Islas Malvinas),

1. *Demands* an immediate cessation of hostilities;
2. *Demands* an immediate withdrawal of all Argentine forces from the Falkland Islands (Islas Malvinas).
3. *Calls* on the Governments of Argentina and the United Kingdom of Great Britain and Northern Ireland to seek a diplomatic solution to their differences and to respect fully the purposes and principles of the Charter of the United Nations.

Adopted at the 2350th meeting
by 10 votes to 1 (Panama), with
4 abstentions (China, Poland,
Spain and Union of Soviet Socialist
Republics).

Importantly, the resolution allowed the UK to invoke Article 51 of the right of self-defence and was supported by members of the Commonwealth and European Economic Community, who later imposed sanctions on Argentina. The Military Junta rejected the demand and the British launched Operations *Corporate*.

In Las Malvinas, the recently arrived chief of the Falkland Islands Police Force Ronnie Lamb had been deported, and several police and several special constables hastily recruited on the eve of the invasion had resigned, leaving local law and order largely leaderless except for Police Constable Anton Livermore, aged 19. Chief Secretary Baker had remained to represent the Islanders for 10 days during the handover to the Argentines and he persuaded Livermore, since he spoke good Spanish, to remain as an interface between locals and occupiers, in the knowledge that he risked treading the difficult line between collaboration and loyalty. Commodore Bloomer-Reeve advised Livermore not to risk his reassuring presence in his British police uniform and to work with 181 Military Police to maintain law and order.

181 Military Police Company arrived on Recovery Day with two main roles of 'population control' and the protection of HQ Commander Falklands Theatre of Operations. Argentine 'population control' had been developed during the seven years of the Dirty War and had become aggressive. Great Britain was also exercising 'population control' during Operation *Banner* in Northern Ireland in a far lesser degree of enforcement than in Argentina, where crime and terrorism were now rife. The company was based at Stanley Police Station. An immediate operational need was for the military police to take over the security of Stanley and allow 25th Regiment to secure the high ground north and west of the airport, two areas that were assessed to be facing amphibious operation and heliborne landings.

In command of the military police for the first month of the occupation was Major Dowling, who regularly carried a British SLR rifle, and conducted the standard internal security and counter-insurgency tactics of snap identity checks, roadblocks, raids on properties – of which some were repetitive – interrogations and deliberate damage to property. He was an example of the 'population control' being exercised in Argentina.

Some Argentine officers disapproved of his strategy in a territory that had hitherto not resisted; indeed, local representatives negotiating with Civil Affairs undermined his authority insisting, for instance, that one speculative property search be deemed sufficient and that formal notices reading 'Searched' be posted on affected properties. Dowling had his sources among resident Argentines and Falklanders sympathetic to Argentina. Alexander Bett (1947–2020), a third generation Islander, had long declared his allegiance to Argentina.

Brigadier-General Menéndez arrived as the military governor-designate on 4 April and moved into Moody Brook Barracks. At the Secretariat, Chief Secretary Baker and Argentine officers and civil servants began to transfer responsibilities through meetings, with the emphasis on incorporating the Recovery into Argentina in a peaceful transfer. Prior to the Recovery, the Argentines had conducted an extensive intelligence operation that examined every aspect of Falklands life, so far as possible, in order to ensure that the rights, uses and customs of the population would be respected and maintained within Argentine laws and customs and, where possible, living conditions improved. Generally, the population were resigned to the nature of the occupation, but not its purpose.

The region outside Stanley was generally known as the 'camp', similar to the Spanish '*campo*' for 'countryside'. On East Falkland (Isla Soledad), the settlement of Goose Green, about 44 miles west of Port Stanley, was important. It had a jetty capable of handling coasters and a grass fixed-wing airstrip. Darwin to the north is smaller, and to the north alongside Wickham Heights is San Carlos Water. Darwin Boarding School had been opened in 1956 with finance provided by the Falkland Islands Company. The two settlements are connected by the Lafonia peninsula, a narrow and treeless expanse interrupted by grassy outcrops, areas of thick gorse and peat bogs. Halfway in between is Darwin Ridge.

The British response to the capture of the Falklands and the rapid assembly of the task force led to Argentina re-assessing the threat and the first steps of converting Las Malvinas into a fortress.

The settlement of Goose Green is midway along the eastern shores of Falkland Sound. In 1982, there were 127 settlers, most of whom were involved in sheep farming. Its deep-water jetty serviced the Falkland

Islands Company coasters. The Argentines knew the Goose Green airstrip was suitable for light fixed wing operations. The 1982 Royal Engineer Briefing Map lists the 400-yard grass airstrip as having a slight slope to the west, otherwise it is 'good, fairly firm'. About 5 miles to the north is Darwin with about 25 settlers. Between the settlements was the 40-bed Darwin Boarding School built at Fish Creek. The unsuitability of the 'camp' for vehicle cross-country movement had been noted and the three settlements had been selected to deter or confine the threat of amphibious and parachute operations.

The Argentine soldiers first went to the farm store, which was managed by Keith Baillie, and asked for the farm manager, Eric Goss. However, Argentine intelligence was inaccurate because Baillie and his family had moved to another house. Staying with Baillie were Mr and Mrs Ray Robson who usually lived at Seal Bay on the West Falkland northern coast and who had planned to stay at Goose Green for the duration of the occupation. Robson offered his Suzuki motorcycle to Baillie to collect Brook Hardcastle, the General Manager of the Falkland Island Company.

Carlos Esteban formally occupied Goose Green by raising the Argentine flag, holding Mass, renaming Goose Green and Darwin collectively to be 'Puerto Santiago', changing the post office number and ordering private weapons and ammunition to be surrendered. Second-Lieutenant Gómez Centurión was appointed to be the main contact for Goss. Second-Lieutenant Reyes commented, 'We treated them as if they were our allies but truly, they never were that. The directives were "They are Argentinians", but they were not and never will be. They always wanted to make perfectly clear the relation of rejection and reticence. In any case, our exchanges were economic only (or limited to trade).'[1] The Argentines were initially accommodated in the centre shed but after a couple of days, Centurión complained that it was cold. Goss wanted to prevent soldiers requisitioning two empty houses and living among the Islanders and offered them Darwin Boarding School. Esteban rationed water and fuel and conducted several searches. During a house search, while the husband appeared calm, the wife seemed nervous and then, without warning, she turned on their record player, opened the windows and turned up the volume for the British National Anthem.

Two days after the Recovery, parents of children at Stanley Boarding School were advised that term was to be finished early. When one father collected his children from their grandmother in the town, the streets were crowded with columns of heavily laden Argentine soldiers en route to the defences to the west and military and civilian vehicles. When the Land Rover of one parent clipped an Argentine war correspondent, he was hustled to the town hall by military police and advised to be more careful. Finlay Ferguson, who skippered the Falkland Island Company schooner *Penelope*, received a message from Brook Hardcastle, who was the Falkland Islands Company General Manager, that the Stanley Boarding School children were being sent home and he was to collect those living on West Falkland, drive them to Egg Harbour and ferry them across Falkland Sound to Port Howard where their parents would collect them. After Ferguson had completed the transfer, the Argentines requisitioned the *Penelope* and dismissed Finlay and his crewman. Both were walking to Goose Green, when they were stopped by a patrol and Finlay's patience snapped and both were locked up in the community hall.

Meanwhile on the 4 April, Corporal York and his Naval Party 8901 section had reached Long Island Farm owned by former Falkland Islands Defence Force soldier Neil Watson and his wife, Glenda. During the defence of Government House, Major Norman had instructed York to evade and establish a point of contact for friendly forces that might land. York explained that he did not have a radio and was sufficiently concerned about the reputation of the authorities in Argentina that he and his section did not wish to risk the lives of Falkland Islanders. Watson contacted Vice-Commodore Bloomer-Reeve and sought advice, then York and his colleagues destroyed incriminating documents, such as radio frequencies and call signs, and buried their weapons. Next morning, Bloomer-Reeve advised Watson that troops were en route. About an hour later, a 181 Military Police platoon arrived by helicopter and although the Royal Marines were prisoners-of-war and protected by the Geneva Conventions, the military police roughed them up, posed for photographs and then flew them to Stanley and locked them up in the police station cells. They were quickly flown to Comodoro Rivadavia and were kept in the General Roca Military College. Some days later, when ARA *Bahía Paraíso* arrived at Puerto Belgrano, they were joined by Lieutenant Mills and his 22 men and Steve Martin's 13-man British Antarctic Survey detachment captured at South Georgia, and all were confined to the base battery and guarded by Argentine Marines.

Two hundred soldiers from the Engineer School reinforced 601 Combat Engineer Group. Typical engineer tasks included general support, including construction of trenches, fox holes, bunkers and provision of reinforcements as infantry; minelaying an estimated 20,000 anti-personnel, with 5,000 mines being laid by Argentine engineers; preparing artillery gun positions and helping to transport equipment and ammunition. The sappers were constricted by the shortage of resources because everything had to be flown or shipped in.

Brigadier Daher advised the commanding officers about the Recovery and, placing his 9th Brigade on very short notice to move, advised Army HQ (Personnel) that it would need to bring the brigade up to wartime establishment.

By 6 April, A and B Companies, 25th Infantry Regiment had been deployed south and east of Stanley. C Company was already at Goose Green. The mobilisation of 8th Infantry Regiment meant that 9th Brigade had landed both of its infantry regiments. 9th Engineer Company was at Fox Bay. Navy ships and requisitioned commercial ships supported the Argentine garrisons.

The average Argentine infantry regiment consisted of three rifle companies each of three platoons and a support company that was equipped with three 120mm mortars, three Czekalski Model 1968 105mm recoilless rifles, three Browning M2 .50-inch Anti-Aircraft Heavy-Machine-Guns and Blowpipe surface-to-air missiles. Some units had received SA-7B Grail missiles from Peru and Libya. Transport to support the regiments was almost non-existent which meant that once the heavy weapons had arrived at their position, they essentially became static. One Jeep fitted with a radio supported Regimental HQ.

In Stanley, Major Dowling continued to disrupt lives. William Luxton could trace his Falklands heritage to the mid-1840s after a relative had developed his farm at Chartres on East Falkland. He and his wife, Patricia, had been in Stanley supporting Governor Hunt during the invasion crisis and when they sought permission at the town hall to return to the farm, Dowling warned Luxton he was one of 500 people of security interest and to avoid trouble. Luxton's reply failed to impress and 36 hours later, Dowling and a military police detachment arrived at his farm in a Puma, surrounded their house and arrested Luxton and his family, flew them to Stanley and confined them to Government House, along with Chief Secretary Baker and his wife and Chief Secretary Ray Checkley. Three days later, on 13 April, they and eight others were deported to Montevideo and flown to London where Luxton became notable for giving his views of the Argentine invasion.

Early the next evening, Major Dowling and a 181 Military Police Company platoon conducted a counter-intelligence sweep in Stanley and lifted 14 allegedly vocal loyalists and their families and gave them 30 minutes to pack. These vocalists included four Falklands Island Defence Company soldiers, Velma Malcolm, the leader of the Falkland Islands Association and part-owner of the Rose Hotel, and Dr Daniel Haines, the senior doctor at King Edward Memorial Hospital, who was accused of objecting to Argentine medical staff using part of the hospital. When military police arrived at Corporal Gerald Cheek's house and demanded that Mrs Cheek and their two young daughters should also pack, Cheek persuaded the Argentines that since his elderly parents lived in Stanley, his family should remain in Stanley. A few days previously, Cheek was summoned to the police station and had a frank exchange of views with Dowling who warned him that if he caused trouble he could find himself 'in a very serious situation'. Cheek was told he did not need his passport because his destination was 'internal' and was hustled into a vehicle and joined the others in a C-130 Hercules loading troops at Military Air Base Malvinas. Cheek had visions of receiving the same treatment doled out to the 'Disappeared', of 'having our stomachs slit and being dumped out over the Atlantic.' The group was then transferred to a helicopter and were flown first to Fox Bay West for the night and then Fox Bay East on the next day where they were met by Major Oscar Minorini Lima, the 9th Engineer Company commander, who welcomed them and admitted he had no idea why they had been sent there. Fortunately, Richard Cockwell, the farm manager, accommodated them and while there was generally enough food, drinking water was short until Cockwell remembered there was a well in his garden.

About a week later at Stanley Police Station, Police Constable Livermore overheard Major Dowling planning to arrest Terry Peck and warned him. Recipient of the Colonial Police Medal and member of the Legislative Council, Peck strongly opposed the proposed transfer of sovereignty to Argentina. When Sir Nicholas Ridley, Minister of State at the Foreign and Commonwealth Office, had visited the Falklands in 1980 to promote leasing the colony, Peck fitted a loudhailer to his Land Rover and invited protesters to barrack Ridley as he was being driven to Stanley Airport on his departure. He had registered as a Special Constable on 1 April. Acting on Livermore's tip, Peck borrowed a motorbike and rode to Long Island Farm, home of Neil and Glenda Watson, where a party celebrating the Queen's birthday was in full swing. Unfortunately, no-one heard the Puma helicopter delivering a search party, nevertheless Peck avoided capture by locking himself in a toilet cubicle and left for Green Patch the next day where he collected some cold weather gear and rations left by sailors from HMS *Endurance* and spent the next 10 days camping in the remote Geordie's Valley. When the cold sapped his morale, he sought help from Gerald and Kay Morrison at Brookfield Farm.

Faced with so many complaints from the islanders about Dowling's attitudes, Vice-Commodore Carlos Bloomer-Reeve and Captain Barry Melbourne Hussey entered the place occupied by Counter Intelligence Section, visibly irritated and shouting. They demanded to know the reason for the actions carried out (breaking into domiciles and detaining members of FIDF), accusing the intelligence personnel of a lack of capacity to discern between the war against subversion and the conventional one. The response these officers received was that they were 'not going to be able to win over the population because they are the ENEMY'. When Bloomer-Reeve and Hussey calmed down, they said they would talk to locals to voluntarily hand over equipment, clothing and weapons. Little was heard about Dowling's disappearance from Malvinas, but he was reported to have re-appeared at Fifth Army Corps HQ in Bahía Blanca during the afternoon of 26 April.

CHAPTER 5

The South Atlantic
Theatre of Operations

Taking into account the political considerations of UN Security Council Resolution 502 and the departure of the British Task Force and its use of Ascension, the Military Junta dismissed the Falklands administration and on 7 April, Brigadier-General Menéndez took office as Malvinas Military Governor in a ceremony watched by Argentine politicians, business representatives and cultural and media personalities flown in as witnesses. Falkland Islander representatives were invited to the ceremony, but none accepted the invitation.

Menéndez was appointed by Decree Number 681/82 as Governor to Malvinas, Georgias and South Sandwich Islands from the National Territory of Tierra del Fuego, Antarctica and the South Atlantic Islands as of 12.00am on 3 April 1982, thus establishing a new province. Under Decree 700/82, the Malvinas Theatre of Operations was replaced by the South Atlantic Theatre of Operations encompassing South Sandwich, South Georgia and the Falkland Islands with Vice-Admiral Juan Lombardo appointed as Commander. Major-General Garcia remained Commander of 5th Corps which included the Coastal Defence of the Atlantic Littoral seaboard and the Argentine Southern Provinces, excluding Las Malvinas. The Military Junta in Argentina issued Communique No. 15 to be adopted by the Military Governor in order to maintain and consolidate the Recovery and for the peace of the nation of Argentina. It stated that all measures to be applied by the Malvinas Military Government are to bring peace to the population, ensure public order, maintain public services and the administration of justice and guarantee the rights of all its inhabitants, and that the commitments assumed by the Argentine Republic with the inhabitants of the Malvinas during the long periods of diplomatic negotiations with Britain will be respected.

Efforts would be made to improve the living standards of the population by:

- Preserving and increasing sources of labour as a result of an increase to the commercial interchange.
- Improving the facilities of supply from the continent.
- Providing such services as the post office and banks on a permanent basis, televisions and radio.
- Better medical services.

It also said that no change would be made in the present sanitary restrictions or the imports of food and animals and that efforts would be made to preserve the population's way of life.

In the medium and long term, the Military Government strategy intended that Las Malvinas should achieve full political and practical integration with Argentina, in accordance with proposals made throughout the negotiations with the United Kingdom – but this was not agreed by the United Kingdom or by the United Nations. Although the majority of the Falklands population regarded themselves as British, hostility was not expected and therefore establishing cordial relations by respecting lives, livelihoods, possessions, customs and human rights and the standard of living was essential, especially when assimilating Argentine economic practices, law and culture. Choices for the population were to leave; remain under Argentine governance; settle elsewhere in Argentina; replace the population with one of Argentine origin; or take mandatory or voluntary Argentine nationality.

Brigadier Daher was appointed Commander Land Forces and Chief-of-Staff. His key staff included:

Staff Ops (Operations G3)	Colonel Machinandiarena
Staff Officer (Intelligence)	Commodore Mendiberry

Staff Officer (Logistics)   Colonel A. Gonzales
Staff Officer (Personnel)   Navy Captain Melbourne Hussey

The Malvinas Military Government appointed Air Force Vice-Commodore Carlos Bloomer-Reeve to be General Secretary. He formed several departments each managed by an officer appointed as Secretary and supported by two Under-Secretaries. An agreement was reached that individuals who held anti-Argentine views would not be invited to apply. One inherent weakness in Argentine military command and control was not adopting the 'Joint HQ' concept and consequently strategy and planning was disjointed.

Supporting the headquarters was the Intelligence Technical Platoon of an officer and seven soldiers who arrived on 11 April. It had a combat intelligence role of collecting and analysing information on the enemy, the terrain and state of roads, locations and cultural 'rural establishments' and conducting a census of communication equipment, machinery and tractors. It also had a counter-intelligence role of unearthing evidence of 'resistance forces' by collecting and collating information on those who could cause mischief, identifying individuals sympathetic to Argentina and vetting Falkland Islanders holding important posts in government, the Public Works Department and other essential services such as Stanley Hospital and Stanley Airport staff. The platoon joined patrols in curfew-related incidents and the monitoring of pamphlets, graffiti, meetings and passive resistance. It was also responsible for the destruction of classified information. It adopted techniques to avoid being detected as intelligence.

By 8 April, Stanley was returning to a degree of normality when the post office was opened under the management of an Argentine employed by ENCOTEL (Empresa Nacional Correos y Telegrafo), the National Postal and Telegraph service that had been providing national postal, telegraphic and monetary services in Argentina since 1972. The distribution of mail to the 'camp' was reliant on the availability of aircraft and the tactical situation. Argentine servicemen were allowed to send and receive aerogrammes free of charge, a system that was in place for the British serving in Northern Ireland. The interception of the telegrams by the British Task Force proved to be a valuable intelligence tool of providing indications of the level of morale and home addresses from which unit localities could be identified. The province of Misiones in northern Argentina provided a TV transmitter that was placed in a studio close to the Falkland Islands Broadcasting Service (FIBS). It was managed by Senor Norman Powell, the announcer, and three Argentines and broadcast between 10am to 12 noon and 7pm to 9pm daily. Falkland Islands Broadcasting Service broadcasts had been suspended to prevent the British using its transmissions as a navigation aid. Since there was no television in the Falklands, colour televisions that had been imported were sold in instalments on a promotional rate and regulated to one set per household. Some sets were placed in air raid shelters and other public places. An account from the Banco de la Nación Argentina (Argentina National Bank) was opened and manned by local staff also using counter services and subject to periodic audits. An Argentine audit in 1982 had concluded the books balanced.

The Ministry of Economic Affairs in Buenos Aires supported converting Las Malvinas into a 'free zone' for the import and export of goods. Compensation was suggested for those who had suffered financial loss from the effects of military operations, damage and destruction to property and theft. Changing the rules of the road to driving on the right inevitably led to incidents and crashes and four highway engineers were transferred from Argentina to work with Public Works and 601 Engineer Company to improve road signage. Inevitably, some Islanders resisted by driving on the left. An Argentine military cemetery added to the town cemetery was managed by an Argentine padre. The provision and purification of water in Stanley improved. Stanley Hospital remained open, however Dr Daniel Haines, the Chief Medical Officer, was interned at Fox Bay in late-April/May for resisting a military hospital wing. Argentine medical staff converted a wing. Empty schools and hostels were later used by unit medical officers. A flying doctor service distributing medicines that began on 10 May was liable to be intercepted by Task Force aircraft flying from the two aircraft-carriers.

President Galtieri and Vice-Admiral Lombardo visited the Falklands on the 23rd and were given presentations based on discussions held two days earlier between Governor Menéndez and Brigadier-General Daher. In relation to the intelligence threat, Menéndez and his senior officers concluded that the British had sufficient experience and freedom of action at sea to be able to land at numerous places, especially East Falkland. They also considered that the enemy would attempt to keep its fleet to the east and reduce the possibility and effectiveness of attacks from our aircraft.

The enemy could head towards Pebble Island and penetrate Falkland Sound from the north or south, although this was considered unlikely given the confines of the waterway. The most likely landing places were Berkeley Sound, Fitzroy, the mouth of Choiseul Sound, the eastern and northern coast of the St Louis Peninsula, Port Salvador and its access, Foul Bay, Concorde. The northern mouth of Falkland Sound of Middle Bay to the east and White Rock to the west, Port San Carlos and San Carlos were also possibilities. The priority was to defend the political and strategic objective of Port Stanley, Goose Green/Darwin and West Falkland sectors.

If a large-scale enemy landing were to occur at other points on the islands, it would be very difficult to assemble a force of sufficient strength. The preferred counter-attack option was to contain the enemy with smaller, mobile resources supported by aircraft and commando troops.

Intelligence assessments suggested the task force would probably be offshore on or after 18 April and therefore the defence needed to be in place by the 15th. The winter weather could restrict fuel supply and refuelling at sea and therefore the task force could be offshore from 25 April. Lombardo and Menéndez agreed that the northern region of East Falklands and the capital of Port Stanley were of the greatest political significance. The Argentine General Staff then produced a current operational assessment. The strategy was to 'Exercise Argentine sovereignty over the Falklands, South Georgia and South Sandwich Islands and ensure that it could be fully exercised in the South Atlantic.'

They also sought to consolidate the defence and prevent the enemy from recovering Las Malvinas as well as using part of the country's military power to capture, consolidate and defend military strategic objectives at the best possible time and under the most formidable circumstances.

Lombardo approved of the assessments and ratified them in Schematic Plan 1/82 dated 26 April – Plan S.

The general strategies were:

Navy

Cause damage, neutralise and/or destroy, when favourable opportunities arise, enemy surface units.

Naval Aviation. Attack surface units and aircraft by using conventional weapons and missiles. Conduct reconnaissance. Provide direct air support, anti-submarine warfare and logistic support.

Marines. Be in a fit state to participate in mining and defence of beaches and surveillance of parachute drop zones and amphibious landing areas.

Malvinas Falklands Military Garrison

Army. Carry out tasks to contain, disorganise, repel, counter-attack and annihilate any attack launched by the enemy ground forces.

Deploy coastal defence role and artillery against amphibious vehicles and/or landing craft.

Exercise surveillance over beaches and maintain strong mobile air reserves ready to intervene in any sectors on the Islands.

Air. Establish an early warning system and contribute to the surveillance of beaches, parachute drops and landing zones.

Co-ordinate and conduct local air defence using the facilities available.

Military Strategic Reserve

Provide two Combat Groups from 4th Airborne Infantry Brigade at Air Force Base Comodoro Rivadavia on permanent standby.

Strategic Air Force operations to be co-ordinated through the Joint Staff.

Enemy Likely Courses of Action

Conduct a landing of men and equipment.

Capabilities

Consolidate any part of the Malvinas that had been Recovered.

Prevent recovery by the British.

Support the Military Government with the aim of 'exercising Argentine sovereignty over the Falklands, Georgias and South Sandwich Islands'.

Contribute to ensure that Argentine sovereignty could be fully exploited in the South Atlantic.

The deployment of the British Task Force led to the Military Committee ordering 1st Corps in Buenos Aires on 8 April to mobilise 10th Mechanised Infantry Brigade to reinforce the mainland Atlantic Littoral Defence. The Brigade was based in La Plata in Buenos Aires Province, 60 kilometres from the capital centre and its role was the internal security of Buenos Aires Province, which was a difficult task. The brigade was commanded by Brigadier-General Oscar Jofre. Born in 1928, he had been commissioned into the Army in 1947 and had studied the role of strategists, including Argentine heroes such as the liberator Juan San Martin. He had also trained as a military pilot, instructed at the Higher School of War, commanded 8th 'General O'Higgins' Mechanised Infantry Regiment and had been Head of Army Aviation before being appointed to command 10th Brigade. The order to the Atlantic Littoral was changed the next day which meant that the brigade was to deploy to Malvinas and would be supported by a company from 601 Combat Aviation Battalion to give maximum helicopter mobility. In order to bring the brigade up to operational strength, conscripts from Class 1962 were recalled.

As the brigade completed mobilisation preparations, on 9 April Brigadier-General Jofre briefed Brigade HQ on the situation and the implications of the Recovery and then at 7.30am, two days later, he issued a warning order to move within 48 hours. Brigadier Daher briefed him that the 10th Brigade tactical area of operations was Sector *Copper* to defend the eastern and southern approaches from Stanley Common and warned him about probable reinforcement plans and re-organisations, including that helicopters could complement foot patrols. The plan was that the troops would be flown from El Palomar to Air Force Base Comodoro Rivadavia with their fighting order and a personal weapon. Guns, vehicles and supplies would be moved by train and transferred by aircraft and included 25 jeeps, an ambulance, a lorry, two Panhard armoured cars and air defence weapons loaded on 12,760-ton Merchant Marine transport *Formosa*. The supplies, as usual, were escorted by a liaison officer and an NCO from Brigade HQ to deal with queries. Late on the 10th, less than 40 hours after 10th Brigade issued its warning order, the brigade began its deployment. In April 1982, Brigade HQ numbered 177 all ranks. The 10th Logistic Battalion played a crucial role in assembling 15 days of rations and 75 days of ammunition for all relevant calibres from depots and controlling issue and supply. 10th Communications Company operated VHF and HF radios.

But a factor within the Argentine Armed Forces was its political nature and such was command dysfunction that the despatch of 10th Brigade had not been shared with Vice-Admiral Lombardo, who was busily planning his defence with his existing resources of ships and Marines and had not yet considered reinforcements. It was therefore something of a surprise early on 11 April when relays of aircraft carrying troops began arriving at Stanley.

The 3rd Mechanised Infantry Regiment was based at La Tablada in Buenos Aires and numbered 930 all ranks and was commanded by Lieutenant-Colonel David Comini. It had been mobilised at 2.30am on 9 April. Their M-113 armoured personnel carriers were left in barracks. The advance party was driven to El Palomar Air Force Base near Buenos Aires and the base of the 1st Air Brigade and then transferred for a three-and-a-half hour flight from Rio Gallegos to Stanley. For many soldiers it was their first flight. Comini reported to Brigadier-General Daher, commander of 9th Mechanised Infantry Brigade, and mentioned there were arrival plans and no reception and the regiment had been moved to bleak and windy moorland near the road to Stanley which sprouted into uncomfortable encampment that became known as 'Tent City'. The 25th Regiment initially supplied food and water from their field kitchens. Such was the frequency of aircraft arriving with troops and supplies that controllers resorted to giving verbal orders for deployments.

6th Regiment was assembled entirely from Class 1962 conscripts and numbered 847 men. At the 7 April meeting at HQ 1st Corps, Lieutenant-Colonel Jorge Halperin, the commanding officer, was instructed to form two heliborne reserves and assembled his best officers, NCOs and men into a company. The regiment received four officers, a captain from the Senior War School, an intelligence lieutenant and two second-lieutenants from the National Military College. On the 11th, the regiment followed the route taken by 3rd Regiment of a road move from its base at Mercedes to El Palomar Airport, where it was joined by C Company, 1st (*Patricios*) Regiment. The regiment was then flown to Rio Gallegos and Stanley and by the 14th was in position on Stanley Common facing east and south to defend the Port Stanley locality against amphibious landings. Regimental HQ was south-east of Look Out Rocks on the eastern fringes of Stanley. With the field kitchens still on the *Formosa*, only cold food was served until B Company, 25th Regiment lent its field kitchen trailer. 1st Regiment company was detached in its place. A company from 601 Engineer Group and two platoons of the 181 Military Police Company were attached.

Attached on the left flank of the Regiment was the 'A' Infantry Company (Buenos Aires), 1st Infantry Regiment Patricios' (*Regimiento de Infantería 1a Patricios'*). The oldest and one of the most prestigious regiments of the Argentine Army, it had been formed as the *Legión Patricia* (Patricians' Legion) by the inhabitants to fight the British 1806 invasions during the War of the River Plate (*Invasiones Inglesa*). Its current role was to provide honour guards and ceremonial escorts for foreign dignitaries. Its title was usually shortened to the Patricians' Regiment (*Regimiento de Patricios*) with the word 'patrician' implying 'sons of the homeland'. The company was attached as C Company to the 6th Regiment, guarding approaches from the east and Stanley Harbour as an airmobile reserve. A Company was placed on the right. About 1,000 metres to the south was C Company. Shortages of equipment meant the soldiers only had infantry entrenching tools and spades for digging in.

Next day, when Lieutenant-Colonel Omar Giménez, commanding 7th Mechanised Infantry Regiment of 562 men, was instructed to occupy Wireless Ridge, a feature to the east of Mount Longdon, he proposed to place C Company on Wireless Ridge as his counter-attack force; however HQ 10th Brigade insisted that it be deployed on the high ground at Point 200 to the north-west. Giménez replaced the loss by combining the Recce Platoon of 15 men and No. 1 Platoon from the Service Company to fill the gap. The lack of entrenching tools and shovels again meant that trenches and bunkers were reinforced by sods of turf and stones. The relative inaccessibility and size of the Wireless Ridge Sector, the lack of vehicles able to negotiate the terrain and the limited availability of helicopters led to the 10 Communications Company signallers and 10 Engineering Company sappers manhandling their heavy equipment from

Ross Road, helped by company fatigue parties man-packing supplies. An insufficient quantity of field communications cable supporting field operations led to three subscribers using one line and the necessity for strict telephone control, which was not always practised during the fighting, nor was repairing cable damaged by shellfire.

The 10th Armoured Cavalry Reconnaissance Squadron was part of the cavalry. The 216 men of the 10th Armoured Cavalry Recce Squadron were also mobilised on 9 April and had the same problem of recalling sufficient Class 1962 conscripts. Its 12 Panhard AML-90s armoured cars were equipped with a 90mm gun main armament and 20 rounds and a 7.62mm turret-mounted coaxial machine-gun with about 3,000 rounds and sometimes a 60mm Brandt light mortar. Fast, long-ranged and crewed by the commander, driver and gunner, the AML-90 weighed 5.5 tonnes, was suitable for airborne deployment, and had an operational range of 370 miles and a top speed of 40mph. The three platoons were flown from El Palomar to Rio Gallegos and spent the night in the barracks of 24th Mechanised Infantry Regiment before being flown to the Falklands one night in mid-April in C-130s that also delivered a Mercedes Benz jeep, two water carts, two field kitchens and 10 per cent of logistic supplies of spare parts and medical equipment. The remainder were on board the *Formosa*. During the night of 15/16 April, HQ 10th Brigade ordered its cavalry squadron to support operations in the Stanley Sector and also provide two dismounted platoons to be located near Moody Brook as a heliborne reserve under command of the squadron second-in-command. Patrols on the tracks were near impassable. The squadron was also designated as the brigade reserve for the defence of Port Stanley and night security for Government House and the Logistic Operations Centre at the nearby racecourse.

In Argentina, 10th Brigade had an internal security role and its lack of artillery was resolved by transferring the 3rd Artillery Group from the 3rd (Jungle) Infantry Brigade. During the afternoon of 2 April, Lieutenant-Colonel Martin Balza, commanding the group at its barracks at Paso de los Libres in Corrientes Province, received a warning deployment order from HQ 3rd Brigade. At 7.30am on 8 April, Balza received a 'prepare to move' warning within 48 hours. The group consisted of four senior officers, 33 junior officers, 75 NCOs and 267 gunners formed into three batteries, each equipped with six Italian OTO Melara 105mm lightweight howitzers, commonly known in the British Army as the Pack Howitzer. The guns had a maximum range of 10,000 metres, were air portable and could be quickly broken into 12 components carried by horses or mules. The reserve C Battery at the School of Artillery in Buenos Aires had been mobilised.

Balza warned his group that the move was the first part of an operational deployment to Las Malvinas from Air Force Base Comodoro Rivadavia. Each man was to take his personal weapon and equipment. The plan was to leave barracks by train on the 9th and be airlifted at 8am on 12 April from Parana. However, the next day at 8.55pm, the orders were changed because of the shortage of aircraft and the group was to be shipped. This required substantial re-organisation for a rail move was achieved within three hours. C Battery and its guns were collected at Buenos Aires and then at 5.30am on the 11th, the train left for San Antonio Oeste, the port city in the province of Río Negro, however during the night, orders were again changed that the Group would embark on a ship at the city of Coronel Pringles in the south of Buenos Aires Province. Brigadier-General Jofre then advised Balza on another change of orders that the train was being diverted to Ingeniero White Harbour on the outskirts of Bahía Blanca in Buenos Aires Province. On arriving at the town, a senior 5th Corps officer, who had responsibility for the defence of the Atlantic Littoral, instructed Lieutenant-Colonel Balza that his group was to be attached to 10th Brigade. They would be flown from Comandante Espora Naval Air Base to Port Stanley and he was to reduce his order of battle by four senior officers, 26 junior officers, 64 NCOs and 110 soldiers. The first aircraft departed at 1.30am on the 13th and within 10 hours the reduced group was in Stanley with its guns and ammunition for three days and a field kitchen and a water cart. The remaining guns, ammunition, heavy equipment, vehicles and 10 days of food were loaded on the *Cordoba* at Puerto Deseado, however at about 10.30am, the threat of submarines led to essential cargo being transferred to Comodoro Rivadavia Air Force Base and flown on aircraft. When the ship arrived in Stanley on 10 April, several vehicles used to tow the guns, two mobile kitchens and other stores and equipment had been left in Argentina in favour of the Navy insisting that containers of rations for the Navy had top priority.

The next day, Brigadier-General Jofre appointed Balza as Artillery Fire Support Co-ordinator, Puerto Argentino Army Force controlling direct fire. By 5pm, the guns were in position and fire plans prepared. The group was later reinforced by 21 officers, 21 NCOs and 21 corporals from other artillery training establishments and in mid-May by two CITEFA M-155mm howitzers each with a range of 20 kilometres, assembled from 101 and 121 Artillery Groups bringing a RASIT ground surveillance radar and two LP-3 laser rangefinders. A third gun was delivered on 12/13 June to replace one which was wrecked during a Harrier attack and a fourth gun delivered during the night of 13/14 June was captured without being deployed in the field.

Great Britain ratcheted the political tension in the South Atlantic by declaring the Falklands Maritime Exclusion Zone on 12 April. Only a few vessels could break the blockade. The ELMA Motor Vessels *Córdoba* and *Río Carcaraña* arrived at Port Stanley on 19 and 26 April respectively. The fear of British submarines immediately led to equipment and troops being transferred by military and civil aircraft using the air bridge. Towing field kitchens was confined to short distances and since distributing fresh food and dry rations to company positions was impractical, it often meant that the food was rarely hot and meal times were erratic. Food had to be rationed and this began to influence the morale of the soldiers. However, the rapid build-up led to the single runway and the tarmac road from the airport to Stanley beginning to feel the strain. Morale dropped even further as troops faced long marches carrying weapons, fighting order and heavy rucksacks to their positions around Stanley. A significant number of troops were neither equipped nor acclimatised to the cold wind and rain of the Falklands. Digging in proved to be difficult. The soft and spongy ground, wet weather and lack of mechanical excavators meant digging in was confined to shovels. It was nearly impossible to construct defensive works of desirable strength and consistency. While soldiers had individual entrenching tools for shell scrapes and shallow trenches, there were insufficient spades for digging in, an absence of trees and limited locally found building material. The sandbags, delivery of timber joists and railway sleepers for trenches and bunkers was undermined by the naval blockade and other priorities, such as ammunition and fuel taking space in aircraft. The impossibility of the terrain of the roads and tracks was also causing significant problems for drivers. For example, on 6 April a column of Unimog lorries using a track to take supplies to C Company at Goose Green became bogged down a short distance after leaving the asphalt road west from Stanley. Tractors could not move the Unimogs, so the equipment was unloaded and man-packed to the road. The lorries were extricated by a Chinook helicopter.

By the 15th, most of 10th Brigade had deployed and since Brigadier-General Jofre was senior to Daher, he took over command of Malvinas Army Force. Daher had developed a strategy of strongpoints and on the day that he returned to Argentina, Malvinas Army Force circulated Defence Plan 1/82 of:

a. Area defence of the Army and Marines with mutually supporting strongpoints of Port Stanley, Goose Green and Fox Bay in order to contain, defeat and annihilate any type of ground attack and thereby prevent the loss of the Recovery and support the Military Government.

b. Port Stanley to be defended by the Outer Defence Zone of Mount Longdon, Mount Challenger and Two Sisters and the Inner Defence Zone of Wireless Ridge and Tumbledown Mount.

c. Reserves for threats against Stanley and Darwin would consist of two heliborne units from B Company, 6th Regiment and the 10th Armoured Recce Squadron providing two Panhard platoons.

d. Reserves on West Falklands to be found from local reserves. With A Company astride Airport Road and covering landings from the south-east, HQ Company, 601 Engineer Group and two 181 Military Police platoons armed with light weapons defended Stanley town.

e. B Company, 25th Infantry Regiment allowed the companies to rotate using its trailers. The airmobile reserve to the South Atlantic Theatre of Operations was replaced by an infantry company formed from 601 Engineer Group and 181 Military Police Company.

When on 20 April, the Air Force asked General Menéndez for troops to defend Military Air Base *Condor* at Goose Green, 601 Air Defence Artillery provided 35mm Oerlikons from B Battery in addition to two Air Force Rheinmetall 30mm twin-guns. The C Company, 8th Infantry

Regiment platoon provided ground defence and 1 Section, 9th Engineer Company arrived with sapper support.

In the background, political and practical judgements by the Junta were emerging as deeply flawed, in particular the belief that the occupation of Malvinas and Georgias would force Great Britain to accept the Recovery and that would be the end of the matter. President Ronald Reagan had told President Galtieri that the US could not and would not remain neutral and would side with Britain, its historical ally and NATO colleague. The British government had gained the right of self-defence at the United Nations. The Junta had failed to anticipate that the US would grant the use of the airfield on Ascension Island, a British territory, and then fail to conduct a plausible assessment of the implication of the decision. Indeed, the Argentine Navy only began planning maritime operations after the Royal Navy had put to sea in early April. Operationally, the British Task Force was highly experienced and built around two aircraft-carriers, HMS *Invincible* and HMS *Hermes*, warships supported by reliable logistic support familiar with operating in the winter weather conditions of the North Atlantic. The two brigades deployed were entirely regulars, most with combat experience, admittedly in Northern Ireland, whilst the Argentine Armed Forces were built around conscripts.

Several visits included the Army Chief-of-Staff on 14 April, the Navy Commander-in-Chief on 19 April and the Air Force Commander-in-Chief on 20 April. When President Galtieri and Major-General Garcia, Commander, 5th Corps arrived on 23 April, the Argentine intelligence assessment was that the most likely enemy option was as an amphibious assault on Port Stanley. Menéndez organised a familiarisation helicopter flight for Galtieri and suggested the assessment was incorrect. He arranged briefings with senior staff officers, some of whom suggested that there were too few troops to defend both Stanley and the countryside of the 'camp'. Menéndez had previously highlighted that should the enemy land at any place that was unoccupied, it would be difficult to oppose because there were no reserves outside Stanley to contain or counter-attack. The nature of the 'camp' of widely dispersed settlements, lack of roads restricting mobility and the difficulties of supporting isolated

Gran Malvina island (West Falklands) bases emphasised the need for more helicopters. One option was to use commando patrols to collect intelligence and attack the British at distance from Stanley and deploy the 5th Mechanised Infantry Regiment as additional infantry.

Galtieri acknowledged the weaknesses and ordered that the 3rd (Jungle) Infantry Brigade, the winter warfare-trained No. 5 Marine Infantry Battalion, the 4th Artillery Airborne Group and the Air Force 3rd Attack Group and its counter–insurgency Pucara aircraft be warned to deploy. Strategic Air Force operations remained controlled by the Military Junta. Brigadier Daher returned as Chief-of-Staff and Colonel Cervo arrived as the chief intelligence officer. The senior command now consisted of:

Chief-of-Staff	Brigadier Daher
Staff Officer	Lt Col A. F. Andujar
Intelligence	Colonel Cervo
Operations	Colonel Caceres
Operations	Colonel F. Machinandiarena
Logistics	Colonel A. Gonzales
Air Force Liaison	Commodore O. Mendiberri
Naval Liaison	Captain J. C. Moeremans and Commander D. J. R. Camiletti

3rd (Jungle) Infantry Brigade, commanded by Brigadier-General Omar Edgardo Parada (born in 1927), was based in the Mesopotamia Region of the provinces of Misiones, Entre Ríos and Corrientes in northern Argentina in an area of forest, jungle and humidity – a far cry from the winter conditions of the South Atlantic. The brigade order of battle was 678 men of 4th Infantry Regiment commanded by Lieutenant-Colonel Diego Soria; 681 all ranks of the 12th Infantry Regiment commanded by Lieutenant-Colonel Italo Piaggi; and 857 soldiers of the 5th Infantry Regiment commanded by Colonel Juan R. Mabragaña. Its 3rd Artillery Group had already deployed. Parada had been trialling a three-monthly call-up system since the New Year and by 2 April, 75 per cent of Class 1962 had completed their training and had returned to civilian life; 25 per cent had completed one year of training and had been released; and 25 per cent of Class 1963 were recently called up in February near completing basic training. Furthermore, a new intake had just been inducted.

When Brigadier-General Parada had learnt of the Recovery on 2 April, his brigade was warned to assemble a company to support the Atlantic Littoral (Coast) Task Force. Four days later, he was ordered to mobilise and called up the Class 1962 conscripts discharged in March; many responded by hitching on buses and troop trains heading east. The Class 1963 conscripts were only partially trained. On the same day, 2nd Army Corps warned the Brigade Logistic Battalion, the Brigade Communication Company and 181 Armoured Cavalry Reconnaissance Squadron to await deployment. At 11pm, 3rd Brigade was ordered to join 5th Corps, and five days later Brigadier Parada and his HQ flew to the Corps Tactical HQ at Comodoro Rivadavia, arriving at 3am – by 9am they were handed the 5th Corps No 1/82 Schematic Plan of Action that the brigade was to secure the Atlantic Littoral between Trelew and Puerto Deseado. The 4th Regiment would detach to transfer to the 11th Mechanised Infantry Brigade and the 3rd Artillery Group would detach to transfer to the 10th Mechanised Infantry Brigade, while the 9th Tank Regiment would attach under command.

To control the deployment, Brigade HQ established an operations centre at Curuzú Cuatiá in the southern Corrientes Province and moved the Brigade Transport Officer to the port of San Antonio Oeste, midway between Buenos Aires and Comodoro Rivadavia, to co-ordinate the moves of men and equipment by road. Parada issued a Special Order that transferred responsibility for security and barrack maintenance to the Brigade Rear Party. The next day, he advised 11th Brigade of his requirements for his scheduled Littoral deployment on the 13th and within three days had received sufficient information to take over the defence of the Comodoro Rivadavia Coast Sector. The road advance parties arrived at San Antonio Oeste on the same day and the remainder of the heavy equipment was moved by rail.

When, on 13 April 12th 'General Juan Alvarez de Arenales' Infantry Regiment, also placed under command of 11th Brigade, was ordered to move from its peacetime location in Mercedes, Corrientes Province and report to Rio Gallegos on the Atlantic coast, it meant a 1,200-mile journey by train across Argentina. The collapse of a railway bridge on the same day in the Rio Colorado region, about 300 miles south of Buenos Aires, led to 3rd Engineer Company leaving the train with all their equipment and continuing their deployment to San Antonio Oeste and Comodoro Rivadavia by any means they could find.

When 3rd Brigade deployed into its Atlantic Coastal Littoral defences on the 16th, it received orders to convert from its jungle warfare role to defending the Atlantic Littoral and received counter-intelligence reinforcements from HQ Military Institutes Command, a training unit that had emerged from the Dirty War with a mission 'to gradually and rapidly intensify the counter-subversive action ... complete the annihilation of the opponent'. Instructors also arrived to support units at all levels of command and conduct counter-terrorist operations. The Brigade HQ Communications Platoon had been reduced to 31 signallers providing a Central Traffic and Messenger Section, five Portable Radio-Telephone Sections, two Radio-Telephone Sections, a Line Laying Section and a Logistics Section to support the detachments at Port Howard and Darwin. This measure was extended to smaller sections needing equipment in order to meet minimum requirements to support their external and internal networks.

Already under 3rd Brigade command at Comodoro Rivadavia were its 12th Regiment and the 5th Regiment Motor Transport Section. The day after 5th Regiment and 3rd Engineer Company arrived by air at Comodoro Rivadavia, 3rd Brigade was instructed to hand its deployments on Coastal Sector to 9th Brigade Rear. On the 19th, Vice-Admiral Lombardo ordered 3rd Engineer Company to join the 9th Brigade Rear. The 3rd Brigade Order of Battle was confusing:

- Brigade HQ, 12th Regiment, Communication Echelon and Logistics Echelon.
- At Peacetime Location – 3rd Armoured Cavalry Reconnaissance Squadron and 3rd Logistic Battalion.
- 5th Regiment and 3rd Engineer Company to remain deployed on the Atlantic Littoral defence under command of 9th Brigade to

detect and neutralise infiltration by 'British Commandos' or small groups of troops evading the vigilance of the Chilean authorities.

- Take under command was the 35th Infantry Regiment, 11th Recce Squadron and 11th Artillery Group for operations in the Rospentek municipality in Santa Cruz Province in the south-west corner of Argentina guarding the border with Chile.
- Parada was to send a liaison officer to 11th Brigade HQ.
- Transfer to 10th Brigade on Falklands – 3rd Artillery Group.
- With 9th Brigade at Comodoro Rivadavia – 4th Regiment.

Three days later, the Joint Malvinas Military Garrison used the deployment of the 3rd Brigade to restructure the defence and include the Falklands in Littoral defence of the eastern seaboard.

On 17 April, the Argentine Army Supreme issued a detailed Intelligence Assessment of several options for an Amphibious Assault.

OPTION 1. Amphibious assault on the Fresinet sector (Stanley east to the Murrell Peninsula)

Method. Deploy SBS and SAS to reconnoitre Argentine positions and deploy amphibious and helicopter guides and attack command posts and other important military installations to disrupt defences.

Open offensive on 18 April and focus on Stanley north to south and Port Harriet south-east to north-west using amphibious operations to secure landings areas, helicopter assaults by 500 men west to east or north to south to seize territory followed by an assault by two battalions of Marines. Supported to include naval gunfire and electronic warfare. Once objectives were secure, reinforcements would include air transport and landing craft.

Purpose.

Advantages. To secure the political objective and recover the islands; neutralise and cause significant casualties to Argentine occupation; reduce the time for political intervention.

Disadvantages. High concentration of defence would cost significant casualties; defence would have acceptable losses; significant air defence. High risk of civilian casualties.

OPTION 2. Amphibious assault elsewhere than Stanley sector.

Deploy SBS and SAS to reconnoitre Argentine positions and use amphibious and helicopter resources to attack command posts and other important military installations and disrupt defences. Mount unconventional operations before or at the same of the amphibious assault.

Open offensive on 25 April in north-east sector of Falklands and establish a beachhead in one of several zones, for instance, north-east of Fitzroy, St Louis and at northern entrance to Falkland Sound and use raiding forces and Royal Marines helicopter assaults to secure zones and deploy amphibious assault to consolidate targets. Reinforcements to include a Royal Marines commando, a para battalion, three battalions of infantry, armoured car regiment, 105mm artillery regiment, two Rapier air defence batteries, a squadron each from the Royal Engineers and the Royal Signals and organise logistic support. Within 48 hours, twenty VTOL (Vertical and Take Off and Landing) Harrier aircraft would be landed from a container ship to an unprepared landing site.

Advantages of the strategy. Advantageous to British political opinion, does not involve an attack on Stanley, makes it difficult for Argentine troops to deploy in sufficient strength for an attack and would place Great Britain in politically advantageous position.

Disadvantageous. An assault on Stanley would result in civilian casualties and significant political criticism. A military operation would be difficult with the risk of not being able to capture Stanley before a diplomatic solution agreed. Absence of roads places a greater reliance on helicopters.

OVERALL CONCLUSIONS. Neither solutions offer rapid success. An assault on Stanley would result in significant civilian casualties, damage and political criticism. *Option 1* of an amphibious attack would be costly in terms of casualty. *Option 2* would necessarily be military methodical and would probably force a diplomatic solution. A British night landing and the grounding of Argentine aircraft would increase the chance of success.

On 19 April, Brigade HQ began planning Operation Order No. 13/82 to transfer 12th Regiment at Comodoro Rivadavia to Commandante Luis Piedra Buena, a small Patagonian township in Santa Cruz Province named after an Argentine naval officer and patriot who had consolidated national sovereignty during the 1880s at a time when the land was virtually uninhabited and not protected by the state. The deployment began on the 21st, however in the atmosphere of order, counter-order and disorder, on the 22nd, Brigadier-General Parada received his third change in orders when General Galtieri, without reference to the Military Committee, cancelled the Patagonia deployment and ordered 3rd Brigade to deploy to Las Malvinas. The regiment was deploying by rail and road to reinforce the border with Chile when a police car overtook the convoy and handed Lieutenant-Colonel Piaggi new orders, he was horrified because most of his soldiers were Class 1963 conscripts with a month's experience and were equipped and clothed for jungle warfare. Private Pablo Vicente Córdoba from the new arrivals (*Soldados Clase '63*) in the 4th Infantry Regiment recalls the accelerated boot-camp training he received under Sub-Lieutenant Oscar Augusto Silva (killed in action on Mount Tumbledown):

> In an outing to Camp Ávalos to carry out practice shooting with live ammunition I had to open fire with an Instalaza 88.9mm anti-tank rocket launcher. He showed me the proper technique of shooting, with me hitting the target 200 meters in front and I was congratulated by the regimental commander, for being the only soldier to hit the target in the first go. From that moment my combat role in the company was that of a rocket-launcher operator.[1]

Five of the platoon commanders had recently graduated from the National Army Academy and hardly knew their men. Fortunately, sufficient Class 1962 reservists responded to provide some experience. First Lieutenant Ignacio Benjamín Gorritti, the B Company commander, recalled the 12th Regiment's departure from Comodoro Rivadavia. 'From the beginning we knew how important the Malvinas were. It was a kind of love; we were going to defend something that was ours. Reaching the "Malvinas" was like a dream to most Argentines. There was no need for speeches.' Matters did not improve when reports of a British submarine lurking offshore closed the sea route to Stanley and flights were prevented from landing due to strong winds blowing across the runway; indeed, some aircraft returned to Argentina, an unwelcome, unnerving experience for the many conscripts who had never flown. When the brigade arrived, the troops were initially confined to 'Tent City' – a chilly and uncomfortable tented camp on the road from the Airport to Stanley. There were still too few vehicles to move troops and equipment and the previous congestion on the one road once again led to frustration and delays moving troops, guns, ammunition and equipment.

The 4th and 5th Regiments and 3rd Engineer Company returned to being under HQ 3rd Brigade command. The 220 engineers of 601 Combat Engineer Company played a crucial role and provided a platoon to reinforce 9 (9th Brigade) Engineer Company, two platoons to 3 Engineer (3rd Brigade) Company and 2 Platoon supported 5th Regiment at Port Howard. Of the 272 all ranks in 10 (10th Brigade)

Engineer Company, 3 Platoon provided general support and military police; 4 Platoon supported Stanley Airport; and other platoons were in direct support of B Company, 4th Infantry Regiment, B Company, 7th Infantry Regiment and 8th Infantry Regiment at Fox Bay.

The 4th Airborne Artillery Group was part of the 4th Airborne Brigade and consisted of three batteries, each with six M-56 105mm OTO Melara howitzers. The regiment was commanded by Lieutenant-Colonel Carlos Quevedo and numbered 362 all ranks. Originally tasked with joining 3rd Brigade on 22 April, 13 guns were tasked to support 10th Brigade and four guns were detached to 9th Brigade at Goose Green. The regiment was limited to 70 tons of artillery ammunition. The first aircraft were en route from Pajas Blancas Airport in Córdoba by midnight on the 23rd; 601 Combat Aviation Company helicopters flew the group to Mount Wall as part of the reserve. There were still too few vehicles to move troops and equipment and the only decent road was prone to traffic jams. Morale among troops unfamiliar with carrying fighting order and heavy rucksacks in the strong, bracingly cold winds dipped. On the next day, the 30th, Brigadier-General Parada ordered one battery and two guns, a jeep and 70 shells to deploy to Port Howard.

Two days after being warned to prepare to fly at 7am on the 25th, it was not until 6pm that the first aircraft took off, however poor weather and high winds at Stanley prevented some aircraft landing. Nevertheless, Brigadier-General Parada, his Brigade HQ and 5th Regiment were welcomed by Major-General Garcia and Brigadier-General Menéndez at Stanley Airport. Garcia explained that President Galtieri had decided, after his recent visit, that a regiment should deploy to Port Howard and Darwin and the Falklands Joint Command heliborne force should support the settlements at San Carlos, Port Salvador and Fitzroy on East Falklands and also on West Falklands. Brigadier-General Daher briefed Brigadier-General Parada that 3rd Brigade would defend West Falklands and it would be transferred on the *Monsunen* and by helicopter; in the meantime, it would remain at 'Tent City'.

Lieutenant-Colonel Soria, commanding 4th Regiment, had expressed concern that the concentration of troops at 'Tent City' was vulnerable to air attack. Indeed, during the early hours of 1 May, the British task force opened its offensive with Harriers bombing and attacking targets, including the 4th Airborne Artillery Group lined up on the road waiting to embark on a ship at 7.40am and losing a jeep destroyed by naval gunfire at the airport. When the group was then ordered to reinforce 3rd Artillery Group, except for a battery to support 4th Regiment, the guns moved to Ramp Head, about 2 kilometres from the airfield. Three days later, Brigadier Daher selected gun positions to support 6th Regiment and 25th Regiment defending the coast south of Stanley.

Between 24 and 29 April 12th Regiment was flown from Comodoro Rivadavia to the Falklands and deployed to the cold, windy heights of Two Sisters and Mount Harriet. On its left was the 7th Infantry Regiment on Mount Longdon and Wireless Ridge supported by a 10th Engineer Company platoon. An officer commanding a detachment of two NCOs and 18 soldiers protected the Mount Challenger helicopter fuel store. The regiment lost B Company when Captain Eduardo Corsiglia, the regimental adjutant, and First-Lieutenant Ignacio Gorritti and B *La Florida* Company were detached to the heliborne reserve under the control of Commander Littoral and renamed Combat Team *Solari*. Tasks included reconnaissance, counter-attack against enemy penetration into the Mount Long Island and Mount Low Sectors and reinforcing the defence of Stanley, especially the sectors defended by 3 and 6 Regiments. On 25 April, the British opened its offensive by recapturing South Georgia.

By the end of April, the three infantry brigades deployed on Las Malvinas were in three areas of responsibility. The Littoral Army Force defended ground outside Port Stanley with orders to deny the enemy any manoeuvre space so as to bolster the defence of Port Stanley, which was assessed as the strategic objective to defend, support Argentine forces on West Falkland and be ready to operate in isolation as ordered. 601 Combat Aviation Company was expected to provide maximum helicopter mobility. 4th Regiment in Port Stanley was tasked to be a helicopter-borne reserve for the Littoral Force and be permanently ready as a rapid reaction force and be prepared to cope with emergencies. When the force was instructed to defend the San Carlos area, C Company, 25th Regiment formed Combat Team *Güemes* of two platoons and a support platoon with two 81mm mortars and two 105mm recoilless guns from

12th Regiment. First-Lieutenant Carlos Esteban commanded the combat team with orders to occupy Port San Carlos and Point 234, usually known as Fanning Head (*Promontorio Güemes*) guarding the entrance into San Carlos Water.

The Puerto Argentino Army Force Area of Responsibility was to prevent the loss of the important Fresinet Peninsula east of the Murrell River and north of Blanco Bay and the area of East Falkland to the east of the general line of Port Salvador, Mount Simon and Fitzroy. The Port Darwin area, which included Military Air Base Goose Green, was the responsibility of the Argentine Air Force.

The Planned Reserve consisted of the Malvinas Army Force, consisting of a heli-transportable company, Combat Team *Solari*, on Mount Kent for rapid deployment to any part of the Islands. An additional proposal to deploy Marines did not take place. While the strategy focused on maintaining the principle of a defensive effort within the area of Port Stanley, providing the reinforcement of Port Darwin and occupying Port Howard and Fox Bay on West Falkland, the armed forces largely operated independently. Supply between East and West Falklands was the responsibility of the Argentine Navy. The Air Force and Navy had the responsibility of delivering supplies to Malvinas and evacuating casualties.

CHAPTER 6

South Georgia: Operation *Paraquat*

Following a request from Navy Captain César Trombetta for support reinforcements at South Georgia, Vice-Admiral Lombardo agreed, in spite of the Military Junta instructing that South Georgia was not to be reinforced. Military Junta member Admiral Anaya authorised the mission, as the garrison there would have to pass the winter without any support. Admiral Edgardo Otero, who formerly commanded the infamous Navy Petty-Officer of Mechanic interrogation centre, was, by 1980, commanding the Argentine Navy's Antarctic operations. He sought to repeat the 1976 Operation *Sol* in South Georgia by establishing a military base in Operation *Alpha*, however Admiral Lombardo feared that such an operation would undermine the Recovery of Malvinas. However, in spite of assuring Admiral Lombardo he would not support Operation *Alpha*, Admiral Anaya had a meeting with Otero and approved it. Among those involved in Operation *Sol* was Trombetta. The Argentines were unaware that lurking under the surface was the powerful nuclear submarine HMS *Dreadnought* conducting periscope surveys and watching for potential threats from the Argentine Navy.

Of the four Argentine submarines, the *Santa Fe* (S-21) was one of the two Balao-class and the other two were German Type 209 class. The *Santa Fe*, formerly USS *Catfish*, had been commissioned in March 1945. It was one of four submarines in the Argentine Navy transferred from the US Navy in 1971 and was commanded by Corvette-Captain Horacio Bicain. Batteries had been fitted in 1945 and it had been converted to a Guppy II in the late 1940s. While the ship's radar was still reliable, the retractable snorkel was liable to betray its presence. On 9 April, the *Santa Fe* departed from Mar del Plata Naval Base with 11 Marine signallers and technicians on board tasked with restoring utility services on South Georgia. Also on board was Group Golf consisting of nine Marines with Swedish BANTAM wire-guided, anti-tank missiles and armed with rifles and machine-guns. Bicain had orders to remain undetected, to break contact if detected and not to attack any ships.

On 20 April, the same day the task force began arriving at Ascension, an RAF Victor was flying an approximately 15-hour mission from Ascension to conduct radar reconnaissance of 150,000 square miles of the South Atlantic. The Argentine Air Force also performed surveillance flights with their Boeing 707 and C-130, detecting the task group on its way to South Georgia, and even HMS *Endurance* hiding in the area. Royal Marines landing parties from HMS *Endurance* probing into Saint Andrews Bay, South Georgia, contacted isolated British Antarctic Survey field parties, including the wildlife film makers Cindy Buxton and Annie Price, who were making a film about king penguins, and elected not to be evacuated. A sailor showed the two women how to use a pistol.

The *Santa Fe* lurked not far off King Edward's Point BAS jetty and landed the Marines in boats during a night of moonless cloud cover. At about 5am on the 25th, the task force declared the South Georgia Exclusion Zone, however a communications failure on *Conqueror* patrolling 70 miles to the west of South Georgia meant that the reported threat was not received. About the same time, Bicain was navigating through Cumberland Bay and had decided to remain on the surface because there was known to be an unchartered submerged rock in the entrance to the bay. He also wanted to keep the submarine close to the steep rocky cliffs from which the radar emissions would bounce and prevent the British detecting him and then he intended to dive.

Meanwhile, British warships were searching Cumberland Bay. At about 9am, the HMS *Antrim* sighted the submarine and attacked with 1943 depth charges – one bounced into the sea from the deck whilst the second one exploded and ruptured the port fuel tank. Captain Bicain decided to return to Caleta Capitán Vago (King Edwards Point).

A petty officer on the bridge lost both legs when a missile passed through the conning tower. A torpedo dropped by HMS *Brilliant's* Lynx passed underneath the submarine. Three Wasps firing anti-shipping missiles (AS-12) and machine-guns also attacked. Argentines ashore provided covering fire as the submarine limped back to King Edward Point at 11am.

Within the hour, a force of Royal Marines and SBS, and the SAS, who insisted on deploying a squadron, landed at Grytviken and, supported by naval gunfire and helicopters, forced Lieutenant-Commander Luis Lagos, the Argentine land forces commander, and Lieutenant-Commander Bicain, commanding officer of the *Santa Fe*, to signal their decision to surrender. That evening, the Argentines signed the Instrument of Surrender followed by Captain Young of HMS *Antrim* and Major John Sheridan, second-in-command of 42 Commando, M Company.

Meanwhile at Leith, Astiz and his *Buzos Tácticos* in booby-trapped buildings had tried to persuade Captain Barker, the HMS *Endurance* commanding officer, to land by helicopter on the mined football field. However, the Argentines were outnumbered and the next morning, Astiz signed the Instrument of Surrender on board HMS *Plymouth* at Leith in front of Captain Pentreath, the commanding officer, with Barker still smarting furiously at Astiz's subterfuge. The recapture of South Georgia allowed a message to be sent: 'Be pleased to inform Her Majesty that the White Ensign flies alongside the Union Jack in South Georgia. God save the Queen.' Astiz was then kept isolated from other prisoners as he was deemed a possible 'troublemaker'. When the British Ambassador in Madrid sent a signal quoting a Spanish newspaper alleging Astiz's record in the Dirty War in Argentina, he was sent by sea to the UK via Ascension Island and held in Royal Military Police custody in Chichester. When Argentina surrendered, he was taken to Ascension Island and was repatriated by an International Committee of Red Cross chartered plane and flown via Montevideo.

By 26 April, the *Santa Fe* was obstructing the use of the jetty and an agreement was reached with Lieutenant-Commander Bicain that he and six crew, escorted by a small Royal Marines escort, should move the boat using battery power. However, as the submarine motored across Grytviken Bay, it developed a list and Bicain obtained permission from Captain Coward, who usually commanded HMS *Brilliant* and was the submariner who had inspected the *Santa Fe*, for the list to be resolved. As Petty Officer Felix Artuso was operating the compressor sticks to level the submarine, one of the Royal Marines thought he was trying to scuttle the submarine and shot him. The control panel had been designated as a 'forbidden' panel. The court of inquiry took statements, including from the prisoners-of-war, and concluded that the Royal Marine had fired at Petty Officer Artuso in self-defence in order to protect the lives of those on board. There was general agreement there were no grounds for military disciplinary proceedings or referring the matter to a civil court. In accordance with Article 121 of the Geneva Convention on the Treatment of Prisoners of War, copies of the report were sent to Brazil, as the Protecting Power, and the International Committee of the Red Cross. Artuso is buried at the Norwegian Lutheran Church Cemetery, Grytviken, South Georgia. He is the only veteran to be buried in the cemetery.

Meanwhile, on the 30th, Cindy Buxton and Annie Price had completed their documentary undisturbed and were collected by a helicopter and flown first to HMS *Antrim*, then to HMS *Antelope* en route to Ascension Island and then boarded a flight to the UK. Meanwhile, the Argentine prisoners and Davidoff's workers captured at South Georgia were kept in RFA *Tidespring* and were then taken to Ascension Island and interned in a prison camp and repatriated via Montevideo after Argentina had surrendered in June.

CHAPTER 7

Waiting for the Task Force

Argentine Air Force and commercial support was efficient with several air terminals and 243 flights managing 13,000 individual transfers to and from the island and 1,200 tons of cargo, much delivered after the imposition of the British blockade.

While the isolation of Ascension Island provided the task force with some defence from Argentine interference, the island was an obvious intelligence and sabotage target and consequently the Argentine Navy took advantage of the expanse of the South Atlantic to task cargo ships and trawlers to scout for the task force and collect intelligence. On 24 April, the 10,409-ton Empresa Líneas Maritimas Argentinas (ELMA) cargo ship *Río de la Plata* was noted loitering off Ascension collecting intelligence. One intelligence report suggested the freighter had recently been in Bilbao, and air photographs taken of the ship near Ascension suggested canoes or mini-submarines beneath tarpaulins and therefore the likelihood of Tactical Divers on board. The next day, after a yellow foreign lifejacket was found floating offshore, 45 Commando conducted a cordon and search operation that concentrated on the fields and woods of Green Mountain. The sabotage threat of divers prompted Operation *Awkward,* in which naval sentries patrolled the upper decks of ships at anchor, seamen in whalers circled their ships dropping small depth-charges, divers regularly inspected hulls of ships and warships patrolled a racetrack from English Bay to the beaches off Wideawake and the horizon. One suspected submarine contact resulted in ships scattering from the anchorage, which then became a nightly routine.

In fact, on 19 April, Captain Carlos Benchetrit, to his surprise, had received an encrypted message from ELMA HQ ordering the *Río de la Plata* to divert its course towards Ascension Island so that, at a distance of no less than 12 miles, it could identify British ships that could be found in its surroundings. As the ship approached the island on 23 April at 5pm, the crew observed about 15 ships and listened to VHF communications, which Benchetrit recorded on a cassette player and that night sent an encrypted message with the result of his observation and identification of the vessels. Argentine intelligence cross-checked that information with that collected by an Air Force Boeing 707. A few days later Benchetrit received a new order to return to Ascension for a new passage around the island about 2 miles away, collecting more information about the ships and noting the intense movement of helicopters. He continued his task until the ship was flown over by Sea King helicopters and was heard on VHF that HMS *Antelope* would come out to intercept him, at which point he decided to move away and return to Argentina.

The British offensive opened early on 1 May with Operation *Black Buck One*, the first of seven long-range air raids on Military Air Base Malvinas by Vulcan bombers operating from Ascension Island, which bombed targets at Stanley. Although 22 freefall bombs were dropped, only one hit the runway and Air Force support ground personnel swiftly repaired the crater, which meant the airstrip was operating again within 24 hours. Further low-level raids by Sea Harriers on the airstrips at Stanley and Goose Green inspired the BBC correspondent Brian Hanrahan to announce to the world, 'I counted them all out. I counted them all in,' and, in so doing, effectively advised the air defence that it was failing. After Royal Navy warships had begun shelling Argentine positions on Stanley Common on 4 May, Civil Affairs formed a committee to survey houses suitable for air raid shelters. Civilians sheltered in a warehouse. On the same day, Lieutenant Nick Taylor RN, of 800 Naval Air Squadron, was shot down and killed attacking Military Air Base *Condor* at Goose Green.

Frequent raids by the carrier-borne Fleet Air Arm Harriers on Argentine ground forces defensive positions and the support and ground attack aircraft and helicopter bases on the Falkland Islands led to the Task Force achieving local superiority and limited the operational capability of the Argentine ground forces to conduct ground operations.

Wing-Commander Pedrozo had ordered the two Air Force CH-47 Chinooks to park close to the Goose Green air defence umbrella. Nevertheless, on 1 May, three Sea Harriers caught the defenders by surprise at the cost of seven Air Force personnel killed, 14 wounded, one Pucara destroyed, two damaged and ammunition exploding. Pedrozo censured Braghini for the unsatisfactory state of air defence, and when the gunners changed to a better position on the ground and were alerted to Sea Harriers approaching up Choiseul Sound, they shot one down. First-Lieutenant Esteban summoned the civilians to a meeting at the community hall to discuss their safety. However, Eric Goss, the farm manager, refused until threatened by a CH-47 Chinook pilot who had spent the night at Goose Green wielding a large hunting knife. Pedrozo announced that since a British landing was imminent, all 113 residents were to be confined to the hall – for their own safety. Lieutenant-Colonel Piaggi gave another reason for protecting the locals from 'the rage of the Air Force men, who had lost so many colleagues.'

Sanitation in the community hall had become distinctly uncomfortable because running water had failed on the third day, the toilets were blocked and consequently there was some dysentery among the internees. The Argentinians agreed to bring seawater in barrels for the toilets; and Mike Robson did sterling work keeping them going. Two young men, Bob McLeod and Ray Robson, both radio hams, found an old broken radio in a junk cupboard. Once they had repaired it, some of the internees listened to the BBC World Service every evening while others made a noise at the windows to cover the crackling of the broadcast. At the end of the first week the Argentines allowed two women to cook up a big meal, with bread and cakes, in the settlement cookhouse which was then taken to the community hall. Considering that internees were cramped together in a small place, everybody remained generally good-natured.

The International Committee of the Red Cross (ICRC) was formed in 1863 primarily to protect civilians. The Swiss government called conferences which agreed:

1. The First Geneva Convention "for the Amelioration of the Condition of the Wounded and Sick in Armed Forces in the Field" in 1864.

2. The Second Geneva Convention "for the Amelioration of the Condition of Wounded, Sick and Shipwrecked Members of Armed Forces at Sea" in 1929.

3. The Third Geneva Convention "relative to the Treatment of Prisoners of War" in 1949, which replaced the 1929 Geneva Convention that dealt with prisoners of war.

4. The Fourth Geneva Convention "relative to the Protection of Civilian Persons in Time of War" introduced the protection of civilians and occupied territory, also in 1949.

While Great Britain had developed a long and profitable relationship with the ICRC, Argentina had no such relationship. Senior Argentine officers appeared to be unaware of the Fourth Convention. For instance, they breached the principles of not supplying the ICRC with details of internees, their location and markings of the community hall as an internment camp. Officers also appeared to have little interest in the welfare of the internees, which included children, a baby aged four months and three octogenarians. No blankets were supplied, the adequacy of the sanitation was not checked and, on the first day, it had not been until the evening that Goss had persuaded a passing Air Force sergeant aircraft-fitter and his four conscripts to allow him and Keith Baillie to 'do a shop' at the farm store. In the darkness, they filled two boxes with Rivita, cream crackers, margarine, spam, tea, coffee, Horlicks, Ovaltine, cocoa, dry powder milk, Marmite and Bovril, and when Goss mentioned that it was hardly enough to feed 113 people, the sergeant allowed four more boxes to be filled and then instructed two of his men to help carry the supplies to the community hall. Suspicious that resupply could be intermittent, Goss rationed the adults to two Rivitas and a slice of spam per day. The children and the elderly had their fill. Fortunately, other 'ration runs' were organised.

Goss eventually won permission for three Spanish-speaking women to cook meals in the galley. When a shepherd and his dogs were given permission to gather in his sheep and some were slaughtered, mutton was stolen by hungry Argentine soldiers restricted to one square meal a day. Goss doubled the slaughter and agreed to ensure that Argentines received water, which gave him the opportunity to conceal two petrol drums under bundles of fencing in the transit warehouse from search parties. Brian Hewitt, a shepherd, was using his motorcycle and his dogs to check the flocks on Goat Rincon, when he was intercepted by an Army Puma, hustled into the helicopter and flown to Goose Green – without his dogs – and confined to a chair outside the galley for an hour until Goss demanded his release. When the Argentines suspected that Harrier raids were being guided by messages passed to the task force, the community hall was searched. Nothing was found. Several detainees were released in the middle of the month. When Goss invited Mr William Bowles, a former legislative councillor, expert carpenter and Spanish linguist and his wife to ride out the war at Goose Green, Bowles built an air raid shelter underneath the community hall floorboards. Nanny McCullum, aged 82, was unable to use the shelter and so he jury-rigged one from a mattress.

At Goose Green, Goss convinced the Argentines that strange lights seen in Falkland Sound were not British Special Forces but moonlight reflecting off seaweed-covered rocks. The imposition of the extension of the Total Exclusion Zone to 200 miles on 6 May led to provisions running short, and military discipline began collapsing as soldiers foraged. Piaggi initiated an investigation and found that a window had been broken in the settlement supply store, and established that some sweets, cigarettes and alcoholic beverages were missing, so imposed close surveillance to avoid repetitions of the event. When Sub-Lieutenant Gómez Centurión demanded provisions from the farm store at gunpoint, Goss insisted he sign for the supplies and then implied that Argentine logistics must be chaotic if the soldiers were expected to fight without adequate rations. Centurión replied, 'No cheek, Goss!' The next day, Centurión said that the jetty warehouse was cold at night and demanded better accommodation. Again, Goss antagonised Centurión, 'What sort of war have you come to fight? First no rations and now no tents or bivouac bags.' The agitated Centurión again threatened, 'Your cheek will get you shot, Goss'. Goss was concerned that the four empty houses in Goose Green and two in Darwin could be converted into defensive positions and suggested Darwin Boarding School as an alternative. School classes could be re-located.

On 1 May, the task force commenced its offensive with air raids. The weather conditions had become wintery. The Argentines were nervous, and every night 601 Commando Company internal security patrols checked areas assessed to be most at risk, such as the racecourse which was identified as a probable landing zone for enemy helicopters and the nearby Government House. Patrols were often accompanied by intelligence officers. A daily psychological warfare campaign broadcast from HMS *Hermes* usually included a daily *Doctor's Hour* suggesting a ceasefire and a helicopter would collect those Argentines who wished to surrender. Meanwhile, the National Guard Santo Patrol was provided the defence of Joint Command Falklands Command Post in Stanley.

It was inevitable that such broadcasts became the subject of chatter in the settlements. Robin Pitulaga at San Salvador suggested that it would be worthwhile advising the Argentines. Inevitably, these broadcasts attracted radio chatter among the farms and Robin, the owner of San Salvador, agreed to reply to *Hermes*. The Pitulaga family had arrived in the Falklands in 1838 from Gibraltar and Robin was the third generation and a farmer, a member of the Sheep Owner Association and a councillor. His intervention resulted in a Puma and Augusta helicopter flying counter-intelligence officers and 1st Platoon arriving at San Salvador where they surrounded the settlement and conducted several searches. Pitulaga admitted to Major Castagneto that he had communicated with HMS *Hermes* not to pass on information but to convey Admiral Woodward's suggestion to Governor Menéndez of a ceasefire. Showing his Union Jack, he said he was English and had no qualms about talking to his countrymen. Pitulaga was then arrested and flown to Moody Brook, arriving in the middle of a naval bombardment. Everyone was nervous. He was transferred to Stanley Police Station where he experienced 'Mutt', the aggressive military police officer, and 'Jeff', the reasonable one suggesting he write a statement, which 'Mutt' then tore up as nonsense. Pitulaga was placed in a cell and that night was joined by a dozen local men arrested after breaching curfew for drinking in a pub until, at midnight, he was interrogated by a counter-intelligence officer who marched him to Victory Green on the sea front and, professing fury, confined him overnight to a trench occupied by two nervous conscripts. The next day, Bloomer-Reeve ordered his release and confined him to the Upland Goose Hotel where his sister was married to the owner, Desmond King, and remained with them until the Argentine surrender.

The next day, Argentine newspapers published Menéndez's answer to Woodward's offer to surrender, 'No way because we are winning. Send in the Little Prince [Prince Andrew] and come to take us!' The response had come from Admiral Otero, who issued that expression in response to the reiteration of the surrender messages heard at the communications centre. Menéndez understood that the issue was trivial and that he would not have given that answer. Later, he was surprised to learn that the answer was attributed to him but thought that there was no point in making a denial.

The invitation to surrender message was also heard on the radio in Fox Bay East by Major Oscar Minorini Lima, in command of 9 Combat Engineers Company, who personally answered the call. The reply came from an officer on board HMS *Hermes*, who radioed a recorded message from Woodward, offering him an honourable surrender and withdrawal to mainland Argentina with all personnel and equipment. Lima asked if that was all and answered to the affirmative with, 'Tell the Admiral to kiss my ass!' Richard Cockwell, manager of the establishment in Fox Bay, was at the scene, and very worried. In a loud voice he said, in English, 'They are going to kill us all!'[1]

One person who represented the Islanders was Monsignor Daniel Spraggon, an Englishman and the papal representative of the Falkland Islands and South Georgia. He wore his formal daytime regalia and regularly intervened, for instance when the prominent citizens were transferred to Fox Bay. He warned Governor Menéndez that the Falklands was not a dictatorship. Menéndez insisted the internees would remain detained. Lieutenant-Colonel Pedrozo and Wing-Commander Piaggi eventually visited them and reiterated that the internees were being locked up for their own protection and denied that they were prisoners.

On 5 May at Goose Green, the Special Order on Civilian Affairs was issued by Piaggi reminding the Army of their obligations. Pedrozo circulated the order among the Air Force personnel. On the same day, the population was subjected to a thorough medical review and the clinical data and medication listed with the signature of each person examined. Special attention was paid to the 30 children, and special measures were arranged for their feeding and care by parents. At the request of some families, some degree of privacy was planned. The next day, Major Frontera, Captain Sánchez and First Lieutenant (Medical) Adjigogovich checked the senior members of the community and found that Mr and Mrs Anderson, aged 82 and 78 years respectively and Mr and Mrs Finlayson, aged 79 and 78 years respectively, were in perfect mental and physical condition.

Brigadier-General Menéndez anticipated special forces incursions, electronic surveillance and naval bombardment prior to a landing. An Argentine intelligence assessment dated mid-May concluded that the British strategy would be to recapture as much of the Stanley peninsula as possible either by a high-risk direct assault against Army Group Stanley Sector or a low-risk amphibious assault north east of Stanley, the aim being to adopt a favourable political bargaining position. San Carlos Water is mentioned as one of three possible landing sites, but its distance from Stanley was considered to be disadvantageous. Berkeley Sound to the north of Stanley was reckoned to be the favoured option because it could be achieved with minimum losses and was thus favourable to British public opinion. It was felt that the British would rely heavily upon helicopters.

Reconnaissance by 601 Commando Company was ceaseless, with patrols checking real and imagined reports, particularly in the northern sector of East Falklands which was considered the most likely approach. 2nd Section searching Windmill Island for a suspected enemy radio station found a Zodiac inflatable fitted with an outboard and lifejackets, one marked 'Hermes'. 3rd Section embarked in the Coastguard cutter *Islas Malvinas* on a patrol from Stanley to McBride Head, but the weather turned unpleasant and the following day the commandos gratefully filed ashore, miserable from seasickness. On 4 May, when Army Group Malvinas ordered Long Island to be searched in Operation *Margarita*, Mirage-III combat air patrols flown from the mainland also provided top cover for Pucaras and Mentors ground attack aircraft from Pebble Island, which were carrying out a detailed recce for an Amphibious Commando detachment landing from the *Las Malvinas* and 601

Commando Company inserted by Army helicopters. Midway through the operation, a deep weather front swept in from the south and it was cancelled. The approaching cold and wet weather attacked the morale of the soldiers in the defensive positions.

The *Narwhal* was one of several stern trawlers hired by the Argentine Navy to be part of an electronic intelligence screen spread across the South Atlantic. The skipper was Captain Asterio Wagata. On board in a cabin was Captain Juan Carlos González Llanos of the Argentine Navy Information Service. An aircraft first sighted the ship on 29 April lurking near the Carrier Battle Group, and HMS *Alacrity* was sent to intercept the vessel and warned it not to approach. However, the trawler continued to show interest and during the morning of 9 May, one of a pair of Sea Harriers bombing targets in the Stanley area diverted and dropped a 1,000-pound bomb on the trawler, but it failed to explode because it had been released below the prescribed height. At about 4pm, an SBS boarding party roped onto the ship from a helicopter and during their search, they found González Llanos and incriminating documents and equipment in his cabin and transferred him to HMS *Invincible*. The 24 crew were assessed to be genuine trawler men, including Omar Alberto Rupp, the boatswain, who had been killed in the attack and was buried at sea. An Argentine Army Puma responding to the distress call sent from *Narwal* was shot down by a Sea Dart missile fired by HMS *Coventry* and the crew of three were killed.

Meanwhile, Argentine ship crews defied the Maritime Exclusion Zone threat and aircrew demonstrated courage and tenacity to prevent the soldiers and Marines from being cut off. In spite of the lack of air cover and shortage of night flying equipment, the helicopter crews of 601 Combat Aviation Battalion overcame poor weather to transport troops, equipment and supplies.

After the *Rio Carcarañá* breached the Maritime Exclusion Zone on 26 April, she sailed from Stanley to Falkland Sound after the British attacks on May 1st, and some of the cargo, which included fuel and ammunition, was transferred to the naval transport ARA *Isla de Los Estados*, which then sailed during the afternoon of the 11th with orders to resupply the garrisons at Fox Bay and Goose Green. Soon after midnight, the frigate HMS *Alacrity,* on orders to penetrate the length of Falkland Sound from the south, located the ship as a radar signature off Swan Island in the middle of the Sound. Although the night was misty and star flares proved ineffective, *Alacrity* opened fire with its 4.5-inch gun and the *Isla de Los Estados* exploded. The Argentine naval authorities ignored reports from HQ 5th Regiment reporting a major explosion and did not mount a search and rescue operation until two days later when the ship did not arrive at its destination. A search for survivors by *Monsunen* located two, including the captain. Rear-Admiral Edgardo Aroldo Otero, the naval commander, analysed the incidents and concluded that there was increased risk in Falkland Sound. Otero had been the director of the Naval Mechanics School between 1980 and 1982 and was head of the Buenos Aires Naval Region. Brigadier-General Menéndez reviewed Otero's findings and ordered Lieutenant-Colonel Piaggi, the Mercedes Task Force commander and Commanding Officer 12th Regiment at Goose Green, to occupy San Carlos and provide warnings of landings in the Falkland Sound. Lieutenant-Colonel Repossi, commanding the Littoral Task Force on West Falklands instructed 5th and 8th Regiments to deploy observation posts to cover the northern and southern entrances to Falkland Sound.

The threat of special forces reconnaissance, the endless chore of repairing and improving trenches, bunkers and gun pits, the inability to dry wet clothing in the cold and rain, the difficulty of keeping weapons maintained and the necessity of maintaining a state of almost permanent vigilance led to about two-thirds of troops being alert each night; opportunities to rest were few. Lieutenant-Colonel Comini, commanding 3rd Regiment covering the Stanley southern beaches, later recorded that in spite of being allocated two warehouses in Stanley to rest his men at 200 per day, the combination of the psychological pressures of the shelling and bombing, the need to remain alert for landings, the jamming of communications and 60 days in foxholes destroyed the will of his men to fight. Air raids and naval bombardment of Stanley Common and the military air base demoralised the troops. 6th Infantry Regiment near the 3rd Artillery Group, a prime target, experienced 50 1,000lbs, 153 500lbs and nine cluster bomb attacks and 1,200 naval shells landing, totalling an estimated 130 tons of high explosive impacting in its sector, with most exploding around the airfield.

Responsibility for military and naval supply lay with Commander, IV (Logistics) at the Argentine Ministry of Defence and provincial logistic centres supporting arsenals, supply services and medical support at all levels. However, such were the security concerns compromising the Recovery during the planning period that Las Malvinas had not been listed in the Strategic Military Directive.

For instance, the Army Transport Directorate was instructed to adapt the plans and procedures developed for deployments in Patagonia to be used for movement centres at Comodoro Rivadavia and Rio Gallegos supporting the Malvinas operation. However, the absence of a joint Army, Navy and Air Force strategy meant strategies to develop the movement of men, transport and cargo did not exist.

There was, for instance, no naval representation locating commercial cranes, allocating space on cargo ships and replacing ineffective port labour. Support was based largely on assumptions and strategies were undermined by inter-service rivalry. The extensive rail network using pre-existing familiar methods gained on exercises filled the gaps to ports and airfields.

The impact of the 30 April Total Exclusion Zone and concerns about logistics led to General Menéndez encouraging Lombardo, when there were disagreements within the Military Committee, that such matters should be referred to the Military Junta.

Morale dived further among the Argentines on 12 May when the Military Garrison Joint Command instructed that prepared meals were to be restricted to one a day.

The Argentine practice of using field kitchens often meant lukewarm or cold food for those at the back of the queue and discipline and morale developed into a serious logistic failure. One commentator noted,

> The breakdown in discipline and morale ultimately derived from the operational logistical failures. One veteran later said to journalists 'Some of us were tortured because we were starving and tried to grab some cookies or to butcher a sheep…' All of this paints a very dreary portrait, revealing a failure of leadership that went well beyond the Junta and the armed forces' planners in Buenos Aires.[2]

The Logistical Operations Centre was responsible for the delivery of groceries and rations usually every three or four days, which was not sufficient to provide hot meals to all of the troops, leading to many receiving substandard rations and eating cold meals in freezing temperatures.

The 4th Infantry Regiment defending Mount Harriet used lorries to tow the standard 250-ration mobile field kitchens to a track below and then along a track up to company quartermaster positions known as 'ranchos'. While troops were encouraged to eat in order to maintain energy reserves in the cold, strong wind and rain, a kitchen pot used for making a chocolate drink could take five hours to heat. Medical officers were encouraged to develop menus to maintain calorie levels.

British observation posts could identify positions from the smoke of field kitchens, the tapping of a triangle summoning troops 'Come to the cookhouse', and the noted timings of the arrival of rations trucks. When the 'ranchos' were shelled, orders were issued that field kitchens were to withdraw at least a kilometre and fatigue parties were assembled to collect the containers. This was onerous and soldiers carrying the heavy containers along slippery clay paths risking falling, spilling onto the ground. In 4th Regiment, soldiers nicknamed this mishap the 'Sapucai Samba', which is an encouragement in Corrientes Province. Platoons then tended to organise two or three ranchos which helped to introduce a fairer distribution of rations and reduced the need to search for food, however the quantity was never enough and patrols raided flocks of sheep and purchased sheep from 'kelpers', and soldiers received food parcels from parents and welfare organisations such as the Rural Society of Buenos Aires. The 12th Infantry Regiment Medical Officer at Goose Green, noted that in the first fortnight of May his Medical Section had observed that the platoons in the North Sector of Goose Green were experiencing ration deficiencies due for several reasons, including lack of containers for the preparation and distribution of food, the lack of thermal containers, spillages along the three miles from Goose Green to the North Sector, and changes in the tactical situation which meant difficulties in calculating appropriate distributions. The consequence was that Argentines were losing about 50 per cent of their body weight which led to loss of energy, sleep and fitness. Infrequent supply, even by air drop, to West Falklands led to short rations. When a field kitchen with 5th Infantry Regiment (Task Force 'Yapeyú') at Port Howard became unserviceable, the shortage of food and accompanying shortage of adequate winter clothing led to complaints and ill-discipline. Punishments included soldiers being staked out and others being buried. At least three conscripts died. A mechanical engineer non-commissioned officer managed to repair the split gasoline of a field kitchen with soap from the settlement store and then converted its tank into two 200-litre bins that supported the Command Post and four infantry companies. However, the taste of fuel in food lingered.

When General Menéndez learnt of the logistic failures on 15 May and several senior officers questioned Army leadership, President Galtieri insisted on the fundamental principle of resolving logistic and command issues before they became major problems and highlighted the need for effective co-ordination between the Army, Navy and Air Force. A fortnight later, 4th Regiment on Mount Harriet and Two Sisters abandoned field kitchens in favour of the issue of US Type C cold-weather ration packs, which raised morale.

Inexperience in expeditionary warfare, poor logistic planning, failure of senior level leadership and planning led to the breakdowns in discipline while poor planning and intelligence failures to recognise that the Task Force had years of operational and logistic experience soon undermined Operation *Rosario*.

In an extensive signal from General Menéndez to Lombardo on 15 May, several senior officers questioned the leadership of the Commander-in-Chief of the Army, President Galtieri and emphasised the basic principle of resolving logistic and command issues before they became major problems. They also highlighted the need for effective co-ordination between the Army, Navy and Air Force and exploiting every opportunity to weaken the enemy before they landed.

For instance, the Comodoro Rivadavia Logistic Operations Centre managed several supporting operations centres, including one that moved supplies to the Falklands. Commanders had learnt to predict air defence and field artillery positions, however the weight of guns, lack of tractors and the characteristics of the soft terrain often meant that the one Chinook helicopter was busy. Ingenuity became a valuable asset.

Few, if any, conscripts had previously experienced naval gunfire and raids. The Military Junta acknowledged the concerns and on 22 May, the day after the British landed at San Carlos, the Centro de Operaciones Conjuntas (CEOPECON; Joint Operations Centre) was formed to co-ordinate operations at a strategic level. The three most senior commanders, Major-General Garcia of Fifth Corps, Vice-Admiral Lombardo, Commander, South Atlantic Theatre of Operations, and Major-General Weber, Commander, Strategic Air Force, agreed that Garcia had the deciding vote. CEOPECON was not a joint command and while it was an initiative to ease coordination, it was too late to be effective. In a damming report written after the war, General Rattenbach commented that,

> ... logistical operations did not unfold in an acceptable manner. It was useless to seek any coherence in the Junta's logistical planning before Operation *Rosario* and thereafter could discern only improvised logistical operations afterward... 5th and 12th Infantry Regiments lacked vehicles and ammunition and there was no internal transportation system to move the supplies they did have. This reduced their combat effectiveness by 40–50 percent before anyone had even fired a shot... Junior officers and soldiers experienced the worst of the inadequate planning in logistics, and this led to their mistreatment... There were deficiencies in the preparation and distribution of food, which had a negative impact on the troops' physical state and morale.[3]

Rattenbach singles out Brigadier-General Parada, who commanded the 3rd Brigade, for special criticism '... seems to have buried his head in the sand and chosen to remain... profoundly ignorant of the state of the forces under his command... He took up residence in a home in Puerto Argentino and was simply "absent".'

Meanwhile, the Argentine Navy conceived Operation *Algeciras* as a plan to sabotage a Royal Navy warship in Gibraltar and encourage the Royal Navy, with its NATO commitments, to remain in European waters rather than join the task force. The plan was developed by Admiral Anaya and was for frogmen based at Algeciras in Spain to swim to Gibraltar, attach limpet mines to a British warship and swim back to Algeciras. Admiral Eduardo Morris Girling, the chief of the Naval

Intelligence Service, was to manage the operation. The operational leader was a former naval officer and expert in underwater explosives, Máximo Nicoletti. His father had served with the successful Italian Navy underwater sabotage unit during the Second World War. Nicoletti had become involved with the Montoneros Argentine terrorist group and in 1974 had placed a remote-controlled bomb on a yacht that killed the chief of the Argentine Federal Police and his wife. After sabotaging the destroyer ARA *Santissima Trinidad* under construction in Ensenada dockyards, Buenos Aires Province, in 1975, he was arrested and sent to the Navy Mechanics School interrogation centre where he agreed to recruit three colleagues from the Montoneros and was moved to Spain. Among several targets selected at Gibraltar was a British oil tanker, however the group believed that an environmental disaster would undermine support for Argentina in Spain. Attacking the frigate HMS *Ariadne* en route to the South Atlantic on 2 May was rejected because Peru had just produced a comprehensive peace plan that Admiral Anaya believed might lead to a peaceful resolution. In the meantime, a car rental owner reported his suspicions of Nicoletti to Spanish police and Nicoletti was arrested. Spain had recently joined NATO and since Spanish Prime Minister Sotelo did not wish to cause tensions with the UK or with Argentina, the police decided to exploit his transferable skills, in particular handling terrorist explosive devices. Nicoletti and a colleague were shelved by the police and quietly returned to Buenos Aires via the Canary Islands – without advising the Spanish security services.

Air defence to prevent, destroy and reduce the consequences of enemy air attack is crucial. The two main targets at risk were at Stanley and Goose Green and the constant threat from the two Royal Navy aircraft carriers meant that after 1 May Argentine air defence was on constant yellow alert of an attack within less than 30 minutes, and red alert meant a raid within five minutes. The constant state of alert brought fatigue among the air defence gunners.

Argentine air defence was concentrated on the 460 men of 601 Air Defence Artillery Group grouped into two 35mm Oerlikon anti-aircraft guns batteries, each with six guns and a Roland Platoon of one launcher. The Roland is a mobile short-range surface-to-air missile with an operational range up to 8,000 metres and an altitude of 5,500 metres designed to engage enemy aircraft flying at speeds up to Mach 1.3 at altitudes between 20 metres and 5,500 metres with a maximum range of 6,300 metres. A pulse-doppler search radar with a range of 15 to 18 kilometres can track targets either by radar or an optical tracker. On 7 April, 602 Mixed Artillery Air Defence Group deployed with a Shorts Tiger Cat launcher in which each missile was capable of a maximum speed of 630mph and a ceiling of 4 miles. The 1st Marine Air Defence Group provided three Tiger Cats and 12 30mm Oerlikon guns. B Battery, 101 Air Defence Artillery Group provided eight 30mm Hispano Suiza cannons. AN/TPS-44 radar with a range of 300 kilometres proved useful in providing early warnings of enemy aircraft and ships positions. Four officers from HQ Air Defence Artillery were advisors.

While 601 Air Defence Artillery Group had early warnings out to 6 kilometres, generally the batteries experienced several obstacles, such as little intelligence, the identification of enemy aircraft and the nature of the environment. The mission, operational restrictions and rules for opening fire were not clear. During January and February 1982, platoon commanders, gun commanders, radar operators and fire directors achieved good results, but the Class 1963 gunners posted to the group had recently left basic training and were unfamiliar with systems, but about 50 per cent of Class 1962 conscript gunners were rejected. When the British imposed the 200-mile Maritime Exclusion Zone on 12 April and the *Ciudad de Córdoba* put into Puerto Deseado to shelter, the next day the battery commander instructed the guns to be unloaded, only for the order to be rescinded three days later as the ship was going to attempt to reach the Falklands. The gunners were issued with duvet winter jackets, goggles, gloves and woollen balaclavas. Although the Air Force loadmasters were unfamiliar with the characteristics of the guns for transportation, on 19 April, the first of 25 Air Force C-130 flights flew the group to Malvinas, but it was a week before it was operational.

Communications with Argentina were first managed by the Argentine Navy, but it was transferred to the Army with the arrival of 44 signallers of 181 Communication Battalion, which had been formed in November 1964 and was originally part of 10th Brigade. It set up in Port Stanley during the morning of Recovery Day with A Company providing the Main Communications Centre for HQ Falklands Theatre of Operations and supporting units in Port Stanley and Darwin in East Falkland and Fox Bay and Port Howard on West Falkland. B Company delivered an External Radio Net of three Multi-Channel Radio Sections, Internal Radio of four Teleprinter Sections and six portable Internal Radio Nets of six Radio-Telephone Sections. The Service Company provided Medical, Arsenal and Service Platoons with logistic support. Restrictions of consignments forced the battalion to reduce its radios to six portable Air Force equipment and four portable sensors, resulting in 11 miles of lines supported by telephone exchanges in Stanley.

The three brigade headquarters were each supported by a Communications Company. For instance, the 3rd Communication Company supporting 3rd Brigade deployed 31 signallers at Port Stanley with Central Traffic and Messenger, five Portable Radio-Telephone Sections, two Radio-Telephone Sections, a Line-Laying Section and Logistic Sections. Nine signallers supported 9th Communications Company. 9th Brigade brought a Special Communications System to support the defence of Stanley. As the number of troops increased, items were not taken to the Falklands, for instance 3rd Communications Company supporting 3rd Brigade was reduced to portable radios and no line. The situation was resolved with small detachments providing signal units in order to meet their basic requirements. The 11 miles of line laid to support communications in Stanley required considerable manpower and resources to repair lines cut in sabotage and from shelling. Two hundred and forty-five signallers supported 10th Brigade in Port Stanley. 601 (Static Communications) Section with six soldiers and 602 Electronic Operations Company, an electronic warfare unit, were both based in Port Stanley.

Concerned at the ease of the piratical penetration that had resulted in the sinking of *Isla de Los Estados*, HQ 3rd Brigade instructed Lieutenant-Colonel Piaggi, commanding 12th Infantry Regiment at Goose Green,

To take up position on Fanning Head to block the north entrance to establish an observation post overlooking the northern entrance to Falkland Sound by fire and to maintain gunfire control over San Carlos Bay and the surrounding area, so as to deny the enemy its use and allow easy access of friendly vessels to Port Howard and Darwin.[4]

Lieutenant-Colonel Piaggi selected First-Lieutenant Carlos Esteban, who had commanded C Company, 25th Regiment on Recovery Day, and explained that Army Group was concerned with the ease with which the ship had been sunk and ordered him under 12th Infantry Regiment Operation Order 12/82 (Block and Control of San Carlos) to establish a military presence at Port San Carlos and occupy Point 234 (Fanning Head) near Port San Carlos, a tussock-covered feature rising steeply to 768 feet which had a good view across Falkland Sound. Piaggi gave him a reinforced company of 60 soldiers. Esteban stated,

> My operation commenced on 14 May… A command post, consisting of a rifle section and a HQ and Supply Section was set up in the community centre and Hill 234 was re-occupied by a strong rifle section. For the next week, Combat Team *Eagle* rarely left Port San Carlos and concentrated on manning the observation post and doing some limited patrolling. There was little contact with the 'kelpers' [Islanders], except to requisition some sheep.[5]

At about 2pm on 15 May, helicopters landed Combat Team *Güemes* at Port San Carlos and Esteban requisitioned the community centre for his headquarters; it was warm and had ablutions. His signallers established communications with HQ 9th Brigade in Stanley, with HQ 12th Regiment at Goose Green and maintained a radio check with Point 234 every two hours. In the event that communications between the two places failed, he organised a route for messengers (runners). Esteban placed Second-Lieutenant Reyes and the Gun Section on Point 234 (Fanning Head). The detachment consisted of two 81mm mortars and two M-40 105mm recoilless rifles, which had an effective range out to 6,870 metres with supercharge ammunition, both from the 12th Regiment Support Platoon. The 25th Regiment provided a defence section from the 1st Rifle Platoon. Esteban imposed a strict regime to ensure that the 114 'kelpers' complied with his demands and confiscated weapons and communication equipment found during a search by the Rifle Platoon. Otherwise, the population carried on with their normal activities.

Pebble Island (Isla Borbón) lies to the north of West Falkland and is about 20 miles east to west and barely 100 metres wide at its narrowest point near the only settlement. The two principal features are the 237ft high Marble Mountain Peak at the western tip of the island and First Mountain, which, at 227ft, overlooks the settlement. The terrain is low, particularly to the east where there are several lakes and large ponds. The settlement lies roughly in the centre of the island. In 1982, it had a population of approximately 25 people mainly shepherding 25,000 sheep. A rough track runs west from the settlement to a croft on the lower southern slopes of Marble Mountain Peak. A jetty on the sheltered south shore is capable of handling the Falkland Islands Company coasters. A Royal Engineers Briefing Map dated April 1982 lists a 650ft grass strip east of the settlement and the other 1,000ft of beach below the high-water mark. Kelp could cause soft spots.

The Argentine Naval Air Command had carried out a detailed survey of all airstrips and when, on 24 April, Pebble Island was identified as having strategic value, Captain Adolfo Gaffoglio, a regular pre-war visitor and senior naval officer, authorised the establishment of Naval Air Station *Calderon*. Lieutenant Ricardo Marega and his 1st Platoon, H Company and a Support Platoon of four 75mm recoilless rifles and a MAG machine-gun group from 3rd Marines provided a defence force. The platoon consisted of 74 men, 21 of whom had served one year and 53 had served just three months. The Marines used the sheep-shearing shed, the guest house and an unoccupied house for accommodation. Lieutenant Marega had placed his command post in a bunker and instructed that weapon pits and trenches were to have overhead protection. 2nd Platoon remained in Stanley guarding naval facilities while 3rd Platoon and the remainder of the Heavy Weapons Platoon protected the Cortley Ridge fuel tanks at Stanley.

The following day, 1st Platoon, an amphibious engineer section and a section of Army engineers were flown to Pebble Island in a Coastguard Skyvan and an Army Puma. The Marines checked the state of the runway, while the Army sappers buried demolition charges into the grass runway. Ground crews checked the facilities. Marega established his command post in the schoolhouse and although insisting that settlement life should not be disrupted, he imposed a daily curfew between 9.30pm and 7.30am, instructed that generators should only be used between 6.30pm and midnight, commandeered all Land Rovers and confiscated Union flags. The requisitioned Falkland Islands Company coaster *Forrest* arrived two days later with the remainder of the equipment, support weapons of two MAG General Purpose Machine-Guns ammunition and aviation fuel.

The arrival of a flight of four 1st Naval Air Squadron T-34C Mentor trainers commanded by Lieutenant José María Pereira Dozo led Naval Air Station *Calderon* to be declared operational. Although slow, the Mentor is a robust aircraft with a steady bomb, rocket and 7.62mm machine-gun weapon platform and can operate from grass strips. The Pucara 3rd Attack Group at Military Air Base *Condor* at Goose Green was expected to join the Mentor, however inter-service rivalry and Navy complaints about the poor state of the Goose Green runway led to two airstrips relatively close to each other. The raid on Military Air Base *Condor* on 1 May led to six Pucara being redeployed to Pebble Island – after Air Force South and Naval Air Command had agreed to use the airstrip as an alternative.

As the winter weather turned nasty with a sharp southerly wind and freezing rain, the Marines struggled to prevent their trenches and 75mm gun pits from flooding. When concerns were raised about their health, Marega centralised the Marines into the sheep-shearing shed. After the runway flooded on the 6th and Naval Air Station *Calderon* was closed to fixed-wing operations, this heralded an unhappy time for the Air Force pilots – grounded, separated from their colleagues and the comfort of Goose Green, confined to an inhospitable windswept island and, worst of all, in a mess of naval aviators. Heavy frost two days later allowed the four Mentors to carry out a patrol to Stanley, much to the disgust of the Pucara pilots.

At about 2.15am on the 15th, flares burst over the island and Lieutenant Marega ordered stand-to and everyone sheltered in the trenches. Marine Javier Ramos recalled, 'There was a heavy bombardment which was probably the softening up for a major amphibious assault on the airfield. Fires were seen burning at the far end of the runway. A patrol then reported that fuel had caught fire and two aircraft were on fire.' Marega sent a fire-fighting party to deal with the burning aircraft and although puzzled when it came under rifle fire, he ordered the runway charges to be detonated, which added to the explosions from the ammunition dump. Still puzzled, nevertheless Marega warned H Company to expect an attack at first light. He recalled:

> When none came, a patrol despatched to clear the area found live and spent 7.62mm and 5.56mm rounds, confirming the enemy had indeed landed. While I requested an air recce of the island, which was refused, Air Force and Coastguard personnel checked the damage. While we were warned to receive reinforcements, the Air Force was told to prepare to evacuate Pebble Island.[6]

Increasing evidence of Task Force interest in Falkland Sound emerged early on 15 May when reports from Naval Air Base Pebble Island, reported that it had been raided the previous night and several Navy aircraft had been destroyed. The next morning, the 1st Rifle Platoon Marines interned the Islanders in the farm house. At Fox Bay, the Task Force *Reconquest* sick list numbered at least 200.

In military terms, the raid, by the SAS, removed a significant air threat to any landings, although there were still aircraft at Goose Green. Of the six Pucaras, one had serious damage to its engine and wing roots, three suffered minor engine and wing damage, another had shrapnel and blast damage and the sixth could still fly. The height of Pucaras made them a difficult target. One Mentor was destroyed, another was badly damaged, the third had minor damage to its engine and the fourth was pitted with small arms fire. The Coastguard Skyvan was totally destroyed by explosive charges, equipment vandalised and wiring ripped out.

The next morning, Marega despatched a patrol to Marble Mount to observe approaches to the settlement. At midday, a 601 Combat Aviation Battalion CH-47 carrying a 601 Commando Company platoon, which had been at Port San Carlos, settled down on the runway. But as the commandos trooped down the ramp, one witness described an 'undignified' stampede as Air Force and Coastguard pilots and ground crew jostled for seats. Not unexpectedly, the garrison was jittery, and that night there were several false alarms and firing at shadows. Next day, the commandos returned to Stanley. On 17 May, an eight-man commando patrol that landed on Pebble Island did not find anything of interest;

nevertheless, when a mixed Marines and commando patrol unearthed an illegal transceiver and sent it to Stanley for technical evaluation, the settlers were detained in the house of Griff Evans, the settlement manager, for the next month. Conditions were difficult. Anyone needing to leave the house had to ask permission. The Rayburn cooker was switched off at night on the grounds that its signature and glow would act as a beacon. When the Argentines cut down the Citizen's Band antenna, Nobby Clarke rigged up a clandestine one and kept everyone up to date with news. Life on Pebble Island became a mixture of boredom, occasional excitement as British aircraft bombed the now useless runway and hopes raised and lowered for evacuation. On 29 May, a Twin Otter evacuated several sick and wounded Air Force personnel from Pebble Island, including a shot-down pilot. Two days later, 1 June, two Naval Air Sea King helicopters were sent from Río Grande to evacuate the remaining naval pilots grounded in Pebble Island and were believed to have been spotted by a Harrier pilot supporting an SBS patrol checking Pebble Island either for a suspected land-based Exocet launcher or helicopters delivering Exocets supplied by Peru. Just in case, HMS *Avenger* shelled the Argentines that night.

601 Commando Company played a key role in the north-eastern sector of East Falklands. On 17 May, Second Platoon was flown to Port San Carlos by two 601 Combat Aviation Battalion Pumas and two Iroquois helicopters to check the derelict refrigeration plant at Ajax Bay. Nothing untoward was found, however an SBS patrol checking the suitability of the Port San Carlos beaches saw the commandos and were extracted the following night. During the next three nights, increased air activity, likelihood of enemy air photographic reconnaissance and the possibility of patrols led to the two artillery groups and air defence changing their positions. The soft ground and poor tracks were keeping the helicopters, in particular the CH-47 Chinooks, busy.

Rio Gallegos Military Air Base had become a centre of intelligence intrigue and a security nightmare for Argentine counter-intelligence officers, largely because the area was well-known for its British and Chilean sympathies. A 20-strong commando patrol raised by the 11th Mountain Infantry Brigade was tasked with searching for British insertions but when newspapers ran a story suggesting that several British commandos had been captured, this effectively compromised Argentine operations.

Argentina had become almost obsessive about protecting its three remaining Exocets and Super Etendard airplanes in the Naval Air Base Admiral Quijada, in Río Grande, Tierra del Fuego, being well guarded by the Fourth Marines Brigade, commanded by Captain Miguel Pita. And then early on 20 May, the burnt carcass of a British Sea King helicopter was found near Punta Arenas, in Chile. As the 11th Brigade commando company supported counter-intelligence officers searching for the infiltrators and the Argentine press ran stories of captured commandos, on 4 June, two suspect backpackers were intercepted by police about to cross the Chilean border near a mining village. One escaped, however his colleague, who was carrying a New Zealand passport, gave contradictory stories and was about to be delivered to the special interrogation centre in Buenos Aires when the senior officer in the area, Brigadier-General Guerrero, ordered his release, possibly under diplomatic pressure.

The helicopter carcass remained a public mystery for over 20 years and only emerged with the story of Operation *Plum Duff* of a reconnaissance for a raid of Air Force Base Río Grande. On 16 May, Lieutenant Richard Hutchings RM and his crew and eight SAS had lifted from HMS *Invincible* in a Sea King and were near the Argentine coast when Hutchings noticed that his on-board radar had been 'pinged'. He later learnt that it was 'pinged' by the destroyer ARA *Bouchard* acting as early warning and defensive screen off Río Grande. When a flare at Río Grande then suggested the Argentines were alert, Hutchings landed on low ground dead to radar sweeps, but when a second flare was fired, the operation and the party split, with Hutchings and his crew evading to Chile. On the eighth day, they had just passed a large army base when a Chilean police captain in a car pulled up and asked, 'Are you the three British airmen?' Arrangements were made to transfer them and the SAS to the British Embassy in Santiago.

Meanwhile, HQ 3rd Commando Brigade preparing to land at San Carlos Water had developed an accurate picture of Argentine units on the Falklands. Information sources included welfare telegrams to and from Argentina that included unit identification, locations and personal information and often indications of morale. An intercepted 'welfare' link indicated that 12th Infantry Regiment had arrived in late April and Goose Green was developing into a major base. The Ministry of Defence collected, analysed, collated and disseminated public and sensitive sources including prisoner-of-war and civilian debrief and a Marine infantry manual captured on South Georgia. Photographic intelligence is important but can be faked. The Argentines persuaded imagery analysts that the runway at Stanley Airport had a bomb crater in the middle, when in fact it was fit enough to take C-130s Hercules. Shortly before HMS *Fearless* left Ascension Island, Brigade HQ received air photographs of Goose Green showing CH-47 Chinook helicopters nestling in the settlement and aircraft dispersed on the airstrip. Assessments suggested an airfield that needed to be defended, aircraft needing to be serviced and repaired, and ground crews and pilots needed rest and food. Fixed- and rotor-wing aircraft require ground crews and the airfield needed to be protected by air defence.

CHAPTER 8

D-Day – 21 May – San Carlos Water Landings: Combat Team *Güemes*

During the night of 20 May, the shelling of Argentine forces at Port Stanley, Darwin and Port Howard and a landing at the St Louis Peninsula in north-eastern East Falklands was designed to distract the defence.

When, at about 1.30am on 21 May, a Support Platoon patrol at Port San Carlos on the beach below Hill 234 (*Promontorio Güemes*) reported shouts, helicopters and the silhouettes of ships in Falkland Sound, Sub-Lieutenant Reyes asked the mortars to fire illumination flares and radioed Esteban at Port San Carlos with a situation report but did not receive a response. He then joined the observation post on Hill 234 position and again radioed Esteban, but there was still no response.

Although he did not have any night observation and ranging equipment, Reyes ordered the mortars to fire two rounds, but these had little effect. At 2.30am, he ordered the two recoilless rifles to fire at the centre of the Sound, which quickly attracted the shelling of Hill 234 from a ship (HMS *Antrim*), which led Reyes to believe the enemy had artillery locating equipment. He ordered the two recoilless rifles to fire again and when this attracted retaliatory fire, he ordered them to move to alternative positions. At about 3.30am, the mortars had run out of ammunition, the rifles were very low and Fanning Head was then bracketed by airburst shells every minute which caused several casualties and persuaded the Argentines to concentrate on survival. Reyes's radio operator was still reporting no communications with

Port San Carlos and at 5am, while still dark, Reyes withdrew from Hill 234 and led his platoon towards the shelter of Partridge Valley, about 400 yards east of Fanning Head and 5 miles from Port San Carlos, but came under heavy rifle fire. Someone then coughed into a loudspeaker followed by a comical splutter and an invitation in Spanish to surrender. Four Argentines did. When Reyes and the remainder of his men were nudged by a creeping barrage back to the shelter of Fanning Head, he divided his platoon into sections and broke through the British perimeter. Shelling convinced four other Argentines halfway up Fanning Hill to wave a white cloth; this signalled the end of the action. Two Argentines later surrendered and four wounded were later found by British troops and evacuated to the *Canberra*.

At Port San Carlos, First-Lieutenant Esteban had reported the shelling of Hill 234 to Stanley, however he had not received any radio transmissions from Reyes, no runner had appeared and there were no retreating Argentines. Unsure and fearing the worst, he ordered Grey Alert to stand-to at 6.30am and deployed observers to overlook the dark and misty surface of San Carlos Water (Bahía San Carlos). All seemed quiet until at about 7.10am (first light), sentries reported a large white ship and three warships entering the narrows into the bay. Climbing to higher ground, Esteban noted three more warships had entered Falkland Sound (Estrecho de San Carlos) and over the next 10 minutes, he watched as several landing craft, larger than he had ever seen, crammed with troops, left the side of the white ship (*Canberra*). Helicopters were very much in evidence. At 7.30am, Esteban's troops radioed HQ 12th Regiment at Goose Green that he had identified Royal Marines (in fact 3 Para) advancing toward Port San Carlos and then, as early morning mist dispersed into a bright day, at about 8.30am, he saw landing craft 'travelling in all directions' and requested an air attack from Lieutenant-Colonel Piaggi.

By first light, six Pucaras of the 3rd Attack Group at Goose Green had drawn up in pairs and as Captain Jorge Benitez and Lieutenant Brest began to roll, the runway was shelled by HMS *Ardent* 12 miles offshore in Grantham Sound, with only Benitez succeeding in taking off. Scouting for enemy activity around Bombilla Hill, he moved his search pattern to the west and upon seeing ships and helicopters in San Carlos Water and troops filing off the beach, he lined up to attack, but his aircraft was hit by two Stinger surface-to-air missiles. Nevertheless, he gained sufficient height and at about 300ft, ejected, watched his aircraft crash near Flat Shanty and then walked south to Goose Green. Meanwhile, Major Carlos Tomba and Lieutenant Juan Micheloud had also taken off and after searching for targets in Port San Carlos and being shot at by Blowpipe missiles, they decided to return to Goose Green. However, after being directed to an enemy patrol directing naval gunfire onto the runway, they were jumped by three Sea Harriers that shot down Tomba, while Micheloud sheltered in cloud and landed at Goose Green. Lieutenant-Colonel Piaggi had been reporting the landing to the Coast Army Force Commander, Brigadier-General Parada, nicknamed '*Capanga*' on the radio net, in Port Stanley.

By 8.40am, Esteban, who was at Port Carlos, realised he was outnumbered and still with no contact from Reyes, he withdrew and while leading Combat Team *Güemes* up the ridge east of Port San Carlos intending to occupy higher ground to the east, a Gazelle helicopter escorting a Sea King carrying an undersling appeared on his intended withdrawal route and hovered. Believing it was about to fire its rockets, his men opened fire and kept firing as the helicopter crashed into the water, however Esteban was unable to stop the over-excited conscripts from firing at the survivors. One person was seen floating and another clinging to a buoy was rescued by a launch. As several local Falkland Islanders pointed out the direction taken by the Argentines, wisps of smoke marking the scene of the short action became an aiming point for enemy mortars. The combat team were still moving to the east towards The Knob and were astonished when a second Gazelle appeared and opened fire with its machine-gun. His men also shot it down. Esteban later reported, 'The helicopters spent sufficiently long in the hover for our men to bring fire to bear. There was little attempt to avoid ground fire. I was pleased that my men had not been paralysed by the fighting.' The British retaliated with a naval bombardment and mortars plastering the Combat Team *Güemes* positions led to Argentines withdrawing from the area. His Platoon Sergeant Rene Martin Colque was captured near Port San Carlos the next day. Meanwhile, 3 Commando Brigade was landing on Red Beach at Ajax Bay, Blue Beach at San Carlos and Green Beach at Port San Carlos. Combat Team *Güemes* at San Carlos now consisted of Company HQ and a Rifle Platoon, a total of two officers, 9 NCOs and 31 soldiers. There was still no sign of Sub-Lieutenant Reyes and his platoon and the 12th Infantry Regiment Support Platoon. Esteban estimated enemy casualties to be about 10 parachutists' dead or injured, two Gazelles shot down and a Sea King and another Gazelle damaged and certainly unserviceable. During the night, Combat Team *Güemes* withdrew toward Port Stanley via Bombilla Hill and Douglas Paddock.

For the next 10 days, San Carlos Water was a battle of courageous flying by Argentine pilots and stubborn Royal Navy defence, with the British eventually gaining the upper hand and the beaches becoming the logistic funnel through which men and supplies were fed into the advance to Stanley with casualties treated at Ajax Bay and on the hospital ship *Uganda*. Argentine observation posts and radar pickets overlooked Blue Beach. On 23 May, HMS *Antelope* was bombed by 5 Group Skyhawks and exploded that night in a spectacular eruption. On the 27th, a first wave of two 5 Group Skyhawks bombed targets near San Carlos Settlement and the second wave bombed the derelict refrigeration factory at Ajax Bay killing five and wounding 26, most of whom were waiting in a meal queue. Lieutenant Commander Dante Camiletti was captured hiding behind a rock observing the British movements in San Carlos.

Evasion is tough, nevertheless, in spite of the relentless wind, low temperatures, rain and pathless 'going', the Argentines had food in their packs and pockets and Combat Team *Güemes* marched at night and rested during the day, concealed from the frequent presence of enemy helicopters. Esteban and his men reached Douglas Paddock after three days and organised rations, ablutions, weapon servicing and resting in shifts and radioed 25th Regiment at Port Stanley and sent a runner with a request for transport to collect them. Esteban held a parade at the settlement to celebrate the anniversary of the revolution in Buenos Aires that deposed the Spanish Viceroy in 1810 (Revolucion de Mayo) and the next day, four Army helicopters transferred his men to Stanley.

Meanwhile, Second-Lieutenant Reyes and his 11 men had breached the San Carlos perimeter, and, hiding by day and navigating by night, had reached New House Settlement but were captured, suffering from trench foot, frostbite and hunger, by a 40 Commando patrol on 8 June. Others cut off by the landings included three airmen from the Air Observation Network (*Red de Observadores del Aire* − ROA) manning a radar beacon on Verde Mountain who tried to surrender to British patrols without success until 30 May when a Sea King crew delivered them to HQ 3rd Commando Brigade at Port San Carlos, bedraggled, but still armed.

CHAPTER 9

The Battle of Goose Green

Although Vice-Commodore Wilson Pedrozo of the Argentine Air Force had been appointed the Goose Green Base Commander, the tactical commander for Task Force *Mercedes*, Lieutenant-Colonel Piaggi, had been given four missions: to provide the Z Reserve battle group to reinforce Army Group Stanley, to prevent occupation of Mount Kent, to occupy Goose Green and defend Military Air Base *Condor*.

Piaggi had developed a 13-mile defensive perimeter around Goose Green and quickly assembled a composite company from Headquarters Company commanded by Sub-Lieutenant Ernesto Peluffo, one of the fourth-year officer-cadets commissioned from the National Army Academy, and 3rd Platoon, 8th Regiment commanded by Second-Lieutenant Guillermo Aliaga. Most of the 12th Regiment's equipment and supplies of radios, support weapons, vehicles, reserve ammunition, field kitchens and other war stores were still on board the *Ciudad de Cordoba*, which was stranded in Puerto Deseado. HQ 3rd Brigade supported with the resupply of ammunition, food and other necessities. The absence of Combat Team *Solari* and B Company, 12th Regiment, meant that Piaggi was 14 MAG machine-guns short and instead of 14 recoilless rifles, he had one. Support Company had three 105mm recoilless guns; of three 120mm mortars, one was damaged; and eight of the 10 81mm mortars were on the ship. In support was a 4th Airborne Artillery Group battery of three M-56 Oto Melara 105 Pack Howitzers. To compensate for the loss of his vehicles, HQ 3rd Brigade loaned Piagga four Mercedes jeeps, but only one was fitted with a radio.

The soldiers spent much of their time preparing defensive positions and keeping weapons clean and serviceable. Digging-in proved to be problematic. Most soldiers had a small entrenching shovel and one spade rationed to one per platoon; it took about two days to dig a decent foxhole. On the high ground, the shelter of firmer peat made life easier. Soldiers had to master the effects of the cold wind, the skills of living in the field on short rations, the darkness and silence of the night, falling asleep and the lack of news. Officers did their best to set examples, for instance not using trenches during air raids and bombardments. The Regimental Chaplain, Father Santiago Mora, wrote, 'The 25th Infantry conscripts wanted to fight and cover themselves in glory. The 12th Infantry Regiment conscripts fought because they were told to do so. This did not make them any less brave. On the whole, they remained admirably calm.'

Argentine intelligence had predicted the British would most likely land in the Stanley Sector, perhaps Berkeley Sound, but the landings at San Carlos had significantly increased the threat against Task Force *Mercedes*. Brigadier-General Omar Parada of HQ 3rd Brigade then extended the Goose Green defensive perimeter to 31 kilometres but failed to provide reinforcements and engineers to improve the defence with, for instance, sangars. Piaggi concluded the most likely approach from San Carlos was from the north and therefore he based his defence across the isthmus from Darwin Hill to the remains of Boca House.

The 104 men of First-Lieutenant Antonio Manresa's A Company were located in the Low Pass-Burntside Sector. Lieutenant Morales' Scout Platoon patrolled as far north as Camilla Creek and sometimes used a corral south of Burntside House, while C Company, 25th Infantry Regiment was at the schoolhouse. First-Lieutenant Ramon Fernandez and C Company, 8th Infantry Regiment covered the southern approaches from Lafonia and 9th Engineer Company laid minefields south of the ruins of Boca House covering Salinas Beach, the north end of the airfield, both sides of the inlet north of the schoolhouse and between Middle Hill and Coronation Ridge.

Under his command, Piaggi had representation from three regiments from two brigades, none of whom had worked together and were rated in quality from good, such as Esteban's 25th Regiment company, to unknown, such as Aliaga's 8th Regiment platoon. On 29 April, 12 Pucara of the 3rd Attack Group, renamed Pucara Squadron Falklands, flew from Stanley and dispersed several civilian and non-operational aircraft around the airstrip to deceive British air photographic interpreters. Sub-Lieutenant Carlos Braghini and his B Battery, 601 Air Defence Group with twin 35mm Oerlikons and the Air Force 1st AA Group Rh-202 twin 20mm sections had a decent ground fire capability. On 13 May, Piaggi ordered Combat Team *Güemes* to establish a block at San Carlos Water. Martín Miguel de Güemes (1785–1821) was a military leader and popular *caudillo* (leader) who defended north-western Argentina from the Spanish interference.

3rd Commando Brigade landed at San Carlos Water on 21 May, however it was not until the 24th that Argentine intelligence accepted that the landings were the main effort, by which time their enemy were secure in their beachhead. The Military Committee formed the CEOPECON at Comodoro Rivadavia to provide strategic direction. While the Argentine Joint Chiefs-of-Staff assessed that an attack on Goose Green was likely, the preferred strategy remained to isolate the landings by attacking Admiral Woodward's ships and the logistic hub on Ascension Island. Consequently, the National Strategic Reserve of the 4th Airborne Brigade was not mobilised except for the 2nd Airborne Infantry Regiment placed on stand-by at Brigadier-General Menéndez's request and the 4th Airborne Artillery Group supporting 3rd Brigade on Las Malvinas. The Joint Operations Centre's suggested strategy was for the Air Force and Naval Air Commands to neutralise the beachhead and that Army Group Malvinas should counter-attack and destroy the San Carlos beachhead. But the Z Reserve of Task Force *Mercedes* was bottled up in Goose Green and the 601 Combat Aviation Battalion hide on Mount Kent had been bombed, and three helicopters were damaged while rescuing two 601 Commando Company sections stranded on West Falkland.

Menéndez argued that dealing with the San Carlos beachhead would expose the weak defence of Stanley, particularly as it was common knowledge that the British 5th Infantry Brigade had left Ascension, and instead proposed that special forces units and 12th Regiment should disrupt the beachhead and the 4th Airborne Brigade should reinforce Stanley and Goose Green. However, a joint assessment by Colonel Pino from the Brigade HQ and Commodore Martinez from the Air Force Air Transport Group stated that an airborne operation would be compromised unless air superiority could be achieved and suggested that troops and equipment should be unloaded at Stanley and transferred to Goose Green.

Such was the bureaucratic inter-service politics rivalry that when Menéndez ordered Brigadier-General Parada to take direct command of operations against the San Carlos beachhead, the duty flight controller refused to authorise a helicopter for him because the orders had not been ratified by Air Force headquarters. Parada instructed Piaggi:

> Task Force *Mercedes* will reorganise its defensive positions and will execute harassing fire against the most advanced enemy effectives, starting from this moment, in the assigned zone, to deny access to the isthmus of Darwin and contribute its fire to the development of the principal operation. The operation will consist of preparing positions around Darwin for an echelon defending the first line and occupying them and from there putting forward advanced combat and scouting forces, as security detachment, supporting the principal operations with harassing fire against Bodie Peak, Cantera Mount and Mount Usborne.[1]

When Piaggi had little choice but to lengthen his perimeter and order A Company to move forward and occupy Coronation Ridge, its company commander, First-Lieutenant Manresa, suggested that deploying half-trained troops from the security and familiarity of their defensive position would unsettle the conscripts, many of whom were ill from the inhospitable climate, while the daily ration of one prepared meal had undermined morale and the inadequate combat jackets, scarves, gloves and underclothes were unable to keep out the rain and biting southerly Antarctic wind. On 10 May, Piaggi had permitted sheep to be butchered. Morale rose nine days later when a C-130 Hercules flying from Argentina parachuted eight tons of canned food and a second drop included Wellington boots.

Meanwhile, events unfolding in London would have a direct bearing on proposals at Goose Green when the BBC World Service disclosed that, 'A parachute battalion is poised and ready to assault Darwin and

Goose Green' and compromised operational planning. While this was yet another blunder in the long history of journalistic and political incompetence and patience, Parada and Piaggi both half-believed the breach to be a hoax because no one in their right mind would broadcast an attack to the whole world.

Meanwhile, A Company and a Scout Platoon section had developed a strong defensive position across the isthmus south of Low Pass and east of Burntside House about 2 miles north of Darwin and when Lieutenant Carlos Morales, the Scout Platoon Commander, reported on 27 May that two sections had clashed with enemy north of Camilla Creek House, Piaggi ordered him to investigate. Morales and three soldiers were using a commandeered blue Land Rover and were ambushed and captured at about 10.30am. Private Esteban Bustamante, of the Scout Platoon, recalled, 'We began to see the English who were coming from the north in columns... Night was falling, and we sent up flares, you see like day.'

At 1.45am on 28 May, HMS *Arrow* triggered the battle of Goose Green by opening fire on Argentine positions. For many of the conscripts it was their first experience of war. The Scout Platoon returned a few shots at enemy seen in a corral near Burntside Pond and withdrew. Following reports that Argentine officers were reported to be using the cottage owned by Gerald and Kay Morrison, the couple, her mother and a friend who had escaped from Stanley lay on the floor as bullets and explosions smashed windows, sieved walls, dislodged the roof and sparked a fire. Shelling from Captain Chanampa's 105mm guns added to the chaos.

First-Lieutenant Manresa lost his radio when his Mercedes jeep was damaged by a grenade. At 4.30am, Piaggi ordered Manresa's A Company to withdraw and join positions on the right flank of Darwin Ridge with Second Lieutenant Horacio Muñoz-Cabrera's platoon on Coronation Ridge. Many of his inexperienced soldiers were shaken by the fighting. Nine had been killed, most in Corporal Pedemonte's section in hand-to-hand fighting. The withdrawal helped to steady the defence and by 9am Piaggi reported to Army Group that the British had been halted and that he intended to defend Darwin Ridge because it had a good view of the ground to the north.

On the right was the 1st Rifle Platoon, 25th Regiment commanded by Lieutenant Nestor Estévez. He had regularly practised counter-attacks and plugging gaps in their positions and during the night had led his men up the reverse (southerly) slope of Darwin Hill and took up a position to the right of Sub-Lieutenant's Peluffo's Service Company Platoon holding the centre. When Estévez explained that his orders were to counter-attack and support A Company, Peluffo thought it was an unwise tactic and convinced him to join the defence of the ridge. Lieutenant Aliaga's 8th Infantry Regiment platoon on the left was anchored on the derelict Boca House. The defenders on the ridge occupied about 25 trenches, bunkers and shell scrapes. To the south of the ridge at Darwin School and near the airstrip were platoon defensive positions. Optimism prevailed. Victory seemed a possibility.

The 4th Airborne Artillery Group was based on Mount Wall as part of the reserve until the afternoon of 26 May when it deployed to support Task Force *Mercedes* and began providing harassing fire at 2.50am on 28 May, supporting A Company, 12th Regiment. As a dull dawn crept across the plain, the defenders watched the enemy advance across the grassy plain from the north and at about 8am as the 1st Rifle Platoon machine-guns and others opened fire, Estévez called for fire artillery and 120mm mortars support and caught the paras in the open. Private Guillermo Huircapán describes the morning action,

> Lieutenant Estévez went from one side to the other organising the defence until all at once they got him in the shoulder. But with that and everything, badly wounded, he kept crawling along the trenches, giving orders, encouraging the soldiers, asking for everyone. A little later, they got him in the side, but just the same, from the trench, he continued directing the artillery fire by radio. There was a little pause, and then the English began the attack again, trying to advance, and again we beat them off.[2]

After Estévez was killed, his radio operator, Private Fabrizio Edgar Carrascul, controlled the guns until he too was killed. Company Sergeant Major Juan Coelho was everywhere encouraging the conscripts. Lieutenant Estévez and Private Carrascul were posthumously decorated for their actions. Thereafter, Captain Chanampa's targets were largely speculative based on his recces and the map. Several enemy attempts to breach the defence failed and then at midday, a small group of the enemy charged up a small gully of Darwin Hill on the Argentine right, leading to the top of the ridge, however three were shot. As the remaining two ran west along the base of the ridge towards a smaller re-entrant, the fourth man fell and the fifth ran up the hill towards a trench and was also shot. The fifth man, Lieutenant-Colonel 'H' Jones, was the 2 Para Commanding Officer. In Argentina, Corporal Osvaldo Faustino Olmos is generally regarded as the person who shot Jones. The historian Hugh Bicheno claims that Corporal José Luis Ríos of the 12th Regiment's Reconnaissance Platoon fired the shot. Ríos was later mortally wounded manning a machine-gun from his trench. The Argentine historian Oscar Téves gathered testimonies and studied the foxholes and trench positions in Darwin Hill and concluded that Conscript Oscar Ledesma manning a MAG machine-gun was responsible.

Throughout the battle, pairs of Pucaras supported the Task Force. At about 11am, two aircraft arrived over Camilla Creek House at the same time as two Scout helicopters had been sent to recover Jones. One helicopter was shot down, killing the pilot and severely wounding his aircrewman. A second helicopter escaped. Lieutenant Miguel Angel Giménez of the 3rd Attack Group was on his second mission of the day with a colleague, and while returning to Stanley had become separated in mist and was listed as missing in action. His aircraft was found crashed into Blue Mountain in 1986 and his body buried with full military honours. The British and Falklands authorities later made arrangements for his father and sister to attend his burial at the Argentine War Cemetery at Darwin. Argentina has refused to repatriate any of their servicemen killed during the Falklands War on the grounds their bodies should remain 'as permanent testimony to Argentine sovereignty.'

12th Regiment kept 2 Para pinned to the northern slopes of Darwin Hill for a further two hours. Many of the Argentine fatalities were caused by mortars. A third assault at 12.30pm was defeated by the 1st Rifle Platoon. In anticipation of a Aeromacchi and Pucara ground attack support, Company Sergeant-Major Coelho spread out white bedsheets marking the Argentine front line when he was severely wounded.

When the weight of the British attack switched from Darwin Hill to the Argentine left flank, Sub-Lieutenant Aliaga and his 8th Infantry

Regiment platoon held Boca Hill until about 2pm when his position was struck by two Milan missiles. White flags appeared at Boca House as the Argentines began running short of ammunition. The 12th Regiment platoon commanded by Sub-Lieutenant Carlos Oslvaldo Aldao and the Argentine Air Force Rh 202 anti-aircraft gunners under Lieutenant Darío Del Valle Valazza were forced to abandon their positions, at the cost of three gunners killed, two guns Rh-202s damaged and the Elta radar lost. Twelve Argentines were killed and 15 captured, including Aliaga with a head wound. Aldao and a corporal escaped in the confusion of an Argentine air strike during the afternoon.

Piaggi planned for Combat Team *Solari* to be flown from Mount Kent to Darwin Ridge to support a co-ordinated counter-attack using Fernandez's C Company and C Company, 25th Regiment. At about 12.30pm, Piaggi reorganised his defence and placed Sub-Lieutenant Gómez Centurión, 2nd Platoon, C Company, 25th Regiment, which had been flown from Stanley to north-east of Bodie Creek Bridge, under the command of Second-Lieutenant Vasquez with orders to defend the airfield. The helicopters left with those who had been wounded including Second-Lieutenant Peluffo who had been wounded in the head and leg on Darwin Ridge. About an hour later, Air Force 20mm gunners and Chanampa's howitzer crews and machine-gunners wounded several British advancing south down Middle Hill. Prisoners included 11 from a command bunker on the edge of the airfield and several Air Force Security Company cadets and anti-aircraft gunners. The day before the battle began, Pedrozo took the opportunity of a break in the rain to evacuate the Army Bell-212 helicopters. The Air Force CH-47 Chinooks had left three days before.

As the enemy advanced toward the airfield and Goose Green, several Argentines near the windsock waved white flags, but as Lieutenant Jim Barry and two of his NCOs walked toward them to take the surrender, they met Sub-Lieutenant Gómez Centurión advancing towards them assuming that the British wanted to surrender. It soon became clear that neither side intended to surrender, and so Centurión and Barry agreed a two-minute break to return to their lines. However, it seems a distant Para machine-gunner on Darwin Hill saw men in the open and opened fire and a short battle broke out which saw Lieutenant Barry killed, and two Paras and an Argentine wounded in the confusion. British newspapers tried to exploit a tragic misunderstanding of the 'white flag incident'. When the Goose Green prisoners were later repatriated to Argentina through Montevideo, Sub-Lieutenant Centurión claimed on arrival that 'I killed the Paras Commander.'

After Darwin Schoolhouse had been overrun, Vasquez and his platoon's withdrawal was covered by Braghini's two 35mm Oerlikons, which prevented British exploitation of Goose Green. When the 25th Rifle Platoon, who were defending the airfield, withdrew to the Darwin–Goose Green track, Sergeant Sergio Ismael Garcia single-handedly covered the withdrawal of his platoon during a British counter-attack and was posthumously awarded the Argentine Medal of Valour in Combat. Under orders from Major Carlos Alberto Frontera, the 12th Regiment second-in-command, Sub-Lieutenant César Álvarez Berro, and his platoon took up new positions and helped cover the retreat of Centurión's platoon along the Darwin–Goose Green track. Argentine 35mm anti-aircraft guns reduced the schoolhouse to rubble after Sergeants Mario Abel and Tarditti and Roberto Amado Fernandez reported sniper fire from it. At about the same time, three Harriers attacked the 35mm guns and although none were damaged, one round damaged a pole holding the generator cable to the guns.

Throughout the battle the Argentine 105mm battery experienced problems with one Pack Howitzer with a damaged wheel being repaired by the armourer and another still beyond repair after being recovered from Choiseul Sound. A commandeered Land Rover helped relocate the guns and ammunition and as 12th Regiment retreated, each bound was usually achieved within 15 minutes but always into unprepared sites. The abandoning of the 35mm Oerlikons after being bombed by three Harriers dropping cluster bombs and firing 2-inch rockets that cut and damaged cables left Task Force *Mercedes* exposed to air attacks. After a Navy MB-339 Aeromacchis had been shot down, with the pilot being killed, three Pucaras approaching from the north-west attacked a British column and dropped napalm bombs. Lieutenant Miguel Cruzado was shot down by ground fire and crashed, drenching several paratroopers with fuel and napalm, and was captured.

During the morning, Combat Team *Solari* was part of a planned move to seize Mount Kent when it was ordered to reinforce 12th Regiment. The platoon consisted of two NCOs and 18 soldiers commanded by Captain Eduardo Corsiglia, the 4th Regiment Adjutant, who had been protecting a helicopter fuel store on Mount Challenger and 20 other men unfit for operations. It had no radios because the batteries of Thompson radios at HQ Task Force *Mercedes* were almost flat. A 105mm recoilless rifle was available, the one 81mm mortar had no sights and two days of ammunition were available. Corsiglia planned that HQ and 1 and 2 Platoons would deploy in the first flight and 3 Platoon on the second. At 3.15pm, the combat team assembled at the foot of Mount Kent and then at 4.30pm, it boarded a Puma, two A–109s, seven UH–IH Iroquois, and a CH–47 Chinook from 601 Combat Aviation Battalion and left for Goose Green. Mid-flight, Brigadier-General Parada cancelled the operation, but it was too late except for Second-Lieutenant Mosterin's platoon, which was escorted by two gunships to a beach several hundred yards south of Goose Green; one Puma with two sections had lost contact. Captain Corsiglia knew nothing about the tactical situation at Goose Green and had no radio. Nevertheless, at about 8pm he found a gap in the perimeter defence and met Second-Lieutenant Vasquez's 3rd Platoon Sergeant who said that Task Force *Mercedes* was practically surrounded and that combat team was to adopt defensive positions. Sub-Lieutenant Centurión's 3rd Platoon, C Company, 25th Regiment was in the centre, men from the Air Force Security Company were at the airstrip windsock and Lieutenant Fernandez was covering approaches from Lafonia.

As Combat Team *Solari* crossed an area being shelled, contact with the Support Platoon was lost for about two hours. There was no news of Second-Lieutenant Carlos Tamini's Platoon and the two Combat Team *Solari* sections ordered to reinforce Task Force *Mercedes* defending Goose Green and be collected from Mount Kent by a Puma in the late afternoon. The Puma was faster than a flight of UH–IH Iroquois also delivering reinforcements and when there were reports of the imminent threat of enemy aircraft, the Puma landed. The aircraft turned out to be an Air Force Pucara en route to Goose Green, where it was shot down and the pilot captured. Meanwhile, Tamini watched as the other helicopters

The Argentine flag consists of three equally wide horizontal bands of light blue and white created by Manual Belgrano in 1812 during the War of Independence. The yellow 'Sun' was added in 1818.

Argentine officers wearing German uniforms in 1930.

Photograph showing the ground east of Stanley including Moody Brook, Mt Longdon, Two Sisters and Mt Tumbledown in 1992.

Capture of Stanley. Air Force Air Comodoro Hector Gilobert approaches Government House to open surrender negotiations on 2 April 1982. He was the Argentine consul.

An amphibious wheeled LARC-5 approaches Naval Party 8901 lying on the road.

Argentine marines disarm Naval Party 8901 outside Government House.

Governor Rex Hunt surrenders to General Garcia. On the right is Major Patricio Dowling, the Argentine military counter-intelligence and security chief.

The Argentine flag that could not be raised on 2 April 1982 at Government House and became a memorial at the Argentine Ministry of Defence.

Second Lieutenant Reyes repairing the damaged flagpole at Government House on 2 April, 1982.

A 601 Combat Aviation Battalion A-109A Hirundo helicopter on the Government House lawn.

The Secretariat in Stanley with an Argentine flag flying.

Major-General Garcia and Marine Vice-Admiral Busser leave Government House after signing the surrender. Behind them is a LVTP-7.

One of several clandestine photos taken by Gerald Cheek, Director of Aviation and member of the Falkland Island Defence Force, of a Navy Electra delivering troops on 13 April.

A Company, 25th Special Infantry Regiment defended Stanley Airport. The insignia on their jackets depicts the seizure of the Las Malvinas (Falkland Islands).

Marine Lieutenant Carlos Bianci, 5th Marine Infantry Battalion, wearing a British Second World War steel helmet and combat waistcoat.

Four conscripts outside of their makeshift bunker.

A mobile field cookhouse at a 'rancho'. Those at the end of queues were often served lukewarm or no food. The British blockade restricted hot meals to one a day.

Faith was important to almost all ranks. Chaplains helped maintain morale and attended to casualties.

Argentine conscripts shopping in a Stanley store.

President Leopoldo Galtieri at Moody Brook, the capital of Port Stanley, where he chaired a meeting of senior military staff and clergy on 22 April.

The shelling of the Military Air Base, Stanley as a FMA IA 58 Pucará ground-attack and counter-insurgency (COIN) aircraft enters the runway.

As winter weather arrived, cold rain flooded this M-56 105mm Pack Howitzer defensive gun position on Stanley Common.

A Royal Marine treats a wounded Argentine lying on a stretcher on 14 June.

The British delegation is escorted by Vice-Commodore Bloomer-Reeve to the Secretariat to discuss the Argentine surrender.

A cartoon found during a search of prisoners at Ajax Bay translated as 'The Six of San Carlos'. Sgt Flores, 602 Cdo Coy, was captured by the SAS during the battle for Mt Kent.

After Argentina surrendered on 14 July, the last of the prisoners are repatriated at Port Madryn. Several senior officers appear to be ignored by the welcoming committee.

Special Category prisoners were retained first at Ajax Bay at Stanley Public Jetty and then embarked on a ship until Argentina surrendered.

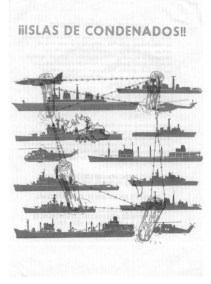

British Psychological Operations. The full text reads 'THE CONDEMNED ISLANDS!! Soldiers of the Argentine forces, you are completely alone. From your homeland there is no hope of relief or help and soon the rigors of a cruel and merciless winter will fall upon you. Your families live in tremendous terror that they will never see you again.'

passed overhead and headed towards Goose Green. Tamini was without communication and over the next three days, he led his platoon towards Stanley and was captured near Estancia on 31 May. It was snowing.

Lieutenant-Colonel Piaggi met with Corsiglia at 10.45pm and briefed him that the chances of relief were slim, he could withstand a siege and that Combat Team *Solari* was to be held in reserve. Major Alberto Frontera, his second-in-command, reckoned that Task Force *Mercedes* could hold out against the 600 British estimated to be surrounding Goose Green. Army Group was less certain and suggested to Piaggi that he abandon Goose Green, make for Lafonia using the Bodie Creek Bridge and wait for the commando-trained Major Oscar Jaimet and his B Company, 6th Infantry Regiment from the Stanley Reserves and continue the fight. After Brigadier-General Menéndez accepted that resistance was futile, Brigadier-General Parada advised Piaggi to take the best course of action and suggested, 'It's up to you', reminding him that pointless resistance would lead to unnecessary loss of military and civilian lives. There is some evidence that Argentine Signals Intelligence believed that Task Force *Mercedes* was outnumbered by a brigade. Equally, the British believed they were up against a bigger fighting force. Piaggi later recalled,

> The battle had turned into a sniping contest. They could sit well out of range of our soldiers' fire and, if they wanted to, raze the settlement. I knew that there was no longer any chance of reinforcements in the form of 6th Regiment's B Company and so I suggested to Wing-Commander Wilson Pedrozo that he talk to the British. He agreed reluctantly.[3]

Eric Goss and his wife had watched the battle from their upstairs bedroom and were impressed by star shells fired by HMS *Arrow*. As the battle crept toward Goose Green, they moved to the sitting room and then sheltered in the below-ground cellars. Old Nan McCallum sat in an armchair in her house between two deep freezers full of frozen meats and covered with a mattress and blankets to protect her from plywood splinters. During the day, Gerald Morrison, a farm worker, left the shelter to check on her and also fetch a jug of water. He encountered a young Argentine soldier stealing food who pointed his rifle at his stomach. Goss also found a hungry and dirty conscript eating powered milk from a tin and took him to his garage, allowing him to slice some mutton from a sheep carcass and braise it on his field cooker. Several soldiers were prevented from seeking shelter in the hall in case they found three 'escape hatches' cut into the floor as shelters.

As the fighting fizzled out, Pedrozo and Piaggi realised Task Force *Mercedes* was trapped and were given permission by Menéndez to surrender. Goss was in his office and answered a knock on his door to the three battle-weary officers who escorted him to Keith Baillie at the store. An Argentine agreed to remain in his house. Goss took Willie Bowles with him and was taken to the dining room in which there were 11 Argentines including Vice-Comodore Pedrozo, Lieutenant-Colonel Piaggi and Navy Lieutenant Gopecevich. Acknowledging the British were close, Pedrozo asked if it was possible to contact them in order to discuss evacuating the civilians, particularly as Darwin School had been badly damaged. When Gopecevich suggested using the international distress frequency on the Monsunen radio but then claimed that Harriers had destroyed the system, Goss suggested using the 2-metre VHF settlement, then reminded the Argentines that they had ordered aerials to be disconnected and radios had been confiscated. When Pedrozo mentioned a radio was upstairs, Goss broadcast, 'This is Eric Goss calling from Goose Green. Is anyone there?' To his surprise, Alan Miller at Port San Carlos answered and Goss replied he was in the presence of 'foreign brass' who wished to make contact with the British. Miller asked 'Are there any British officers? Do you have many little men in green uniforms?' Goss replied that it would be an indiscretion to reply to the first question and to the second he replied, 'In excess of 1,000.' He then spoke to a British officer and told him the Argentines wished to meet the next morning. HQ 3 Commando Brigade then issued an ultimatum and arrangements were made that two Argentine NCOs who had been captured during the day would take the ultimatum through Argentine lines with an answer expected no later than 8.30am. The ultimatum read,

> That you unconditionally surrender your force to us by leaving the township, forming up in a military manner, removing your helmets and laying down your weapons. You will give prior notice of this intention by returning the POW under a white flag with him briefed as to formalities no later than 08.30 hours local time.

You refuse in the first place to surrender and take the consequences. You will give notice of this intention by returning the POW without his flag (although neutrality will be respected) no later than 08.30 hours local.

In any event and in accordance with the terms of the Geneva Conventions and Laws of War, you shall be held responsible for the fate of any civilians in Darwin and Goose Green and we shall, in accordance with these laws, give you notice of our intention to bombard Darwin and Goose Green.

Signed C Keeble, Commander of the British Force

The night was quiet, and well before dawn next day the two NCOs returned with a message from Pedrozo and Piaggi: they wished to discuss terms. Taking advantage of the ceasefire, Sub-Lieutenant Gómez Centurión and two Air Force stretcher-bearers, Privates David Alejandro Díaz and Reynaldo Dardo Romacho, and the Air Force medical officer, Lieutenant Carlos Beranek, were tasked with searching for casualties and found the severely wounded Corporal Juan Fernández behind British lines.

When agreement was reached at 7.30am local time that representatives from both sides would meet at the Goose Green airfield wind sock at 9.30am, Eric Goss gave Pedrozo a note written on a page of Amateur Radio logbook paper:

With your concern you show for the safety of civilians, can I now ask you to take this a step further and in view of the brave and courageous way your soldiers fought; in the interest of saving lives of such valiant soldiers on both sides – will you consider an honourable surrender? Britain and Argentina need these young men? 29 May 1982.[4]

29 May is Argentine Army National Day and is normally a time for parades and celebration. But not in 1982. After the Argentines formally surrendered to Major Keeble, Wing-Commander Pedrozo held a parade of Air Force, Coastguard and Navy, and after the 12th Regiment had burnt their flag, Piaggi led out Task Force *Mercedes*. Two hours later, British troops entered Goose Green and released the interned Falkland Islanders. Pedrozo and Piaggi were then flown to San Carlos and met Brigadier Thompson. Piaggi was proud of Task Force *Mercedes* and later said, 'It would have fought until the last man if Parada had demanded it.' Goose Green was the first battle of the Falklands War and lasted 14 hours, fought over featureless and windswept ground.

The Argentine Junta was slow to admit defeat, but did broadcast that 'Contact is lost with Goose Green'. While Venezuela and Guatemala offered to send airborne units to 'smash the British in the Falklands', the US encouraged Argentina to consider a solution to the war.

The Argentines had forced 2 Para to fight a tougher and longer battle than any other Argentine commander would do and yet Piaggi, bitter that his men had been sacrificed, suffered the consequences of defeat and was dismissed from the Army in disgrace. His men were not tough Germans, hardy Middle Eastern tribesmen or clever Irish republican terrorists, but barely trained and hungry conscripts let down by their senior commanders and had confounded Jones's theory, 'Hit them really hard and they will fold'. In 1986, Piaggi wrote the book *Ganso Verde* (*Goose Green*) in which he criticised the lack of support from Brigadier-General Menéndez. He estimates that Task Force *Mercedes* disposed of just 28 per cent of the available artillery, mortars and heavy machine-gun firepower. In February 1992, after a long fight in the civil and military courts, Piaggi was promoted to full colonel and then retired immediately. He died in July 2012. Major Alberto Frontera faced similar charges but these were also eventually dismissed and he was promoted to lieutenant-colonel prior to his retirement. Alberto Frontera and Chris Keeble met in person for the first time in May 2015.

Task Force *Mercedes* lost 145 killed and wounded, with 12th Regiment losing 31 killed, 25th Regiment 12 killed, five from 8th Regiment, two from 1st AA Group, four Air Force and one Navy pilot. Not since October 1975, had the Argentine Army suffered such a loss when 19th Infantry Regiment lost 12 killed to an attack by 500 left-wing rebels in Tucumán Province. Estévez was posthumously awarded Argentina's highest gallantry award for supporting his platoon by directing artillery fire. Two days after the surrender, the seriously wounded Private Ruiz was found still alive in a waterlogged trench and evacuated to Ajax Bay and nursed back to health.

The Argentine prisoners helped clear up the battlefield. In a tragic accident, four 12th Regiment conscripts were moving artillery shells piled near a warehouse when there was a massive explosion. Although a British medical orderly hauled two men from the inferno, a third suffering horribly could not be reached and was shot to relieve him of his agony. The fourth man lost both legs and although flown to Ajax Bay died on the operating table.

A major problem for the British was that the prisoners were protected by the International Committee of the Red Cross and now needed to be sheltered and fed. The loss of the prisoner-of-war camp equipment and Chinooks on board the *Atlantic Conveyor* added to the logistical difficulties. Practice at managing large numbers of prisoners was rare, and consequently interrogating and handling large numbers of prisoners had never been rehearsed. An initial plan to march the prisoners to San Carlos was rejected as impractical, particularly as the weather was wintery. When most of the prisoners were embarked on LSL *Sir Percivale*, Argentina filed a strong protest invoking the Geneva Convention, forbidding a protective party to keep prisoners in a military ship and a battle zone. Arrangements were made with the Red Cross to repatriate the prisoners and while they waited in two sheep-shearing warehouses at Goose Green, intelligence concentrated on updating Argentine tactical philosophies, organisation and weapon systems, the tactical situation in Stanley and answering why 1,000 prisoners had been captured. It emerged that the day before the battle about 400 logistic troops had been flown from Stanley to reduce the risk of casualties from bombing and naval bombardment. None took part in the battle. One prisoner who unwittingly helped solve the issue was an immaculate Air Force warrant officer, complete with a briefcase, who had been despatching troops at Comodoro Rivadavia Air Force Base. He had been checking the numbers on a C-130 when the ramp shut, and he found himself in Stanley and was posted to the Air Force Post Office in Goose Green. A session with a resistant parachute gunner officer was interrupted when two members of the Brigade Defence Troop entered 'the cell' to check the window blackout and piled two chairs on top of each other. One of the Royal Marines climbed this precarious contraption, and it was inevitable that it wobbled and crashed to the floor. The tension in the 'cell' was converted to laughter, made worse when the pair propped a ladder against a wall, only for the first few rungs to break. It was the perfect, if unintentional, demonstration of the 'Incompetent Approach' to interrogation.

British intelligence assessment of Argentine positions of Task Force Mercedes at Goose Green

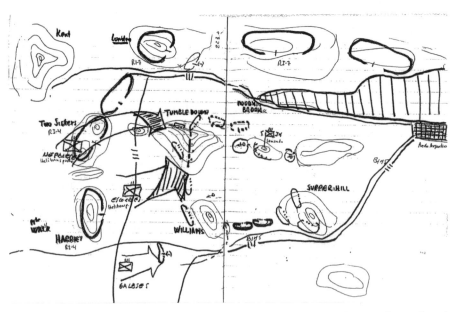

Map seized at the prison camp at Red Beach (Ajax Bay) showing the British attack and Argentine defence of Stanley

CHAPTER 10

Battle for Mount Kent

The origins of the Argentine Special Forces can be traced to the 1978 Football World Cup when the Junta dictatorship believed that a widely televised event, such as the World Cup, was a likely target for a terrorist incident. This resulted in Major Mohamed Alí Seineldín, who commanded 25th Infantry Regiment in 1982, forming the counter-terrorist team, the Brigada Especial Operativa Halcón (Special Operations Brigade Falcon), a military organisation under the direct command of the Buenos Aires Police Department on 5 January. Seineldín was born into a Lebanese-Argentine family who had converted from Druzism to devout Roman Catholicism with a philosophy of nationality and Christianity. He formed Special Team Eagle 8 (Equipo Especial de Lucha contra la Subversión Halcón, shortened to Equipo Especial Halcón 8) which reformed as 601 Commando Company on 5 April 1982. It consisted of 64 men selected after a bespoke Commando aptitude course and three weeks of intensive training that included intelligence and knowledge of the environment. It consisted of a headquarters and three assault platoons and was commanded by Major Castañeto. Seineldín was now commanding 25th Special Infantry Regiment. He deployed with a small advance party on 24 April and reported direct to Governor Menéndez. Commando units wore a green beret with their unit badge.

In addition to the Commando units, the Argentine Air Force Special Operations Group (Grupo de Operaciones Especiales; GOE) had also formed a company-sized counter-terrorist unit that had its origins in the Air Force parachute school formed in 1947. This led to the formation of 13th Parachute Regiment, which was manned by the Air Force but controlled by the Army. The Army later formed its airborne force. 601st National Gendarmería Special Forces Squadron (Escuadrón de Fuerzas Especiales 601 de Gendarmería Nacional) raised four patrols to support the National Gendarmería (Border Guards) for internal security operations. The squadron, nicknamed *Alacrán* ('black-coloured scorpion'), was commanded by Major José Ricardo Spadaro and worked closely with the 181st Military Police and the Military Intelligence Company carrying out counter-intelligence and cordon-and-search operations in Port Stanley, particularly searching for British agents that may have infiltrated into civil population. Port Stanley resident John Smith recalls the surprise inspection his family received on the night of 9–10 June by a Gendarmería patrol under Captain Hugo Díaz:

> We were just about to set the table for supper when the security police arrived at the back door to check that all of us in the house had documents. A most odd sensation to hear a knock on the door after dark. We shouted to ask who it was before opening the door; all very sinister, rather like the sort of things you read about in books but never expect to happen to you.[1]

A Summary of Special Forces Operations

30 April. 1st Platoon, 601 Commando immobilised a lighthouse, conducted several helicopter patrols in the Estancia area and laid an ambush at Green Patch. 2nd Platoon checked the population in the north-west of Pebble Island. 3rd Platoon carried out a reconnaissance of Fitzroy.

1 May. The day that the Task Force began its offensive. The Argentines were nervous.

3 May. After reports of enemy activity, 1st Platoon recced beaches south on the Murrell Peninsula and found a Zodiac inflatable fitted with an outboard engine, equipment and several life jackets, one identified from the aircraft carrier *Hermes*. 3rd Platoon laid an ambush on Tussac Islands.

4 May. While 1st Platoon laid an ambush on the Murrell Peninsula, 2nd Platoon defended the command posts of 3rd, 9th and 10th Brigades against the possibility of an attack. Third Platoon embarked on a Coastguard launch and recced Sand Grass Bay south-east of Pebble Island.

5 May. Following reports that strangers had entered, the West Store was searched. After reports of weapons being fired, 1st and 2nd Platoons commanded by First-Lieutenant García Pinasco embarked on a Coastguard cutter and reconnoitred the north-east coast of East Falklands, without anything to report.

6 May. In a combined operation with the Amphibious Commandos and supported by the Argentine Air Force, 1st Platoon recced Bougainville, Lively Island and Sea Lion Islands to the east of East Falkland, 2nd Platoon conducted helicopter and ground recces of East Falklands.

7 to 9 May. 601 Commando. Captain Ricardo Frecha and First Sergeant Sergio Fernandez used motorcycles to reconnoitre the Murrell Bridge and assess the feasibility of transporting a Blowpipe by motorcycles.

8 May. Captain Llanos, 601 Commando Medical Officer, and First-Corporal Calgano delivered correspondence, medicine and other items to the residents at Fitzroy.

13 to 15 May. 601 Commando conducted recces and a check of the people in the San Carlos area to detect any evidence of infiltration and assess the conditions for deploying 25th Regiment patrols. Search and rescue equipment was recovered from an Argentine helicopter brought down south of Port Howard. Anti-aircraft ambushes were established but no enemy aircraft appeared.

16 May. 601 Commando deployed to Pebble Island after the SAS raid on the Military Air Base.

17 May. 2nd Platoon recced the derelict refrigeration plant in Ajax Bay, San Carlos Water.

19/20 May. 1st Platoon, the reduced 2nd Platoon and an anti-aircraft ambush group recced Port Howard.

21 May (British landings at San Carlos Water). First Lieutenant Sergio Fernández and First-Corporal Martinez laid an anti-aircraft ambush group with First Platoon and claimed to have shot down the Harrier flown by Flight-Lieutenant Jeff Glover; the pilot was rescued from the water by First-Lieutenant García Pinasco. An ambush was laid north-east of Howard in case an attempt was made to rescue him. Corporal Martinez claimed that he brought down a Harrier with a Blowpipe.

22 May. Captain Frecha and Lieutenant Llanos rescued two Air Force pilots who had ejected south of Port Howard. Anti-aircraft ambushes were set but no enemy aircraft flew within effective range. Equipment from a shot-down helicopter was found. The next day, after the defeat at Goose Green and a British advance to Stanley expected, a strategy was devised to deploy all special forces to occupy the high ground north and south of Mount Kent in order to force enemy helicopters to be within range of air defence and oblige the enemy to engage in fighting. In the event that Mount Kent was by-passed, they planned to attack the enemy rearguard.

During the morning of 21 May, the day that the British Task Force had landed at San Carlos Water, the School of Infantry had ordered the Special Operations Group to form a second commando group and for the next 12 days, a special aptitude course was run for applicants and former commandos whose skills had lapsed. The successful candidates were formed into 602 Commando Company under command of Major Aldo Rico. After intense training between 15 and 26 May that included a study of the Falklands, the advance arrived in Stanley on 28 May, the day of the battle of Goose Green, and was followed three days later by the remainder of the company.

Mount Kent is 1,093ft (333m) high and, with several other features, dominates 5 miles to the west of Stanley. It dominated the British advance from San Carlos Water and became the focus of skirmishes and ambushes between the opposing special forces.

Lieutenant-Colonel Diego Soria, commanding 4th Regiment, had been ordered to prevent the British advance from San Carlos and had placed C Company on Mount Challenger and Two Sisters. On 28 May, the Combat Team *Güemes* (B Company, 12th Infantry Regiment) heliborne reserve on Mount Kent as a reaction force rejoined 12th Infantry Regiment at Goose Green during the battle and was captured. That Mount Kent was undefended was soon spotted by both sides. Soria also deployed his C Company from Mount Challenger and placed it on Mount Two Sisters and Mount Harriet. On the saddle between Two Sisters and Mount Longdon was B Company, 6th Infantry Regiment and Support Platoon from B Company, 12th Regiment left behind by Combat Team Güemes and commanded by Major Jaimet.

While 601 Commando Company supported the defence of Stanley, Goose Green and West Falkland, the recently arrived 602 Commando led by Major Rico was ordered to seize Mount Kent prior to the insertion of Major Jose Ricardo Spadaro's 601st National Gendarmería Special Forces Squadron and Major Oscar Ramon Jaimet's heliborne-trained B Company, 6th Infantry Regiment, which had undergone night-combat training the previous year, and the Air Force Special Operations Group.

26 May. The special forces operations began with 3rd Platoon, 601 Commando conducting recces of the ground between Mount Kent and Mount Simon and dumping caches of food and ammunition. The next day, the patrol occupied Big Mountain.

27 May. Soon after 3rd Platoon had taken over from 2nd Platoon, increased helicopter activity to the west was noted and a second observation post was established that night.

28 May (Battle of Goose Green). 1st Platoon, 602 Commando Company commanded by Captain Jose Arnobio Vercesi, was dropped by two Argentine UH-1 helicopters on Mount Simon with orders to observe, recce and set up anti-aircraft ambushes. The section numbered eight commandos, including the scout, First-Sergeant Helguero from 601 Commando Company, two soldiers with a Blowpipe missile launcher and the medic, First-Sergeant Pedrozo. The commandos reported to HQ 10th Brigade that the enemy had created an air corridor between San Carlos and Mount Kent but then lost contact.

29 May. During the night, Captain Andres Ferrero's 3rd Assault Section, 602 Commando Company was flown to a landing site on the lower slopes of Mount Kent. It was about 11pm and was snowing. As the helicopter had delivered the patrol and was leaving and the patrol began climbing a hill, it unexpectedly came under enemy fire, including tracer, from three directions. Surprised by the ambush, the Argentines began to return fire. First-Sergeant Raimondo Viltes was on his knee firing his rifle when a bullet hit him on the heel and he collapsed, unable to get up. First-Lieutenant Lauria saw that Viltes would need assistance and after the patrol distributed their rifles and backpacks, Lauria lifted Viltes, a big man, in a fireman's lift. When the patrol reached a stone run under fire, First-Sergeant José Núñez helped the pair across. Fourteen hours later,

when the patrol rendezvoused with another patrol on Mount Estancia, Viltes was placed in a sleeping bag in a cave and joined by someone else to keep him warm. However, Viltes was thirsty from the continued loss of blood. The next night, Lauria moved Viltes to another cave. By now, their only food was rice pudding, which Lauria gave to Viltes. Lauria ate nothing and was concerned because he had not eaten for two days and was out of strength to carry him. Confined to watching British helicopters moving guns and supplies, the next day three officers and a sergeant from 602 Commando on motorcycles rescued the two men and took them to a medical unit where Viltes assumed he would soon be cured. The first person he saw was his brother, an orderly, but he did not recognise Viltes. Viltes was immediately sent to the operating theatre on the *Bahia Paraíso* where surgeons removed ammunition embedded in the wound.

During the day, 601 and 602 Commandos, 601st National Gendarmería Special Forces Squadron and the Air Force Special Operations Group were ordered to occupy the high ground north-east of Mount Kent and 1) prevent the movement of enemy helicopters; 2) slow down the enemy advance to Stanley; and 3) if cut off, to disrupt the enemy. However, Second and Third Platoons found the feature was occupied by enemy and were ambushed. They withdrew from the immediate area and were directed to occupy other ground, but the action had cost three killed, one wounded and one taken prisoner.

30 May. During the mid-morning, the Army's last operational Puma helicopter crashed north-west of Murrell Bridge. Throughout the day, Royal Air Force Harriers had been supporting ground operations on Mount Kent and it was assumed that it had been shot down by a Stinger SAM near Murrell Bridge, on the eastern slope of Mount Kent, with the loss of six Gendarmería killed and eight injured from *Alacrán* Squadron. A Harrier was hit by ground fire from Sub-Lieutenant Llambas-Pravaz's platoon during a raid and crashed into the sea. A radio operator had passed a short transmission to HQ 10th Brigade that the security of the air corridor from Stanley to Mount Kent had been compromised. The British believed that the helicopter had not been shot down with a missile but had been hit in an Argentine 'blue on blue'.

Captain Tomas Fernandez, of 2nd Assault Section, intended to withdraw at about 5am on 30 May, however a battery of guns was being deployed using helicopters and it was not until about 11am that his section emerged from their hide now intending to seize Bluff Cove Peak. First-Lieutenants Daniel Oneto and Rubén Márquez and Sergeant Humberto Blas were scouting ahead, and after about 500 metres they heard an unusual noise. Captain Ferrero joined Marquez and Blas to investigate and they had hardly covered 50 metres when they came under machine-gun and mortar fire. Blas was killed. Marquez threw a grenade, but he was wearing gloves and was unable to use his FAL rifle. The patrol had stumbled into a hide occupied by 15 SAS. At about 5pm, First-Sergeant Vicente Alfredo Flores, the radio operator, sent a contact report from Bluff Cove Peak. 'We are in trouble' and then 40 minutes later: 'There are English all around us... you had better hurry.' Fernandez broke contact and in the scramble down the hill, Sergeant Flores fell, was knocked out and woke up a prisoner-of-war and a guest of 'Hotel Galtieri' interrogation centre at San Carlos farmyard where he joined prisoners captured at Goose Green.

31 May. Major Castagneto, who commanded 601 Commando Company, was leading a patrol to extract 2nd Platoon from Mount Simon when the helicopter returning to Stanley came under friendly fire. 3rd Platoon, 601 Commando Company occupied Mount Estancia.

Meanwhile, Major Rico was leading a patrol assembled from 601 and 602 Commandos using Land Rovers and seven motorcycles conducting a recce in the direction of Moody Brook intending to collect intelligence on Mount Kent. The patrol then left Two Sisters on foot while the seven motorcyclists commanded by Major Castagneto reached the northern ridge of Mount Kent and became engaged in a firefight and were mortared, which damaged one machine.

Meanwhile 3 PARA had reached Estancia House and found field dressings used to treat the two commandos, Marine special forces wounded and National Gendarmería commandos before they were evacuated. Lieutenant-Commander Camiletti's Marine special forces patrol, minus Camilletti and Corporal Carrasco captured at Verde Mountain and Teal Inlet respectively, were returning from reconnoitring San Carlos Water and ambushed on the lower slopes of Estancia Mountain. Sergeants Jesús Pereyra and Ramón López were seriously wounded and captured along with Corporals Pablo Alvarado and Pedro Verón, both unwounded.

Captain Verseci had listened on his radio as 2nd Platoon clashed with the enemy and decided to abandon Mount Kent and link up with the 601 Combat Engineer detachment at Fitzroy. The previous night, his patrol had endured a snowstorm without proper equipment and with more bad weather predicted, he decided to shelter in a deserted shepherd's cottage known as Top Malo House near Bull Hill. Shortly after a gloomy dawn the next morning, the Argentines heard helicopters and quickly gathered their equipment and prepared to leave the house using the cover of a stream bed. But the British had deployed a seven-man fire support team on a hillock 150m from Top Malo House and a 12-man assault group, all wearing combat uniforms.

Lieutenant Espinosa was on guard on the first floor at about 10am and when he saw British soldiers, he raised the alarm and opened fire. The British fired a green Very flare, pulverised the cottage with six M72 LAW 66mm rockets and then charged, with two more rockets exploding in the stream. The Argentines were caught unprepared and as they sought the cover of the stream, Lieutenant Espinosa was killed by a 66mm and Sergeant Mateo Sbert was shot dead giving covering fire. As the British assault group advanced towards the burning building, the Argentines in the stream were screened by the smoke but trapped, and within about 45 minutes, low on ammunition and with six wounded, Captain Vercesi had no alternative but to surrender. After the battle, Captain Rod Boswell, who commanded the attacking Royal Marines Arctic and Mountain Warfare Cadre, commented to Vercesi 'Never in a house...' The battle had been watched by members of Red de Observadores del Aire or ROA (Argentine Air Force forward observation teams) on Malo Hill and Mount Simon.

HMS *Glamorgan* shelled the Skyguard fire-control radars at Stanley Airfield, almost hit close to the base of the 40-strong Air Force Special Operations Group (GOE) and fired a Sea Slug missile. First-Lieutenant Luis Castañari was killed and Corporal Juan Chiantore and Corporal (Mechanic) José Francisco Guastalla were both wounded taking cover.

That night, the Gendarmería Santo Patrol provided the defence of the Joint Falklands Command Post.

1 June. Lieutenant-Colonel Soria had become exasperated by the one meal a day policy that he gave his men permission to use their combat rations.

After the loss of Mount Kent, Argentine Air Force Canberras bombed British positions from information and a map provided by Captains Ferrero and Villarruel. In the hills to the west of Stanley, 4th Infantry Regiment experienced nightly patrol clashes. The section commanded by Corporal Elvio Alberto Balcaza detected an enemy presence on Mount Wall.

2 June. Captain Carlos Patterson, the 4th Regiment Operations Officer joined two inexperienced platoon commanders on Two Sisters to advise on maintaining morale. Second-Lieutenant Lautaro Jiménez Corbalán, the B Company 3rd Platoon Commander in 4th Regiment, ordered Corporal Nicolas Víctor Odorcic and his section to investigate. At about 11am, the patrol clashed with the enemy on the ridge and Privates Celso Paez and Roberto Ledesma were shot dead and Odorcic was concussed when a bullet hit his helmet. Second-Lieutenant Marcelo Llambías Pravaz, commanding 3rd Platoon, A Company on Two Sisters, ordered Corporal Walter Ariel Pintos and his section to counter-attack, which they did by using rifle grenades. The RAF Primary Forward Air Controller, commando-trained Flight Lieutenant Dennis Marshal-Hasdell, remembers,

> We were separated from our heavy bergens with the radios and all our gear. The patrol was spread over quite a large area, with lots of shouting, noise and firing going on. The Marines abandoned all their equipment, and although no one told us, it became clear that we were to withdraw. With no information and the likelihood of having to fight our way out, Dave Greedus and I decided to abandon our equipment, destroying as much as we could. The two radio sets (HF and UHF) were tough enough, but the HAZE unit of the laser target marker was designed to withstand the weight of a tank![2]

Technical analysis of the target marker suggested that a 1,000-pound GBU-16 Paveway II laser-guided bomb was to be delivered on Argentine bunkers on Mount Harriet by RAF Harriers.

By profession, Captain Carlos Túrolo was a doctor. He was also a reservist in 602 Commando Company and was armed with a .300 Magnum rifle.

> We appropriated anything they had abandoned. The good thing was that they also left food, which we tried. Once we reached our position, we opened the backpacks. In one, probably from a Royal Marines officer, we found a typically English leather box and in it, we found polished shoes, corresponding brush and a cloth. Therefore, the owner travelled 14,000 kilometers to be in the middle of a lost mountain in the Falklands. He also had his battery-powered shaver, another very important object in combat. As soon as we arrived, we had grown a beard because every night we mask our faces with polish or mud and wore black balaclavas. The next day we gave the shaver to the non-commissioned officer who had stood out the most in the patrol at the discretion of the section chief.[3]

4 June. 45 Commando advanced to Bluff Cove Peak on the lower of Mount Kent and linked with the SAS.

5 June. Harriers attacked Two Sisters with rockets. A 45 Commando patrol used heavy mist shrouding the Murrell River to penetrate the C Company 3rd Platoon, 602 Commando position.

Captain Carlos Túrolo commented that:

> At about 4pm in the evening on the 5th, we moved up to First-Lieutenant Carlos Alberto Arroyo's command post on Mount Harriet. Major Aldo Rico commanded the patrol. We were as glad to see Arroyo as he was to see us. Dirty, bearded and a little thinner, he gripped Rico in a bear hug. A gallant Commando, Arroyo volunteered to go with us to Mount Wall. Several conscripts came to see us. There was a lot of laughter, some of it nervous, perhaps adrenaline-driven. We had a chance to get a scrumptious and – let us be honest here – very fatty barbecue going and look at the enemy positions at Bluff Cove Rincon and tried to pinpoint the observation post on Mount Wall. A 4th Regiment patrol had been out in the area the night before. Distances were deceptive. In the thin air Mount Kent seemed close at hand. In nearly every other direction rose outcrops of limestone. Their slopes were not sheer; rather they spread themselves, rugged and inhospitable. It was a very humbling place. We watched 155mm fire falling on the British paratroopers at Bluff Cove Rincon. The weather was appalling, cold and wet with high wind. Few people are aware that we also had the ugly experience of being shelled by the 3rd Artillery Group at one point. It was human error. The plan was to take Mount Wall from the rear. Two artillery batteries were on call, because our route up the feature was very open – a perfect killing ground. By 4pm it was almost dark and the temperature had sunk. Moving past

shell craters and remnants of cluster bombs to the base of Mount Wall, we lay up among boulders while First-Lieutenant Lauria cleared a path through the minefields. Altogether it must have taken three hours to get there. It was a moonlit night and cold. I lay there frozen, not moving. Argentinian artillery fire started coming down on Mount Wall at approximately 10.30pm. Crouching in silence, we waited for the fire to end. Some shells fell only 150 metres from us. Then – sudden silence. It ceased and Major Rico screamed to us to go and we advanced uphill through the rocks. A fit commando, if anyone was going to get to the mountaintop first it would be Lauria, but as he swept round a boulder, he came across a straggler or so he thought. It was Major Rico. Who says age slows you down? On the way up we passed the body of a 4th Regiment conscript. Captain Hugo Ranieri knelt down to examine the body and removed the rosary from the young soldier's neck before moving on. We found a laser target designator and several rucksacks. It was the first indication we'd had of how well they had been equipped. There was even a 42 Commando beret.[4]

3rd Platoon, 602nd Commando Company reached the summit of Mount Challenger after a difficult approach and then returned to Port Stanley where Major Rico and First-Lieutenant Jorge Manuel Vizoso Posse (second-in-command of the patrol), tried to convince Brigadier-General Jofre to fly a rifle company to attack the British artillery batteries. But Jofre was irritated and told them to leave the decision-making process to 10th Brigade. Captain Tomas Fernandez and his 2nd Platoon, 602 Commando Company were on Bluff Cove Peak intending to seize it and noted at 5am that British helicopters had delivered 105mm guns.

The increase in enemy activity led to 602 Commando Company deploying to Mount Wall and Mount Harriet to reinforce 4th Regiment. During the day, the Artillery Group of Army, Para and Marine gunners was formed to support Argentine units manning the Outer Defence Zone, now under frequent shelling from enemy artillery and naval gunfire. First-Lieutenant Hector Domingo Tessey, who usually commanded C Battery of the 3rd Artillery Group, received two guns manned by airborne gunners, bringing his battery to eight guns.

During the night of 6/7 June, Corporal Nicolás Albornoz led a 4th Regiment patrol of eight conscripts that crossed Murrell River and reached the slopes of Estancia Mountain and spotted several British vehicles, but came under mortar fire and had to withdraw.

Ten commandos from 1st Platoon, 601 Commando established an OP overlooking Port Howard on West Falkland. A fighting patrol from the Gendarmería and 602 Commando laid an ambush on Mount Wall, forward of positions occupied by 4th Regiment on Mount Harriet. The following day, the centre position was mortared and machine-gunned and, as an attack developed, 602 Commando deployed onto the enemy flanks and, covered by the guns from the 3rd Artillery Group, counter-attacked. It claimed the enemy had lost a complete patrol with two killed and one wounded.

Raids, sniping and naval gunfire harassed defenders and denied them any sleep. During the night of 8/9 June, at the same time as an enemy patrol probed the sector defended by 3 Platoon and killed Corporal Hipólito González and Private Martiniano Gómez, two large enemy fighting patrols attempted the same on Two Sisters, but the Argentine RASIT ground surveillance radar on Mount Longdon detected the activity and artillery fire dispersed the force. Lieutenant Roberto Francisco Eito's platoon from the 601st Combat Engineers Company laid a large minefield around Mount Harriet. There was another smaller one between Mount Challenger and Mount Harriet. Lieutenant-Colonel Soria stated,

> In the second week of June we received a platoon of the 12th Infantry Regiment, which had been unable to link up with the bulk of its unit and recovered two rifle platoons from A Company, which had been supporting Two Sisters defences. We also got reinforcements in the form of MAG machine-guns from the Mounted Grenadiers Regiment along with their crews.

Also reinforcing the defence were machine-gunners mortar crews and riflemen from the 1st 'Patricios' Infantry Regiment and the 17th Airborne Infantry Regiment. Second-Lieutenant Corbalán reported a total of six killed and 14 wounded during the fighting on Mount Wall and during the battle of Mount Harriet.

At dusk on 9 June, 4th Regiment had noted that British troops had occupied Port Harriet House to the south of Mount Harriet. The Reconnaissance Platoon commanded by Sub-Lieutenant Pasolli was flown to the area and, supported by the 120mm Mortar Platoon on Mount Harriet, forced a Scots Guards patrol to withdraw across soft ground with three wounded, but abandoning their bergens and radios. When an Argentine platoon pursued the patrol down the hill, although out of range, the Scots Guards opened fire with their two Bren light machine-guns.

A fighting patrol from the National Frontier Force and 601 and 602 Commandos supported 4th Regiment on Mount Harriet and laid an ambush on Mount Wall but lost two killed and one wounded in a patrol clash. On the following day, the centre position was mortared and machine-gunned and as an attack developed, 602 Commando deployed onto the enemy flank and directed shelling from the 3rd Artillery Group, which forced the enemy to withdraw. The Argentines launched a counter-attack and claimed that the enemy was neutralised.

10 June. At 2.10am Captain Andres Ferrero's 3rd Platoon's position was attacked by an enemy (45 Commando) fighting patrol. A 66mm projectile exploded close to Major Rico. Sergeant Mario Cisnero and Captain Miguel Santos of the National Gendarmería section were killed and Sergeant Ramon Acosta wounded in fierce action near Murrell River after seizing equipment, forcing the Royal Marines platoon to withdraw, with Major Rico calling for fire support from the 3rd Artillery Group. Lieutenant Horacio Lauria and Sergeant Orlando claimed to have destroyed an enemy machine-gun with rifle grenades. Two Argentine Special Forces deployed to ambush the enemy patrol as it withdrew were wounded. During the same night as a 'blue on blue', a 45 Commando patrol returning to its base was mortared with the loss of four Royal Marines killed and three wounded. The next day, a patrol sent Sub-Lieutenant Llambias-Pravez to recover the bergens and several weapons left by the Royal Marines. They were then subsequently photographed as trophies by war correspondents.

First-Lieutenant José Martiniano Duarte, in charge of the 1st Platoon on West Falkland, was leading a reconnaissance patrol with three NCOs, and clashed with an enemy observation post on a ridge near to Poke Point Hill, close to Many Branch Point overlooking Port Howard. Captain John Hamilton, D Squadron, SAS was killed providing automatic covering fire for his colleague, Sergeant Fonseka, who was captured with a substantial amount of material, including radios and code settings and naval gunfire targeting equipment. Two other SAS men withdrew from the second OP close to Hamilton's position without being noticed.

In late May, Marine Corps Major Raul Cufre, of the Tactical Divers, had devised a plan to install 601 and 602 Commando Companies, the 601 Border Guard Special Forces Squadron and a 1st General San Martin Cavalry Regiment squadron behind British lines to link up with a parachute drop by the 4th Airborne Brigade. Operation SZE-21 was approved by the Junta, Cufre flew to Stanley on 10 June to finalise the details and returned to Comodoro Rivadavia, reporting that the plan was ready to be implemented. The two Argentine Air Force CH-47 Chinook helicopters in the Falklands returned to the Argentine mainland. The plan was to collect Major Armando Valiente's 75-strong 603 Commando Company together with petroleum shaped charges which had been seized from a French company operating in southern Argentina and insert this force behind Mounts Kent and Challenger in order to attack British artillery.

On the night of 12/13 June, Captain Andres Ferrero's 3rd Assault Section of 602 Commando Company took up ambush positions in the vicinity of Mount William in support of the 5th Marine Infantry Battalion.

Although the Argentines were on the back foot by early June and withdrawing to their fortress at Stanley, there was no question of negotiating a truce or ceasefire. Indeed, Vice-Admiral Lombardo of the Military Junta had approved of a counter-attack.

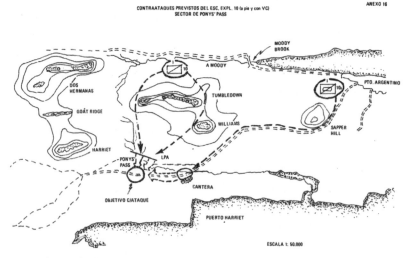

Argentine plan to deploy 10 Armoured Car Squadron to defend the southern approaches to Stanley from the south at Pony Pass. 'Dos Hermanos' is the Two Sisters.

CHAPTER 11

Defence of the Outer Defence Zone: Mount Harriet

After the battle of Goose Green, the Argentines switched from defending landings to the defence of Port Stanley based around the high ground of the Outer Defence Zone of Mount Longdon, Two Sisters (Dos Hermanas) and Mount Harriet and the Inner Defence Zone of Mount Tumbledown, Mount William, Sapper Hill and Wireless Ridge – a perimeter of 48 miles. However, the Argentines could only defend about 40 per cent of the ground, therefore gaps and weaknesses had developed. To the north, east and south was the South Atlantic Ocean and the Royal Navy. By 31 May British patrols had considerable success that included capturing a document in a command post showing the Argentine order of battle and arrangements for the defence of Stanley. Royal Engineers collected intelligence on minefields. The ground war developed in sharp patrol actions and ambushes, such as the ambush at Top Malo House. By the morning of 12 June, Army Group, Stanley had three choices – fight, swim or surrender. Even though the odds were stacked against him, Brigadier-General Menéndez chose to fight.

Lieutenant-Colonel Diego Soria's 4th *Monte Caseros* Infantry Regiment (RI 4) could trace its history to 1810. The Argentine defence was entrusted to B Company commanded by Captain Carlos Alberto Arroyo, a former Army Commando. Most of the passive night goggles were with his company. During the second week of June, Soria received reinforcements from 12th Infantry Regiment of two A Company platoons, which he allocated to the defence of Two Sisters and several MAG machine-guns from the Mounted Grenadiers Regiment.

Mount Harriet is a hill of 873ft on East Falkland to the west of Stanley and is linked to Two Sisters by Goat Ridge to the north. Two thousand metres to the west is Mount Wall. Between Mount Harriet and Stanley is Mount Tumbledown. Like all mountains in the Falklands, the lower slopes consist of frosty white grass or bog, and wind-battered hard rock summit and stone runs litter all sides. The feature is strategically important because it guards the approaches to Stanley from the west and the south. The regiment hosted artillery and Air Force forward observation officers and they had alerted commanders in Stanley of the British advance to Port Pleasant. Captain Tomás Fox, the Artillery Observation Officer on Mount Kent, directed the 155mm battery to shell enemy reported to be in the Bluff Cove area.

The 42 Commando attack was preceded by several days of observation and nights of patrolling looking for approaches from the south of the feature. When two landing ships arrived at Bluff Cove on 8 June and were seen from Mount Harriet, Major Rico, of 602 Commando Company, sent Private First Class Argentino Foremny from his Commando Company Blowpipe Team forward with his built-in/zoom-in sight of his man-portable surface-to-air missile launcher to confirm the reports. Major Rico stated,

> In the area of Port Pleasant, about 35 kilometres from our position, we were able to make out the silhouette of two ships that appeared to be transports. No way could they have been Argentine for the British were predominant; we later found out they were *Sir Galahad* and *Sir Tristram*. We alerted our headquarters and three hours later the first air attack took place. The day ended up being the blackest day for their fleet, as was admitted by the British, with 56 British and three Argentines killed.[1]

Lieutenant-Colonel Soria, commanding 4th Regiment, wanted to exploit the disruption of the raid but was denied permission to attack the beachhead.

At 11pm on 8 June, Mount Harriet was bombarded by ships that cost two Argentines killed and 25 wounded. The first that 4th Regiment knew of an assault was when B Company on the left flank came under sustained pressure from the south – and not from the direction of Mount Wall to the west, as was expected. John Witheroe, a British war correspondent, was attached to 42 Commando.

> Sporadic shellfire slowed our progress tremendously. Eventually, we made the base of Mount Harriet, which was coming under incredible fire from a frigate offshore. The whole mountain seemed to erupt in flame. It seemed impossible that anybody could survive an attack like that. This went on for well over an hour, shell after shell whistling over our heads and hitting the mountain.[2]

When the 120mm Mortar Platoon position near B Company on the eastern heights was attacked, its commander, Sub-Lieutenant Mario Juarez, drew his pistol, but was badly wounded. First-Lieutenant Jorge Alejandro Echeverria, the 4th Regiment Intelligence Officer, assessed that the attack was not a diversion and assembled the Reconnaissance Platoon, the Reserve Platoon and the 12th Regiment Platoon attached to the regiment to prevent the enemy gaining a foothold on the ridge. Corporal Roberto Baruzzo, a sniper, and a machine-gunner picked off targets. When a Royal Marine charged him, Baruzzo shot at him twice. The shock and flash of night fighting quickly destabilised the conscripts and increasing numbers surrendered. However, officers, including Lieutenant-Colonel Soria and First-Lieutenants Rubén Cucchiara, the Medical Officer, Francisco Pablo D'Aloia, Esteban Guillermo Carlucci and Luis Oscar García and senior NCOs resisted. The heavy machine-gunners and protecting riflemen also mostly remained in their positions.

A second assault from the south aimed at the centre of the ridge was contested for nearly five hours by Sub-Lieutenant Pablo Oliva's 3rd Brigade Security Platoon and Sub-Lieutenant Eugenio César Bruny's 4th Platoon, who were equipped with seven machine-guns as rifle teams were deluged with Milan anti-tank missiles and shelling from Mount Challenger. The British war correspondent Kim Sabido described the stiff Argentine resistance as follows:

> For a couple of hours, it seemed as if it might all go wrong. Pinned down on the slopes by heavy machine-gun and sniper fire, progress was painfully slow. I saw several men fall with bullet wounds, others were hit by flying fragments from the constant barrage of long-distance, high-explosive shelling. The men in front of us were not giving up without a bitter fight.[3]

Oliva lost four men killed and five wounded, including the B Company second-in-command and his signaller. Lieutenant-Colonel Soria personally organised the shelling of the British advance and brought it very close to his headquarters. A Royal Marine described the battle:

> The enemy fire came under lots of effective fire from 0.50 calibre machine-guns. At the same time, mortars were coming down all over us, but the main threat was from those machine-gunners who could see us in the open because of the moonlight. There were three machine-guns and we brought down constant and effective salvoes of our own artillery fire on to them directly, 15 rounds at a time. There would be a pause, and they'd come back at us again. So we had to do it a second time. There'd be a pause, then 'boom, boom, boom,' they'd come back at us again. Conscripts don't do this, babies don't do this, men who are badly led and of low morale don't do this. They were good steadfast troops. I rate them.[4]

Sub-Lieutenant Oscar Augusto Silva and his platoon resisted on Goat Ridge until shelling, white phosphorus and machine-guns pushed them off, at the cost of Privates Juan José Acuña and Carlos Epifanio Casco killed and three captured. At first light, Lieutenant-Colonel Soria ordered the remaining troops on Mount Harriet and Goat Ridge to withdraw. However, as enemy then advanced across the open ground towards Goat Ridge, a young Guarani conscript, Private Orlando Aylan, continued to harass L Company until he was blasted from his position by an 84mm Carl Gustav rocket fired at short range. Sub-Lieutenant Corbalán and his 3rd Platoon were covering the Argentine withdrawal to Goat Ridge under cover of the pre-positioned machine-guns. Corbalán commented,

> When we had them about 600 metres, I ordered the rifle grenades to be fired at an angle of 45 degrees in order to obtain the maximum possible range. Several explosions fell in close proximity to the British, but we could not assess in detail the effects of our distant fire. We were sure that we encouraged him even more to leave the place.[5]

3rd Platoon lost two killed to mortar fire as it withdrew though a defensive minefield to a new position on Mount William; Corbalán was temporarily blinded when he triggered an Argentine booby-trap and was rescued by Privates Teodoro Flores and Carlos Salvatierra, two conscripts who were decorated for their bravery. However, Lieutenant-Colonel

Soria had little option but to surrender, 'It hurt me a lot to have to take the decision to surrender, but the situation then gave no alternative, and all I could have achieved was further casualties in my command, who were already in a bad state.' The fighting lasted longer than anticipated. Eighteen Argentines were killed defending Mount Harriet, including those killed in earlier patrol battles and shelling. Over 300 Argentines, a considerable amount of intelligence and masses of ammunition had been captured. Enemy bunkers were simple shelters, some with foam rubber mattresses and ration packs. In one near the summit was a battlefield radar still in its unopened crate. Lance-Corporal Tony Koleszar was trying to remove the 'desirable' boots of two 'dead' Argentine soldiers when they proved to be very much alive and more than willing to surrender. The battle had lasted longer than expected and left 42 Commando no time to assault Mount William under the cover of darkness as had been planned. An Argentine journalist commented on the imaginative tactic, seemingly with little tactical knowledge,

> Evidently, it was a clever infiltration. From the reports I have so far, I cannot specify exactly where they [42 Commando] entered, but I do know that they entered through the flank that we had completely covered, which was the coast that went to Puerto Argentino [Stanley]. We had it mined. That minefield cost a lot of time, sweat and casualties, and those mines that were laid weighed 20 kilos. Even if they put minefields on one, if we have to attack, we would attack the same and we will see where we pass. That same determination, I think, was theirs.

Several British journalists depicted the Argentines as hapless teenage conscripts who caved in after the first shots were fired. Warrant Officer 2 John Cartledge, serving with L Company, 42 Commando was more realistic and gave the young conscripts due credit:

> They used the tactics which they had been taught along the way very well. They were quite prepared for an attack and put up a strong fight from start to finish. They were also better equipped than we were. We had first generation night sights, which were large cumbersome pieces of equipment, while the Argentines had second generation American night sights that were compact and so much better than what we had. The one deficiency which we exposed was that they had planned for a western end of the mountain attack and therefore had not bothered to extend their defensive positions to the eastern end, where we ultimately attacked.[6]

The Argentine defeat of the Outer Defence Zone, in particular the loss of Two Sisters, which overlooked Stanley, appalled Brigadier-General Menéndez and he signalled the Joint Operations Centre in Buenos Aires demanding immediate air and navy bombardment and insisted the National Reserve must be deployed.

Defence of the Outer Defence Zone: Mount Longdon

The 7th *Coronel Conde* Mechanised Infantry Regiment was part of the 10th Brigade, could trace its history to 1813 and was based in the tough districts of Lanus and Bandfield in Buenos Aires. Many of the soldiers knew each other well and indulged in Hollywood movies and American swearing. It used the San Miguel del Monte training camp on the outskirts of Buenos Aires.

The regiment was based at Arana (La Plata), Buenos Aires Province and was usually prepared for war against Chile and carried out helicopter drills with the 601st Combat Aviation Battalion. In October 1981, Brigadier Jofre had organised an exercise in central Argentina in which the brigade advanced to the General Acha Training Area in La Pampa Province on the lower slopes of the Andes and about 1,000 kilometres from Buenos Aires. The climax was a mechanised infantry assault supported by Skyhawks representing friendly and enemy air support strafing hulks with rockets. The Argentinian Army Commander-in-Chief, Lieutenant-General Leopoldo Galtieri, paid close attention to the performance of the brigade. Some suitable soldiers completed a commando course organised by commando-trained Major Oscar Jaimet, the Brigade Operations Officer, an Army commando who had fought against the People's Revolutionary Army in Tucuman province during the 'Dirty War'. He was a thoroughly professional and a dedicated soldier who expected high standards and exercised rigid but fair discipline.

The 7th Mechanised Infantry Regiment was deployed in Sector *Plata* to the north of Stanley, east of Murrell Bridge. A Company was to the north of Longdon and B Company and C Company covered Wireless Ridge and Cortley Ridge in reserve.

Jorge Alberto Altieri was born in Banfield and lived in Lanús, a province of Buenos Aires. After completing his military service in 1981, he was discharged in March 1982 and was training to be a martial arts instructor when on 9 April, Good Friday, a police officer arrived at his parents' house and informed him that he had been mobilised. His mother was distraught because her younger son had just been conscripted. Nevertheless Jorge advised his mother that, 'I preferred to go and die in the Malvinas.' After she found some warm clothing, he returned to the barracks and joined his friends who had also received re-enlistment papers. Jorge was due to depart to the Malvinas on the 13th and when his father came to say goodbye and reminded him to write, Jorge replied, 'I don't know if I'm going to have time, because I'm going to be fighting there in the Malvinas.' Poor weather prevented flying for two days.

On arrival at Puerto Argentino (Stanley), the troops were issued with weapons, ammunition and other equipment and after spending the first night in a school, the next day they negotiated the soggy, peat track to the summit of Mount Longdon. Sub-Lieutenant Juan Baldini, a B Company platoon commander, assigned the soldiers to tents and issued each man two ponchos, a sleeping bag and a blanket. The next day, trenches were dug, which was a daily fatigue until the Royal Navy started bombarding the Argentine positions. A radar team attracted bombardment. When one of his mates was wounded by bombing, Jorge and friends made a stretcher with their rifles, as there were no actual stretchers, for the long carry to the road. Altieri was later elected head of the National Commission of Former Combatants of the Malvinas, which now represents Argentine veterans.

The defence of Mount Longdon was entrusted to Major Carrizo-Salvadores, the 7th Regiment second-in-command. In 1974, he was serving in the 17th Airborne Infantry Regiment as a captain when about 16 guerrillas from the People's Revolutionary Army attacked a military barracks. Part of the group escaped, another person was arrested nearby and the remainder sought refuge in the Capilla del Rosario and resisted until they ran out of ammunition and then surrendered. A senior officer ordered that since they failed to comply with the Geneva Convention and were disguised in Army uniform they should be shot. Carrizo-Salvadores was accused of being a secondary participant in homicide, however a Federal Court acquitted him on the grounds that the incident had been committed before the 1976 to 1983 dictatorship.

B Company consisted of three platoons. 1st Platoon commanded by Sub-Lieutenant Baldini were deployed among rocky outcrops on the western feature known to the British as 'Fly Half', a position in rugby union, a sport well known in Argentina. To the south was Second-Lieutenant Enrique Neirotti's 3rd Platoon and to the north was First-Sergeant Raúl González's 2nd Platoon. Captain Sergio Andrés Dachary of the Marines arrived in early June with a detachment of six 0.50-inch M2 Browning machine-gun teams and protecting riflemen numbering about 100 ranks. Lieutenant Diego Arreseigor's 10th Engineer Company platoon laid a protective minefield along the western and northern slopes. The total number of defenders was 278 all ranks. Private Altieri described the B Company training organised by Drill-Sergeant Pedro Reyes:

> I was issued with a FAL 7.62mm rifle. Other guys were issued with FAP light machine-guns Argentine PAMS sub-machine guns and FN MAG 7.62mm general purpose machine-guns. The main emphasis was making every bullet count. I was also shown how to use a bazooka, how to make and lay booby-traps, how to navigate at night, did helicopter drills and practised night and day attacks and ambushes.[1]

Morale was reasonably strong. Private Fabián Passaro in 1st Platoon recalled:

> Most of us had adjusted to what we'd been landed in and adjusted to the war. But some boys were still very depressed and, in many cases, were getting worse all the time. Of course, we were very fed up with wearing the same clothes for so many days, going without a shower, being so cold, eating badly. It was too many things together, quite apart from our natural fear of the war, the shelling and all that. But I think some of us were adapting better than others. There were kids who were very worried, and I tried to buoy them up a bit. 'Don't worry,' I told them. 'Nothing will happen, we're safe here. Don't you see they could

never get right up here? There's one thousand of us; if they try to climb, we'll see them, we'll shoot the shit out of them.'[2]

A section of five conscripts commanded by Corporal Geronimo Diaz of 1st Platoon tasked with guarding supplies brought forward by helicopters were relaxing on a sunny day drinking several cans of beer on the eastern end of Mount Longdon when an Islander arrived on a motorbike claiming he was lost. In fact, the visitor was former Falkland Islands Defence Force and Chief of Police Terry Peck who was wanted by Major Dowling after he had evaded capture in Stanley. He joined one patrol as a guide that had a friendly fire 'blue on blue' with another patrol.

As 3rd Commando Brigade headed toward Stanley, the weather turned increasingly wintery. Private Nick Rose of 3 Para stated,

> The terrain dictated exactly how we advanced. A lot of the time if we were going along on tracks – what few we did go on – we used Indian file, which is a staggered file on either side of the track, like a zig-zag. But there are great rivers of rock – big white boulders – and you have to cross them and then there's the heather and the gorse and its constantly wet. The wind chill factor was – I think somebody said minus 40 degrees – and storm force winds and horizontal rain – a nightmare scenario… It was horrible, we're miserable as sin, all of us – we're missing home, want a dry fag [cigarette], warm, dry boots, a cheese and onion sandwich and a bottle of blue top milk. I used to dream of these.[3]

By 3 June, 7th Regiment patrols were encountering evidence of enemy activity in the Murrell Bridge area, including a mine exploding. During the night of 4/5 June, 1st Platoon on the western slopes of Mount Longdon was raided by a small patrol, including a sniper, probably seeking a prisoner. After firing a 66mm missile at the mortar pit used by Corporal Óscar Carrizo, the Argentines retaliated with machine-gun, mortar and artillery fire. When the Reconnaissance Platoon commanded by Sub-Lieutenant Francisco Ramón Galíndez Matienzo based on Wireless Ridge was attached to the Force Reserve, it was replaced by 601st Commando Company sections. During the early hours of 7 June, the 3rd Assault Section, 601st Commando Company commanded by First-Lieutenant Gonzalez Deibe and the 601st National Gendarmería Special Forces Squadron commanded by Second-Lieutenant Miguel Puente investigated intelligence reports from Major Jaimet that the enemy were active around the Murrell Bridge. Shortly before dawn, the patrol clashed with enemy on the bluff overlooking the western banks and recovered a radio and packs. Sergeant Rubén Poggi was slightly wounded. A 3 Para patrol checked the site of the clash next evening but there was no sign of the packs or radio, which meant the battalion radio communications could have been compromised.

The capture gave 7th Regiment valuable intelligence including radio frequency settings and codes. Expecting the enemy to recover their lost equipment, 3rd Platoon laid an ambush south of the bridge, without results.

During the early evening of 11 June, the Argentines were alerted to intense enemy activity and then at about 10pm, a mine exploded on the upper slopes of Mount Longdon and the battle began. The low esteem held by some British units of the Argentines was quickly undermined when 1st Platoon reacted quickly and with determination. Private Victor José Bruno recalled that Baldini was removing the mechanical jam of the MAT-49 sub-machine-gun when he was shot in the stomach and First-Corporal Rios picked up the gun to provide him with covering fire but was also killed. Cavalry-Sergeant Jorge Alberto was killed as well. Marine Corporal Carlos Rafael Colemil was a sniper and commented:

> A British soldier climbed over the rock which supported the accommodation bunker of the 105mm gun crew and was silhouetted. He screamed like he was giving out orders. I aimed and fired and he fell, then Conscript Daniel Ferrandis alerted me to the approach of three British soldiers on the flank. I observed them with a night sight; they were very close. I saw one of them was carrying a gun with a bipod; he fell at the first shot and shouted. Another man approached him and I fired again and also got him. The enemy soon became aware of my presence and every time I fired a shot, I received a great deal of fire in response. I was then wounded. I heard the cries for help from the wounded Rasit radar operator, Sergeant Roque Nista. I could hear Sergeant Omar Cabral, a sniper, giving targets.[4]

Corporal Carrizo was wounded and later recovered by British stretcher-bearers and transferred to Ajax Bay. On the right, Second-Lieutenant Neirotti's 3rd Platoon claimed to have killed six enemy attacking the B Company right flank. The last message of the artillery forward observation officer Lieutenant Alberto Rolando Ramos was that his position was surrounded. A radio operator at Company HQ also warned that Mount Longdon was surrounded. In the centre, Marines Jorge Maciel and Claudio Scaglione were manning a .50 heavy machine-gun in a bunker; Marines Luis Fernández and Sergio Giuseppetti had rifles with nightscopes. Using the testimony of Major Andino Luis Francisco Quinci, a medical officer based at *Logistics Operation Centre* in Stanley, Simeoni describes the treatment of a seriously wounded casualty at the Military Wing at Stanley Hospital:

> I remember the name of a soldier who died, whom I buried myself. His name was Rito Portillo, a *morochito* [dark skinned] from Marines. He came very badly injured with a deep wound in his abdomen with exposure of viscera. We took care of him but… I got to talk to him quite a bit. The only thing he told me was that it hurt him a lot. He didn't cry, he didn't scream, he didn't complain excessively. He died meekly, meekly… He didn't say any heroic phrases or anything. He only died meekly, saying that it hurt him. It wasn't Sergeant Cabral or anything like that. He died, but he did it without shouting, even without demagoguery. Humbly, as his life must have been… So I would like to die in the same way.[5]

First-Sergeant Raúl González's 2nd Platoon, on the northern half of the mountain, was under pressure until Second-Lieutenant Hugo Quiroga's 1st Platoon, 10th Engineer Company arrived as reinforcements, some with night sights fitted to their FAL rifles. When Neirotti and his platoon sergeant were both badly wounded, Captain Lopez took over 3rd Platoon and gave an enemy platoon a difficult time after they missed a large bunker in the darkness. Major Carrizo-Salvadores moved his headquarters from the eastern summit when a Milan missile exploded against rocks just behind him:

> At about midnight I asked RHQ for infantry reinforcements and was given a rifle platoon from Captain Hugo García's C Company. First-Lieutenant Raúl Fernando Castañeda gathered the sections of his platoon and hooked around First-Sergeant Raúl González's 2nd Platoon that was already fighting, and counter-attacked at about 2am local time. The platoon fought with great courage in fierce hand-to-hand combat and the battle raged for two more hours, but gradually the enemy broke contact and withdrew while being engaged by artillery strikes.[6]

Carrizo-Salvadores ordered Castañeda's reinforced platoon, now led by Corporal Jorge Daniel Arribas, to advance towards a position that turned out to be an abandoned first-aid post and came under fire from enemy withdrawing from the summit.

Savage, Miguel, an Argentine-Anglo conscripted into the 7th Infantry Regiment in Buenos, wrote an account of the Battle of Mount Longdon on his website *Viaje al Pasado (Journey to the Past)* in 2000 in which he writes 'We were still in our teens, we were still like bewildered children'. Jon Cooksey gives reference to 'teenagers' in his *3 PARA – Mount Longdon* in 2004. Major-General Julian Thompson does not mention 'teenagers' in his *No Picnic*:

> The fighting on Longdon lasted until just before daybreak, about ten hours of what someone described as 'gutter fighting, conducted at close quarters with grenade, rifle and bayonet and 66mm LAW, with support from guns, naval gunfire, mortars and bayonet. It was a battle in which junior officers, NCOs and private soldiers fought with tenacity and aggression.[7]

As 3 Para shelled Mount Longdon and then counter-attacked, the resistance weakened as the 21 surviving soldiers of Castañeda's 46-man platoon withdrew, Corporal Julio Nardielo Mamani and his section provided an effective rearguard. Corporal Manuel Medina in the Czekalski 105mm Recoilless Rifle detachment fired along the ridge, killing a para who took the full force of a 105mm anti-tank round and wounding three others. Corporals Julio César Canteros and Jorge Norberto González of the Recce Platoon on Wireless Ridge also fired a recoilless rifle. Private Leonardo Rondi was a runner delivering messages to the section leaders and upon finding a dead para behind a rock, took his red beret and rifle which he later gave to the Argentine commanders as trophies. Altieri was waiting for the enemy to arrive when 10th Armoured Cavalry Recce Sergeant Jorge Alberto Ron asked for volunteers to recover Mount Longdon – after all, 'Mount Longdon was Argentine'. Altieri and a friend, Fernández Rito, volunteered – 'three Argentine soldiers against 500 English soldiers', as recalled by Altieri. As the three advanced up the hill, Altieri threw 10 grenades and then they were mortared. Sergeant Ron was wounded in his legs and Altieri was severely wounded, with brain damage that affected the use of his arms, legs and speech and blinded his left eye. Rito took Altieri to the road and were picked up by a lorry driver who offered to take them to hospital. When an officer said there were higher priorities than the severely wounded Altieri, the driver insisted on taking both casualties to hospital and Altieri was evacuated on the last Hercules to leave the Falklands before the Argentine surrender. Altieri's battered helmet seems to have been taken as a souvenir to the UK and in January 2022 it was for sale on eBay. The Argentine Embassy in London were alerted and arrangements were made to return the helmet to Altieri. His wounds led him to being unable to find work after discharge.

Swearing in 'Americanese' had been heard during the battle and the discovery of several dead Argentines dressed in US camouflaged uniforms led the British to believe they were mercenaries from the United States. They were, in fact, Argentine Marines. Two days of shelling directed by Sub-Lieutenant Marcelo de Marco of the 5th Marines between Tumbledown Mountain and Sapper Hill and directed by the Argentine Forward Artillery Observation Officer, Major Guillermo Nani, on Wireless Ridge during the night of 13/14 June caused more casualties.

CHAPTER 13

Defence of the Outer Defence Zone: Two Sisters

The twin peaks running west to east about 2 miles south-east of Murrell Bridge is known as Two Sisters. About half a mile to the south-west is a pile of rocks running east to west and 800 metres to the south is Goat Ridge. To the north is the track from Murrell Bridge east to Stanley. Throughout 30 May, Royal Air Force Harriers were active over Mount Kent with one pilot responding to help from the SAS attacking the eastern lower slopes of Mount Kent. Two Harriers operating from Sid's Strip attacked Two Sisters with rockets.

The Defence of Two Sisters

Lieutenant-Colonel Diego Soria, commanding 4th Regiment, had entrusted the defence of Two Sisters to Major Ricardo Cordón, his second-in-command, and when he withdrew C Company from Mount Challenger, the field kitchens were left behind.

A Company, 1st Platoon (Sub-Lieutenant Juan Nazer), and Support Platoon (Sub-Lieutenant Luis Carlos Martella) were on the saddle between the two features. 3rd Platoon (Sub-Lieutenant Marcelo Llambias Pravaz) was on the southern peak named Long Toenail. B Company was reinforced by Second-Lieutenant Marcelo Dorigón's Support Platoon, B Company, 12th Regiment which had been left behind on Mount Kent after the remainder of the company had been helicoptered forward as

Combat Team *Solari* reinforcements during the battle of Goose Green. C Company, 1st Platoon (Sub-Lieutenant Miguel Mosquera-Gutierrez), and 2nd Platoon (Sub-Lieutenant Jorge Pérez-Grandi) were on the northern and eastern peaks of Two Sisters. On 2 June, the 4th Regiment Operations Officer, Captain Carlos Alfredo López Patterson, arrived on Two Sisters to assess the defence.

> In those visits, one thing that always moved me was that, while I saluted Second-Lieutenant Llambias-Pravaz, the platoon would clap and cheer. It must have been because they noticed that I was recognising the valour they were acquiring in that place. Because they were very isolated, waiting for the enemy, just them and their souls. Or, perhaps, because seeing their commander sharing a few words – a brotherly gesture of a young man towards other young people – they felt their desire revived to fight. One day, a lad approached me and said 'Since we have got to dance in this one, we are going to do it well. We are going to support the Second-Lieutenant who has fallen sick and still remains with us. We have got to help the one whose feet get cold or the one who freaks out. Because from here we all leave together or no one leaves at all. What could I say?'[1]

The next day, soon after dawn, Sub-Lieutenant Aldo Eugenio Franco's Rifle Platoon had a short exchange of fire alongside Captain Patterson, and a patrol dispersed the enemy with the help of Lieutenant Luis Carlos Martella's 81mm mortars. After the British occupied Bluff Cove Peak the next day, Major Oscar Jaimet's heliborne B Company, 6th Regiment arrived and he placed patrols around the saddle near Murrell Bridge between Two Sisters and Mount Longdon to the west. On the 5th, two Harriers attacked Two Sisters with rockets.

On the 3rd, when the enemy were seen in the area of the Murrell River, Major Castagneto, commanding 601 Commando Company, tasked First-Lieutenant Fernando García Pinasco, commanding 2nd Platoon, and two 601 National Gendarmería to cross the river and attack the enemy when they least expected it. Major Ricardo Mario Cordón, the 4th Regiment second-in-command, provided the fire-power of Corporal Oscar Nicolás Albornoz Guevara and eight soldiers, including Private Orlando Héctor Stella, a C Company radio operator on Two Sisters. Captain Rubén Teófilo Figueroa, the 601 Commando Company second-in-command, linked up with Major Jaimet to finalise the details. First-Lieutenant Pinasco left one of the radio Land Rovers with Sergeant Alarcón Ferreyra to serve as a liaison officer with the 3rd Artillery Group.

After Jaimet confirmed no enemy activity had been detected, Castagneto launched the operation after dark on 6 June. Lieutenant Marcelo Alejandro Anadón led the patrol through a minefield and followed the River Murrell for about 2 miles until they reached a bend where the patrol then split. A recce group of Anadó, First-Sergeant Ramón Vergara and Sergeant José Rubén Guillén crossed the river downstream and continued on the western (enemy) side, while the main body crossed the river intending to make contact with the enemy. After an hour and a half, Anadón saw something shining in the distance, which Guillen suggested was the moon reflecting on the river surface or reflections from a waterproof poncho. Meanwhile, Pinasco had sent four commandos across the river to form a rearguard and reserve while the remainder crossed the bridge and gathered around a mound of stones where they agreed to rendezvous and were later joined by the recce group.

As First-Sergeant Vergara left with the advance guard and Pinasco and Guillen moved some stones for fire support, the enemy opened fire from high ground above the river about 70 metres from the bridge. It was 6.45am. The Argentines reacted quickly but as Pinasco, Assistant Sergeant Rubén Poggi and First-Sergeant Miguel Ángel Tunini ran across the bridge, Pinasco was shot in the leg and was helped by Tunini, who was supported by Sergeant Guillen giving covering fire with a MAG and others using their rifles. Anadón radioed Pinasco that the situation was under control. Meanwhile, First-Sergeant Ramón Vergara had found a higher position from which he fired a rifle grenade into the middle of the British position and covered Pinasco, Anadón, Vergara, Suárez, Quinteros and Gendarmería Assistant Sergeant Natalio Jesús Figueredo and Sergeant Miguel Víctor Pepe as they charged the enemy machine-gun. Lieutenant Luis Carlos Martella on Two Sisters supported by dropping 81mm bombs onto the British position, which was soon abandoned. The Argentines found eight sleeping bags and backpacks, two steel helmets, a Parachute Regiment beret and badge, a camera with a half-used roll, a Clansman PRC-351 radio still switched on and a Union Jack flag. In a radio conversation with Medical Captain Pablo Llanos, Anadon learnt from intercepts that the Paras had sent a desperate request for a helicopter to rescue them. Indeed, several minutes later they fired a flare and a Sea King evacuated them but not before a 'blue on blue' as two British patrols fired on each other. The Argentine commandos moved the captured equipment to a hide about 500 metres from the position. When everything was quiet, Pinasco, Anadón and Tunini returned to the area to search for other abandoned equipment; nothing was found. The only casualty was Assistant Sergeant Ruben Poggi, who was evacuated by motorcycle and was treated by Captain Llanos. The patrol remained in place the next morning, observing enemy activity on Mount Kent and at Estancia and directing artillery fire onto enemy positions.

During the night of 6/7 June, Corporal Oscar Nicolás Albornoz-Guevara, Private Orlando Héctor Stella, the lead scout, and eight conscripts crossed the Murrell River and upon reaching Estancia House noted several British vehicles but were seen and withdrew. The next day, Corporal Hugo Gabino MacDougall, from 6th Regiment's B Company, was credited with shooting down a Harrier with a shoulder-launched Blowpipe missile. The 12th Regiment Support Platoon under Sub-Lieutenant Dorigón attached to Major Jaimet's B Company were living off the land. Rations were often short and soldiers would barbecue sheep over turf laid in a hole and set alight using petrol.

Shortly after dark, the 3rd Platoon Section, 601 Commando Company commanded by Captain Jorge Eduardo Jándula crossed the Murrell Bridge and while setting up another ambush on the night of June 7/8 discovered a British position. Marine Andrew Tubb of the 45 Commando Recce Troop recalls:

> We were actually inside the Argentine position, so we ended up shelling ourselves. We did a lot of patrols up to Two Sisters. That time we fired 66mm rockets for about 400 metres during a counter-attack by Platoon Sergeant Ramón Valdez. We got artillery again to smoke us out. It took us well over an hour to get away and it seemed like a few minutes. We killed seventeen of them, Privates Jose Romero and Andres Rodriguez and three sappers Cisneros of a Marine mine-laying party.[2]

In another patrol, Sub-Lieutenant Llambías-Pravaz found a green Royal Marine beret left behind during the Argentine counter-ambush.

At about 2.10am on 10 June, a strong enemy fighting patrol probed the 3rd Platoon position and during the clash Special Forces Sergeants Mario Antonio Cisnero and Ramón Gumercindo Acosta were killed and two other Argentine Special Forces lying in ambush were wounded. One British patrol installed a position among rocks in front of the Argentine trenches, however at about 4am, an Argentine machine-gunner opened fire as the enemy launched an attack that left three Argentine and two Royal Marines dead. On the left other figures could be seen running on the hill. Four more Argentines fell to the Marines' accurate fire. The troopers further up the slope were now wide awake, and put down heavy fire trapping the British patrol in the rocks until their withdrawal was covered by a machine-gun. Major Rico, commanding 602 Commando Company, had a lucky escape when a 66mm projectile exploded uncomfortably close to him. First-Lieutenant Horacio Fernando Lauría and Sergeant Orlando Aguirre both claimed to have destroyed a British machine-gun with rifle grenades. Captain Hugo Ranieri proved to be a useful sniper. After two Royal Marines patrols clashed in a 'blue on blue', Sub-Lieutenant Llambías-Pravaz recovered enemy rucksacks and weapons that were shown the next day to war correspondents in Port Stanley.

Command-detonated barrel mines buried on the saddle and eastern half of Two Sisters by Argentine amphibious engineers were discovered by a British patrol patrolling against Two Sisters from Goat Ridge. At 11pm, the Outer Defence Zone was bombed and then attacked.

Two Sisters

The company attack of the western peak of Two Sisters was stoutly resisted by 3rd Platoon C Company, 4th Regiment commanded by Sub-Lieutenant Llambas-Pravaz and his Guarani Indians and Lieutenant Mario Pacheco's 10th Engineer Company section supported by the 3rd Artillery Group and their fixed bayonets. For four hours, the platoon defeated efforts to close with them and won the respect of the Royal Marines. The X Company, 45 Commando Company Commander Captain Gardiner, later commented: 'A hard cadre of some twenty men had stayed behind and fought, and they were brave men. A lone rifleman on "Long Toenail" held out long after resistance had ended on the mountain.'[3] At about 12.30am, enemy attacking the easterly peak were driven back by the platoons commanded by Sub-Lieutenants Mosquera-Gutierrez and Pérez-Grandi, but Lieutenant Martella, the Argentine Mortar Platoon commander, used all of his ammunition and was killed. A British officer led a bayonet charge that recaptured the eastern peak at the cost of two platoon commanders wounded in his company. Second-Lieutenant Aldo Eugenio Franco and his RI 6 Platoon planned to counter-attack the saddle of Two Sisters supported by Major David Carullo and his Panhard 10th Armoured Car Squadron until it emerged that both peaks and his platoon formed the rearguard. When HMS *Glamorgan*, about 17 miles offshore, was using its guns to clear Franco's determined resistance, a RASIT detected the warship taking a short cut and although HMS *Glamorgan* launched a deterrent Seacat, at 3.36am, a land-launched Exocet skipped onto the flight deck and exploded in the hangar, killing 14 members of the crew.

Private Oscar Ismael Poltronieri, of 6th Regiment, held up the enemy with accurate shooting with his machine-gun and was awarded the Argentine Cross to the Heroic Valour in Combat. Sub-Lieutenant Nazer, of A Company, was badly wounded during the withdrawal. His platoon was then led by Corporal Virgilio Rafael Barrientos, who guided it to Sapper Hill. Sub-Lieutenants Mosquera-Gutierrez and Pérez-Grandi were wounded in the British bombardment and the survivors of their platoons were placed under the command of Captain Carlos López Patterson, the 4th Regiment Operations Officer, who had formed a block position between Mount Tumbledown and Wireless Ridge, alongside the dismounted 10th Armoured Cavalry Reconnaissance Squadron under Captain Rodrigo Alejandro Soloaga; he had been engaging enemy on Mount Longdon with heavy machine-guns and mortars throughout the daylight hours of 12 and 13 June. With the telephone lines to the command post in shreds, Llambías-Pravaz and his men joined M Company, 5th Marines on Sapper Hill. During the fighting he had nearly been killed by a rock after a Milan missile exploded close behind him; fortunately he was wearing his helmet.

Argentine mortaring and shelling of Two Sisters led to some members of the 45 Commando sheltering in the captured bunkers amid near misses from 105mm and 155mm shells. Sergeant-Major George Meachin of Yankee Company later praised the fighting abilities and spirit of the Argentine defenders and the leadership of such officers as Pérez-Grandi and Mosquera-Gutierrez.

CHAPTER 14

The Inner Defence Zone: Mount Tumbledown

Brigadier-Generals Menéndez and Jofre both realised that if Tumbledown and Wireless Ridge were to be lost, there was nothing to stop the British from entering Stanley.

Commanded by Lieutenant-Commander Robacio, the highly motivated 5th Marine Infantry Battalion knew that Tumbledown would be attacked next. His 700-strong battalion was trained and equipped for cold weather operations. It was supported by 'Bravo' Battery from the 1st Marine Field Artillery Regiment of six M-56 Oto Melara 105mm Pack Howitzers, three batteries of the 1st Marine Anti-Aircraft Regiment equipped with three Tigercat surface-to-air missiles, three Hispano-Suiza 30mm anti-aircraft guns and platoons from the 2nd and 3rd Marine Infantry Battalions, an Amphibious Engineer Battalion, a Marine Police platoon and a dog platoon. The difference with Army battalions is that they do not have a M-30 107mm mortar platoon.

M (Mar) Company defended Mount William. 1st Platoon, under Marine Second-Lieutenant (Guardiamarina or Midshipman) Carlos Bianchi, was dug in the south side of Mount William, covering the road between Fitzroy and Stanley.

N (Nácar) Company defended Tumbledown and the eastern end of the feature. 2nd Platoon, led by Marine Second-Lieutenant Marcelo Oruezabala, was dug in between Tumbledown and William on the west side of the feature. Two Sisters was to the west. 3rd Platoon, under Marine

Sergeant (Suboficial or Chief Petty Officer) Jorge Lucero, was dug in on the northern slopes of Tumbledown overlooking Mount Longdon, Wireless Ridge and Moody Brook. 4th Platoon, led by Sub-Lieutenant Carlos Daniel Vázquez, dug in on the southern slopes of the summit of Tumbledown covering the western approaches to the peak, consisted of 27 Marines, most drafted from other duties within the battalion, 16 4th Regiment and several Marine engineers. He had too few radios and was therefore relying on runners relaying orders to keep his men near to him.

O (Obra) Company under Lieutenant (IM) Carlos Alberto Calmels, had held a defensive position on Wireless Ridge between 8 and 16 April, and with the arrival of 10th X Brigade held a position in the centre of the battalion deployment east of Tumbledown, as a reserve, between 17 April and 8 June until it blocked the British advance at Pony Pass.

5th Amphibious Engineer Platoon commanded by Second-Lieutenant Miño was behind 4th Platoon defending the highest point of the western peak and covering approaches from the north-east. There was also a detachment of Browning 12.7mm heavy machine-gun teams.

Marines police included German Shepherd Dog Squads (from the Puerto Belgrano-based Headquarters Battalion) and were also present on Mount Tumbledown and Sapper Hill.

Marine Tigercat Surface-to-Air Missile (SAM) launchers and anti-tank gun and missile teams were also part of the defences, with one anti-tank team located on Mount William in support of Bianchi's men and another anti-tank team supporting Lucero's men. The Marine SAM Platoon equipped with British Blowpipe and Russian SA-7 shoulder-launched missiles were positioned on Sapper Hill.

The 81mm Mortar Platoon was split in two detachments. On Tumbledown, the mortars were placed near the summit and controlled by Marine Sergeants David Ramos and Lucio Monzon, mostly in support of Vázquez's 4th Platoon. The 120mm Mortar Platoon was on Sapper Hill.

B Company, 6th Infantry Regiment (Major Jaimet) and two platoons of 10th Armoured Reconnaissance Squadron were in a blocking position covering the Estancia track. Second-Lieutenant Óscar Silva and Second-Lieutenant Marcelo Llambías-Pravaz's depleted 4th Regiment platoon and the remnants of Second-Lieutenants Celestino Mosteirín's and Marcelo

Dorigón's 12th Regiment platoons had recently fought on Two Sisters, Goat Ridge and Mount Harriet. Their arrival brought the defence to 92 men. A Company, 3rd Infantry Regiment (Major Guillermo Berazay), was in layered defence at Moody Brook with orders to support Tumbledown and Wireless Ridge. When Lieutenant-Colonel Comini, of 3rd Regiment, was instructed by Brigadier Jofre to reinforce the 5th Marines on Tumbledown Mountain with his reserve company, Major Berazay, the operations officer, assembled A Company and was ready to move at about 3am on a frosty and cold morning. However, some lorry batteries were flat and drivers could not start the engines. When the convoy eventually left for Stanley, there was mist and drivers skidded on the icy roads near Moody Brook. Berazay ordered the soldiers to debus from the lorries, however some soldiers slipped on the ice, which further slowed progress. At about first light, British gunners started shelling the column as it climbed Tumbledown. Very few soldiers, if any, had been under fire and virtually everyone took cover. Berazay eventually met a 5th Marines guide, who led A Company to their position north and north-west of Tumbledown. It had taken A Company five hours to move 4 miles.

After Robacio had instructed his operations officer, Major Antonio Pernías, that the road through Pony Pass was to be blocked, O Company and the 1st Amphibious Engineer Platoon moved to the lower slopes of Mount William.

A strong wind was carpeting the slopes of the bleak mountain with snow and froze the 'camp' which was now pitted with peat banks and littered with minefields. Robacio assumed the British would attack at night and consolidate at dawn. If they failed, the British were expected to withdraw.

At about 10.30pm, the battle for Tumbledown began when an infantry company and an enemy troop of light tanks attacked O Company in the first tank action of the war. Marine First Class Private Jose Luis Fazio recalls:

> At about 10.30pm our battalion had its first intensive gun battle with British companies which appeared out of nowhere. I heard Private Roberto Barboza yell 'The English are here!' I remember our operations officer requested the artillery to assist at 11pm with starshells. The close quarter battle was such that

the Argentine artillery was unable to drop shells on to the British attackers. I was shooting, doing my work. I don't know if I killed anyone. We just fired our rifles, that's all. Contact was maintained for over an hour before Battalion Headquarters ordered our company to fall back. We did not realise at the time that a wounded Marine made his way to the Amphibious Engineer platoon position and hurled a grenade, wounding a major. Simultaneously, the major opened fire, killing him.[1]

For the next two hours, O Company defended 11 positions arranged in depth in fierce fighting, some held by the Amphibious Engineers who were not best pleased to find themselves under crossfire. The 81mm Mortar Platoon on Mount William and the 120mm mortars with M Company on Sapper Hill opened fire on the minefield, a barrage that lasted about 40 minutes and trapped the attackers into debating what was a mine and what was not. One mine lifted a Scorpion into the air. The Argentines had not been distracted toward Mount William and Pony Pass from focusing the main attack. Captain Eduardo Villarraza's N Company from the 5th Marine Battalion would defend Mounts Tumbledown and William.

At about 11.45pm, flares soared into the snowy darkness, bullets cracked overhead and rock splinters whined into the darkness. Vasquez later described that he believed the enemy was overconfident:

> The British soldiers crept up on the platoon position just before midnight. Before long the platoon was completely surrounded and on the verge of being overrun, I instructed that the 81mm mortar platoon of Ruben Galliusi should fire on our platoon. He had no other choice. The British had to withdraw and we started swearing at them. That was how the British were driven out during that first attack. I lost five of my own men.[2]

At about 1am, Vasquez called for supporting fire to shell his position but this was refused. Half an hour later, a B Company, 6th Infantry Regiment platoon arrived at the N Company command post and was tasked with reinforcing a 5th Platoon counter-attack. Snow clouds rushing across the full moon cast eerie shadows across the battlefield. The cold slowed down body metabolisms and helped the wounded to survive. For the next three hours, the Marines kept the attack pinned down. It was not unusual that British paras might be taking cover behind a rock just a few dozen meters from an Argentine Marine behind another rock. Just out of grenade range, they would take pot shots at each other. Armed with 7.62mm FAL rifles that could fire on automatic, the Argentine Marines did always wait to be shot at and often attacked the flanks of the enemy to the extent that by dawn, the assault was very slow.

Vasquez commented:

> It was now around three in the morning and we had been trading fire off and on for nearly three hours. The British were now amongst the rocks above us. I found out that if I started to give out orders, I would draw machine-gun fire and that was the biggest shock to me. I discovered that the Amphibious Engineer platoon had withdrawn too soon and their position was quickly occupied by the British. We asked for our artillerymen to shell our position, which provided a useful breathing space, but it was evident that reinforcements would still be needed to beat the attackers off. In the fight that followed, five Army and two Marines died. We were alone now, with nothing around except us and the British. It was about then that Second-Lieutenant Oscar Silva of the 4th Regiment was killed after he had carried a wounded Marine machine-gunner to safety through heavy fire. He then returned to the position with one of his soldiers.[3]

O Company then clashed with the Welsh Guards intent on passing Mount William and withdrew to Sapper Hill where it was reinforced by linking with the 3rd Regiment. At 2pm, 4th Platoon was attacked from several directions and gradually overran trench by trench. When Brigadier-General Jofre learnt that the Marine Engineers had withdrawn, he radioed Robacio and Lieutenant-Colonel Giménez, then on Wireless Ridge, and warned, 'Anyone seen to transmit an unauthorised order to fall back should have their head blown off.'[4] Lieutenant-Colonel Robacio ordered Major Jaimet to reinforce Vasquez, who had taken up positions about 250 yards from the summit. Leaving his Mortar Platoon with the Marines, Jaimet moved on to the saddle between Tumbledown and Mount William at about 3am. By this point Argentine machine-gunner were beginning to run out of ammunition. Again, Vasquez asked for artillery to shell his position.

By about 4.30am and aware that the summit had been captured, Major Jaimet instructed 1st Platoon commanded by Second-Lieutenant Esteban La Madrid to reinforce Vasquez, but the radios and night-sights of the platoon were not fully charged and had mortar and machine-gun ammunition not been supporting Wireless Ridge, B Company could have counter-attacked and bought M Company time to be moved from Mount William to Mount Tumbledown for a battalion counter-attack. This missed opportunity probably cost the Argentines the battle.

Expecting Lieutenant Miño's 5th Amphibious Engineer Platoon to join him, with his customary enthusiasm, Second-Lieutenant Vilgré La Madrid issued quick orders – advance, allow no one to pass and recruit stray conscripts. Several of his men had helmet-mounted night-vision devices and all were willing, but none of them had seen the ground over which they were about to advance. La Madrid recounted:

> We moved off through a gap in the rocks; I spread my men out behind the men who were still fighting. My orders were not to let anyone pass, not even Argentine soldiers. I went forward to make a reconnaissance and could see that the British had two machine-guns and a missile launcher in action. I went through another gap in the rocks and was surprised by three men speaking in English behind and above me and firing over the top of me. I could see them with my night binoculars; there were about twelve of them in all. I was anxious to get back to my platoon. I took a rifle grenade and fired at where I had seen the first three men. I heard it explode and some shouts and cries of pain, and the sound of someone falling down the rocks. I ran back to my position and ordered my men to open fire. We stopped them, but they thinned out and came round our flanks; their deployment was good. They also engaged us with light mortars and missile launchers [more likely 66m light anti-tank projectiles]. This went on for a long time, and we suffered heavy casualties; we had eight dead and ten wounded. We started to run short of ammunition, particularly for the machine-guns.[5]

So far, the battle had lasted seven hours of hard fighting amid snow. While Argentine resistance was fierce, it was unable to halt the assault. Corporal Marco Palomo's section briefly held up the enemy in the saddle between the centre and eastern summits but were unable to withstand the enemy tactics of machine-gunners and riflemen advancing across open ground in an extended line and halting to allow an assault time to gain a foothold and then fight through the objective crag to crag, rock by rock.

By 5.30am, Commander Robacio informed HQ 10th Brigade that the western sector of Tumbledown had been captured and he was intending to use M Company and two 6th Infantry Regiment companies on Sapper

Hill to counter-attack. Within half an hour, 6th Regiment came under fire from enemy who had infiltrated into the rocks. La Madrid believed he was at risk of being cut off from Major Jaimet and instructed Palomo's section to cover his withdrawal. La Madrid recalls:

> I could see that we were outflanked, with the British behind us, so we were cut off from my company. Some of my men had been taken prisoner. I reorganized and found that I was down to sixteen men and started to retire. The British above me were firing machine-guns but we passed close to the rocks. I left six men in a line with a machine-gunner to cover our retreat, but we could not break contact. They came on us fast, and we fell back; it was starting to get light. The whole hill had fallen by then, and we were on lower ground, just south of Moody Brook. We eventually got through to Stanley, through what I would like to say was a perfect barrage fired by the Royal Artillery. We had to wait for breaks in the firing, but I still lost a man killed there.[6]

The casualty was Sergeant Eusebio Aguilar, a popular drill instructor. Private Montoya is reputed to have wrestled with a guardsman.

When Lieutenant-Colonel Robacio reported that La Madrid's counter-attack on Tumbledown was in trouble, Brigadier-General Jofre's frustration was amplified when he learnt that Miño's amphibious engineers were again withdrawing without any authority and he had no alternative but to order Colonel Felix Aguilar, his Chief-of-Staff, to instruct Robacio to break contact and regroup on Sapper Hill. Robacio and Jaimet were both furious because they believed the 5th Marines were holding the enemy and were in a position to counter-attack. It would be six years before they openly criticised the decision. Robacio states:

> On the last day of the war, 14 June, at about 6.30am I thought that we were still winning. My unit hadn't suffered any real losses. We hadn't given up any of our positions. All we had lost was a very, very small part of Mount Tumbledown. I knew that we were running out of ammunition, so I asked my headquarters for more. We were concentrating our efforts on Mount Tumbledown because that was the battle that would seal the fate of Port Stanley. Unfortunately we never received the ammunition we needed. At about 7am, I received the order to withdraw prior to surrender. Our military code states that for an Argentine military unit to surrender it must have spent all its ammunition or lost at least two-thirds of its men. It was awful to have to ask the units that were still fighting to withdraw. It was a very bitter moment.[7]

The Argentine defence then began to crumble. Private Jorge Sanchez, in Vasquez's 4 Platoon recalls:

> The fighting was sporadic but at times fierce as we tried to maintain our position. By this time we had ten or twelve dead including one officer. I hadn't fired directly at a British soldier, as they had been too hard to get a clear shot at. I can remember lying there with all this firing going over my head. They were everywhere. The platoon commander then called Private Ramon Rotela manning the 60mm mortar and Rotela fired it straight up into the air so that they landed on ourselves. At this point I had been up and in actual combat for over six hours. It was snowing and we were tired. Some of the guys had surrendered, but I didn't want to do this. I had only twenty rounds left and I decided to continue the fight from Mount William. I popped up, fired a rifle grenade in the direction of eight to ten British soldiers to keep their heads down, then ran for 2nd Platoon. I can remember saying some type of prayer hoping the British wouldn't shoot me in the back. You could see the battle coming to an end.[8]

One of Lieutenant La Madrid's men nicknamed the Scots Guards 'The panthers in the dark'. By 7am, three positions were still resisting but ammunition was very short. Jofre later wrote in *Gente* weekly magazine,

> Robacio came on the air to advise me that his command post, near Felton Stream, was under direct attack. There are varying accounts of the report time, but I am sure it was around 7am. 'We are encircled', Robacio told me in a hurried call, 'All around us are British forces firing at us; at least 150 troops and more than a dozen tanks. We are not in a good position.' This came as a shock to me. To us it was apparent, at the time, that Special Air Service personnel dressed in Argentine Army uniforms had mixed in with the 7th Regiment soldiers and under their cover infiltrated to the rear of the 5th Marine Infantry Battalion. Now we did have something to worry about.

Major Jaimet, 6th Infantry Regiment describes,

> Just as dawn was breaking, Robacio came up on the air to advise me that he would not come to our assistance and that he had orders to withdraw the companies. I was gutted more than anything because I wanted to play the rest of the company. That was the only thing I was thinking of really. I was a commando and it was a matter of personal as well as national pride, to go on fighting regardless of the consequences. I considered Malvinas my paradise. When I got through to HQ 10th Brigade and made it clear that my company should be going forward. The orders puzzled and dispirited us. Many looked on the big break of contact as running away and did not like it at all.[9]

Vasquez states,

> As dawn approached, I spoke to 'Habana' – that was the battalion commander's call sign – to get reinforcements. Robacio said that no reserves were available, and that fighting was also taking place all around the headquarters of the battalion. At 07.15 sharp, I remember I looked out and three British soldiers were up there, pointing their weapons at me. That finished my platoon, but we had lasted more than seven hours of actual fighting, longer than any other Argentine platoon in Malvinas.[10]

Jaimet instructed Second Lieutenant Franco's platoon to cover the withdrawal of 5th Marines from Mount Tumbledown. It had already successfully covered the withdrawal of C Company, 4th Regiment, from Two Sisters on 12 June, at the cost of three killed. Robacio recollects,

> The unit withdrew in orderly fashion, under intense enemy fire and with the help of God, because God exists on the battlefield. Then as my men prepared to resist on Sapper Hill to the last man, we were told that our commanding officers had already surrendered and I had to give my units the order to withdraw yet again.[11]

At about 7am, the Argentines watched with incredulity as two Sea Kings appeared from the west dropping troops onto the track below Sapper Hill, and a firefight rolled backwards and forwards and slowed down when Argentine troops withdrew from Sapper Hill, at the cost of three men killed. The skirmish convinced Brigadier-General Jofre that further resistance was pointless,

> Things went from bad to worse. No sooner had Jaimet reached Sapper Hill, Colonel Dalton, the brigade operations officer, told me, 'Many soldiers are in a strange state and the kelpers are bound to get hurt. One 3rd Regiment platoon has been told to go into the houses by a fanatical lieutenant, who has also ordered the men to kill the kelpers – something awful is happening.' I'll never forget that moment. It was like a lightning bolt had hit me. It was becoming evident to me that I was no longer at the control. 'We've had it. The lives of the kelpers are being risked.' I told General Menéndez and he realised that there was no question of fighting any further. Menéndez told me that he wished to talk to Galtieri to arrange a ceasefire. I agreed. It was all over. Fighting on Sapper Hill was out of the question.[12]

As the enemy reached the eastern slopes of Tumbledown and Mount William, Robacio planned for M and N Companies to counter-attack, but this was refused at Brigade HQ at 8.45am and he was ordered that 5th Marines was to abandon any heavy equipment and join the defence of Mount William. Meanwhile British stretcher bearers had been collecting the wounded and when mortar bomb wounded another casualty, it was later suggested that the Argentines had deliberately targeted stretcher-bearers on Mount Tumbledown. It is of interest that Argentine medical personnel were clearly identified with the Red Cross on brassards and helmets.

Throughout the 12th, the 3rd Artillery Group had supported the defensive shelling of the west slopes of Mount Kent to neutralise a suspected Blowpipe and marking artillery targets for the Pucaras of the 3rd Attack Group, which with the 4th Airborne Artillery Group was also supporting the defence of Mount Longdon. B Battery reported shooting down an enemy helicopter. Enemy shelling forced C Battery to rejoin the group with both groups firing 10 to 15 guns per mission. The 13th saw intense counter-battery fire. Two Harriers attacked the two 155mm guns and silenced the 5th Marine Artillery Group. First-Lieutenant Juan Caballero, of the 3rd Artillery Group, was tasked with locating the enemy batteries from a helicopter, however when it was hit, the group lost its locating capability. At 1pm, 3rd Group came under intense shelling that saw a gunner killed and two wounded. The shelling decreased at 8.30pm when the British guns opened fire on 7th Regiment and 5th Marines withdrawing from their defensive positions held during the night of the 13/14 June. Enemy activity decreased between 4pm and 9.45pm and then increased. The 155mm were running out of ammunition. Nevertheless, the group and the Para gunners covered the withdrawal of 7th Regiment and 5th Marines and then at 5am, the Para gunners shelled Moody Brook over open sights while the 3rd Artillery Group supported the 10th Armoured Cavalry. At 6am, Commander Port Stanley offered vehicles to help the Para gunners move their guns nearer to Stanley, however enemy shelling prevented any support being provided.

By 8am, enemy troops were about 700 metres from the Para gunners position and the group was down to one gun still firing, so the group ordered the gunners to withdraw. Meanwhile, a considerably depleted 3rd Artillery Group was still supporting the 5th Marine Battalion to withdraw and was brought down 100 metres in front of the Marines at the order of Navy Captain Moeremans to allow the troops to withdraw. By about 10.30am, the field artillery had become largely ineffective. Robacio still believed that the 5th Marines could recapture Tumbledown and telephoned Captain Villarraza of O Company to organise a counter-attack from Mount William. Brigadier-General Jofre recalls:

> When I got back to Robacio, I emphasised he was to regroup on Sapper Hill. Apart from re-opened communications in the rear and an abundance of ammunition, there would be a dozen Army radar-guided anti-aircraft guns and 'C' Company, 3rd Regiment to support him. In his earlier reports he had reported a shortage of belt-fed ammunition for the machine-guns and a pressing requirement for casualty evacuation. It would be very loathsome to somehow suggest that I was a quitter, that somehow I misled and that we did something wrong. That is nonsense. To stay would have necessitated re-organising our deployment in broad daylight. There was no immediate response to this. Obviously he had more confidence in the situation than I did. I patiently chewed at my fingernails for as long as I could tolerate it. I then got on to battalion headquarters for an explanation. I was told that O Company was planning to counter-attack. From my point of view we had already lost too much time and I was anxious to get the companies off Tumbledown and the withdrawal under way while we still had darkness. It was still dark outside. I asked Jaimet if his company could hold out for another hour as we were planning to pull the 5th Marine back onto Sapper Hill. Jaimet agreed. Villarraza waited for artillery to open up to signal that he could get away. At 9.45 am Jaimet was ordered to withdraw and although hindered by British fire his company was able to break contact.[13]

Most of the 5th Marines had reached Sapper Hill by 10am. Despite the fact that it was made up almost entirely of conscripts led by inexperienced young officers, it was still highly motivated. Vasquez had shown the same commitment as First-Lieutenant Esteban had shown at Port San Carlos and Second-Lieutenant Baldini on Mount Longdon. Robacio believed Brigadier-General Menéndez had not reacted aggressively enough to the British landings. Criticised by some British officers who did not understand the culture of military conscription, he had total command of his battalion and the Army units under his command and deserves credit for doing all that was possible to limit British gains. His positioning of heavy weapons on Sapper Hill was a formidable defensive barrier. In the 44 days since 8 April, 5th Marines had suffered 16 dead and 64 wounded. Vasquez's stubborn defence had cost seven Marines and five soldiers killed, several wounded and others missing. Of the Amphibious Engineers, Lieutenant Miño was wounded. Between them, the 4th and 12th Infantry Regiments platoons lost five killed in the battle. When La Madrid reorganised, he mustered 16 from the 45 who had started the counter-attack. Five had been killed and several others had been captured. Lieutenant Franco's 6th Regiment platoon lost three killed. About 50 Argentines were wounded, some of whom were recovered by the Marines Medical Officer, Captain Ferrario, and a medical party. Most were from Jaimet's infantry company.

As a grey dawn filtered into daylight, two British brigades had bitten further into Army Group Stanley and the defeat of the Inner Defence Zone, Wireless Ridge and Cortley Ridge had opened the door to Stanley. Argentine prospects were bleak. The Royal Navy commanded and a Dunkirk-style evacuation by sea was most unlikely. Annihilation by naval and artillery bombardment or the surrender of the 12,000 men was a distinct possibility. During the early afternoon, electronic warfare identified the location of HQ 3 Commando Brigade and four Skyhawks dropping and then machine-gunning the position, forced the brigade to move.

CHAPTER 15

Defence of the Inner Defence Zone: Battle of Wireless Ridge

Lieutenant-Colonel Giménez had responded to intelligence assessments that a landing at Berkeley Sound was probable and therefore instructed 7th Regiment to face north toward the Murrell River and the Hearnden River, as well as face the British threat from the west. He knew that after the loss of Mount Longdon two nights before, Wireless Ridge was next and later commented, 'We had the doubtful honour of fighting the British twice.' While his regiment was considered to be the best infantry in 10th Brigade, his men were dirty, hungry, tired, wet and demoralised by the shelling from warships, artillery, mortars and tanks.

On 12 June, men of the 601 Commando occupied an air defensive blocking position to the north-east of Moody Brook, however the position was shelled by enemy artillery fire that destroyed the Moody Brook Barracks. It was not until the night of 13 June that the British launched the second phase of their assault on Port Stanley on a bitterly cold night, with snow showers shielding a bright moon. There was still plenty of fight left in the Argentine commanders, but more realistic conscripts told interrogators they realised the war had been lost.

Wireless Ridge is a rocky feature north of Moody Brook with three distinct features. Spot Height 250ft, nicknamed by the British as 'Rough Diamond', was a mile east of Mount Longdon and defended by C Company, commanded by First-Lieutenant Hugo Garcia. Spot Height 250ft, nicknamed 'Apple Pie', to the east was occupied by A

Company, commanded by First-Lieutenant Jorge Calvos. Spot Height 300ft, nicknamed 'Blueberry Hill', to the south of 'Rough Diamond' is a long ridge west to east occupied by a C Company platoon and the Recce Platoon. To its east was a small feature overlooking the Murrell River known as Position X. Command Company was located in rocks above Moody Brook Barracks and defended by a 2nd Airborne Infantry Regiment platoon commanded by Second-Lieutenant Gustavo Alberto Aimar. In reserve at Moody Brook Barracks was A Company, 3rd Infantry Regiment commanded by Major Berazay on call to 5th Marines and 7th Regiment.

Firepower support included a 105mm Pack Howitzer battery and the Mortar Platoon, 6th 'General Juan Viamonte' Regiment's 'B' Company on the north-east shoulder of Tumbledown. Soon after dark on 13 June, British artillery pounded the Argentine positions with about 6,000 shells and ripped apart Lieutenant-Colonel Giménez's carefully laid defence plan.

At about 1.40am, British tanks (Blues and Royals) and an infantry company captured 'Rough Diamond' only to find it abandoned. Two A Company platoons commanded by First-Lieutenant Jorge Calvo and Hugo Garcia resisted fiercely and withdrew. The feature named 'Apple Pie' was heavily shelled, forcing a trapped platoon to surrender. The 7th Regiment Command Post was hit several times by artillery and Lieutenant-Colonel Giménez was nearly killed and Captain Carlos Ferreyra, the operations officer, was badly wounded. Battle planning collapsed as other officers were wounded, including Lieutenant Ramon Galindez-Matienzo of the Reconnaissance Platoon, and in A Company the two senior officers had been evacuated to hospital with severed tendons and deep lacerations from shelling. The three platoon commanders, First-Lieutenants Antonio Estrada, Jorge Guidobono and Ramon Galíndez-Matienzo, were wounded to a greater or lesser degree. Private Felix Barreto was sent to evacuate a wounded officer:

> I was told one of our officers, a lieutenant-colonel, had been wounded. Major Salvador-Carrizo told me to go up there and get him. I was to avoid the fighting and get him back to Moody Brook. We made our way up, but the battle was everywhere. The gorse was on fire and we had to fight our way to the command post. When

we got there and found the officer (Major Nani) he said he had no intention of withdrawing to Moody Brook with us, so we turned round and went back.[1]

Major Emilio Guillermo Nani was an experienced Forward Artillery Observation Officer. The command post was being defended by the Signals Platoon and the Argentine 2nd Airborne Infantry Regiment Platoon commanded by Lieutenant Jorge Guidobono, who had also been wounded. British tanks advanced onto the ridge and, encountering fire from the defence, the airborne platoon faced a company attack. Giménez admitted to Brigadier Jofre that 7th Regiment had been destroyed and rumours were undermining confidence. Private Jorge Abdul states,

> There were thousands of rumours. I was even told that some English commandos had infiltrated Argentine troops, that they spoke perfect Spanish, and that some had even made a company retreat, saying that they had orders from the commander. The unit may have been First Lieutenant Hector Miño's 1st Amphibious Engineer Company platoon on the centre of Tumbledown Mountain that, at about 0200 local time, sought safety on the eastern end of Tumbledown. I don't know if it was true, but a lot of people in the town were afraid that there were English mixed in among us. Until then, when someone approached we said, 'Halt', and asked for identification. But there was so much fear that the system was no good anymore.[2]

Discipline was wavering and there was nothing to stop the British pouring through the defence. Jofre refused an offer for Skyhawks to bomb Wireless Ridge with napalm on the grounds that the British response would be commensurate. As demoralised and leaderless conscripts began to abandon their positions, many collected at Felton Stream on Stanley Common.

When C Company, 3rd Regiment reported an attack developing north of Moody Brook, a counter-attack force consisting of B Company, 6th Regiment and First-Sergeant Jorge Lucero's 3rd Platoon, N Company, 5th Marines was placed under command of Major Berazay, the 3rd Regiment second-in-command. He planned for the 25th Regiment and the 10th Armoured Cavalry Reconnaissance Squadron to counter-attack. The squadron was commanded by Captain Rodrigo Alejandro Soloaga, but communications in the two platoons were poor and therefore Berazay drove to HQ 10th Brigade to collect radios and explain the seriousness of the situation to Brigadier-General Jofre. When he returned to his regiment and C Company reported an attack developing on the left flank, Berazay assembled the 81mm Mortar Platoon commanded by Lieutenant José Luis Dobroevic and the Armoured Cavalry Reconnaissance Squadron in a counter-attack. He sent Captain Soloaga to liaise with the 4th Airborne Artillery Group but the gunners were having problems registering targets and Soloaga resorted to using only the Mortar Platoon. Major Roberto Berazay, commanding 3rd Mechanised Infantry Regiment, described the attack:

> It was like a theatre. I had never seen anything like it before. After the artillery fire came the fire of the infantry action – a lot of tracer. I could actually see the British working their way along the ridge by the light of the star-shells. Between 3am and 4am, I heard Commander Robacio of 5th Marines telling Brigadier-General Jofre on the radio to release 'Guillermo' (that was my call sign) to help the 7th Regiment. Thanking Robacio for that doubtful honour, Jofre first told me to prepare my men to cross the valley and then, fifteen to twenty minutes later, ordered me to meet guides at Moody Brook from the armoured cars and a 25th Regiment company which Jofre was sending. I arrived at Moody Brook to find there were no guides from the armoured cars, they were already in action, and no-one from the 25th Regiment. I reported all this to 'Oscar' (Jofre's call sign). 'Okay,' he said. 'Just go up the hill and you will meet Colonel Giménez.' The tracer fire seemed to have died down, so I presumed that the British had taken all of the hill. I placed the company commander and the heavy weapons under Lieutenant Jose Luis Dobroevic in a fire support base among the trees around a small house. Nothing happened for a few minutes, so we moved forward with the machine-guns but got no more than a hundred metres when the British opened up. Captain Soloaga, arrived at 'Blueberry Hill' at about 4am, just in time for 40 minutes of shelling, during which Sergeant Adolfo Cabrera and Corporal Alberto Chavez were killed and several others wounded to enemy shelling. A further five were killed and 50 wounded by 'friendly shelling' from the airborne gunners.
>
> I ordered Captain Soloaga to take assault in single file. The two platoons were illuminated by flares, and most of Second-Lieutenant Aristegui's men dropped themselves on the ground and kept calm, some no doubt fearing more artillery. One problem was that there was no real cover at all and after several minutes, the platoon advanced, however Second-Lieutenant Aristegui was wounded in the neck and Platoon Sergeant Juan Vallejos was seriously wounded in the stomach. First-Lieutenant Victor Hugo Rodriguez-Perez's 1st Platoon then passed through 2nd Platoon and in spite of heavy fire, reached a British platoon and managed to sneak into the rocks and opened fire, causing some confusion among the enemy and in the enemy command post bunker. After losing half its strength, the Argentine platoon withdrew.[3]

Private Patricio Perez was in the platoon and recollects:

> As we climbed up the ridge we came under heavy fire. The worst thing was the cries of the wounded, shouting for help. You felt a lot of pain but you also wanted to avenge them. I remember thinking how important it was to cover my legs. I always thought that if I was hit in the arm or chest or stomach I could always walk out. The main thing was to keep the legs covered. I didn't want to lose my legs. At one point I took cover behind a rock. I was carrying two rifles and I noticed that there was a sniper who was pinning me down. I wanted to come out of the rock and kill him but I couldn't because the firing was so intense. At that moment I heard somebody shout that he had seen the sniper. I came out, saw that he was leaning over the rock and shot at him and his gun fell silent. I saw him fall but I don't know whether he was wounded or dead. That kind of combat among the rocks is like a western, but it all happens so fast that you don't quite realise what is going on.
>
> What I felt at that moment was mostly hatred. I wanted revenge. I had forgotten fear by then, what sort of risk I was taking; the only thing I wanted to do, my obsession, was to avenge my fallen comrades. Whenever I saw one of my friends hit it was worse, it just made me want to continue fighting, it didn't matter for how long or at what cost. I didn't care about death at that time, the main thing was revenge. Looking back, I now think it was all quite mad, very strange. I once heard a Vietnam veteran talk about the 'drunkenness of war'. He was quite right, it is like being drunk and I enjoyed it at that moment. As children we all play at war because we have seen it on television or films, so as a child you play up to this role with a wooden gun, only this time I had a real gun in my hands and perhaps I forgot that I could actually kill and be killed. Some of us went looking for the wounded. We thought they could make it back. I heard they had killed my friend Private Horacio Benitez, and the feeling for revenge came over me again.
>
> We evacuated the wounded and, returning to the battle, fought on for four hours. Luckily after the surrender I found out that Horacio had survived. People greeted the surrender with relief. They were all crying. That wasn't how I reacted. I had been fighting for many hours and I was not prepared to give up my rifle until forced to do so. It's different for those who had been in actual combat. I couldn't give my rifle back until they took it away from me, and when I did give it back, I made sure it was completely unusable.[4]

Privates Julio Ruben Cao, Jose Reyes-Lobos and Julio Cesar Segura were killed and casualties among the NCOs and soldiers were high.

Near the church, Major Carrizo-Salvadores, whose 7th Regiment had already suffered grievous losses, and Chaplain Father José Fernández called for one final effort and mustered about 50 soldiers. The commando-trained 7th Regiment conscript Santiago Gauto, whose heritage is Guarani, describes the counter-attack:

> Outside the church they gave us a magazine each for our rifles and told us to gather at the artillery positions on the edge of Stanley. Major Carrizo was organising a counter-attack. I met Felix Barreto and we watched and listened to what was going on. There had been other attacks and they had failed. Major Carrizo asked a colonel [Eugenio Dalton] for a radio and was refused. We stood watching them arguing. Carrizo told him: 'We'll never win a war like this.' He was right. Then he turned to us and said: 'Those who've got balls, follow me.' We advanced. Around me guys had tears running down their faces. Inside we knew we were not going to get very far, we were going to die, we were marching to death. The British were firing down on us with machine-guns mortars, artillery. It was like advancing through the gates of hell itself. It was a suicidal mission. We were about 50 against a company of the British red berets. It was to me the greatest counter-attack of the war. For the first time I saw British paratrooper faces. We got that close.[5]

The counter-attack advanced up Wireless Ridge singing 'The Malvinas March' until it was discouraged by artillery and machine-gun fire. While the attack was a forlorn hope, it won the admiration of Major Philip Neame who described it as 'quite a sporting effort'. The Argentines withdrew at about 9.15am and not a moment too soon. A napalm strike on Wireless Ridge was in progress as the Argentine force moved into the area: hardly a good omen. Meanwhile, another counter-attack force of Lieutenant-Colonel Comini and his 3rd Infantry Regiment, the 25th 'Special' Infantry Regiment and others, totalling about 1,000 Argentinian troops, formed up near the 35mm anti-aircraft artillery battery on Stanley Racecourse. Fortunately, Brigadier-General Jofre knew the war was nearly lost and cancelled the move.

With the two British brigades literally at the gates of Stanley, Argentine command and control disappeared as the Inner Defence Zone collapsed and thousands of troops poured into Stanley, some in units, others as individuals. Lieutenant-Colonel Carlos Quevedo, commanding the 4th Airborne Artillery Regiment, had noted a sense of hopelessness as soldiers streamed past Wireless Ridge. This infuriated Major Antonio Perez-Cometto, the 7th Regiment Operations Officer, who is reported to have cursed the retreating conscripts. Private Miguel Savage and others from C Company, 7th Regiment were among the first to reach the relative safety of Port Stanley only to be greeted with disdain by immaculately dressed staff officers,

> They had been sleeping in houses, in warm beds. They had shiny shoes, pristine ironed uniforms and waxed moustaches. They even had heating in their cars. I was so furious with them.[6]

Nevertheless, there was still resistance. The 155mm howitzers of D Battery posed a threat to the Scimitar light tanks firing their 30mm Rarden cannons. The guns of the 3rd Artillery Group also gave some respite. Lieutenant-Colonel Eugene Dalton, a 10th Brigade staff officer, used a jeep to collect about 100 weary soldiers from various units who had been on Wireless Ridge and formed them into a company, and led them to Stanley's western sector in a last ditch stand in front of the silent guns of the 4th Airborne Artillery Group near the racecourse.

So far, the Argentine troops had been reasonably disciplined, but with defeat beckoning and with no chance of a rescue there was a risk of a breakdown of discipline. Commando operations during the defence of Stanley included, on 10 June, 602 Commando carrying out several operations in the Port Stanley to prevent enemy infiltration. The National Guard provided internal security patrols to deter and detect enemy agents who had infiltrated the town. On 12 June, an anti-aircraft ambush covered the 4th Airborne Artillery Group near Moody Brook. 2nd Platoon, 601 Commando occupied a blocking position west of Stanley. The next day, 3rd Platoon, 601 Commando provided the defence of the Joint Falklands Military Garrison Command Post. After reports of possible British landings, small patrols from 601 and 602 Commando Companies recced north of Stanley and laid an ambush to cover the 101 Air Defence Artillery Zone. 602 Commando also laid an ambush covering the ammunition dump north-east boundary of Stanley. In response to intelligence reports of a probable landing north of Stanley, a recce patrol scouted Cortley Hill, north of Port Stanley. Another ambush was established close to the position of 101 Air Defence Artillery Group. On the 14th, 601 Commando's last operation established a block east of 7th Regiment to deny the enemy access to the high ground north of Stanley Common. Rumours of British infiltration, which were rife, emerged among leaderless soldiers sheltering at Felton Stream on Stanley Common and the risk of the breakdown of discipline emerged; Major Berazay ordered that anyone spreading disinformation was to be shot. Brigadier-General Jofre ordered 181st Military Police Company, the 5th Marines Military Police and 2nd Assault Section, 601st Commando Company to maintain law and order and shoot on sight British Special Forces wearing Argentine uniforms. For over two hours, 7th Regiment regulars, the military police and commandos debated the tense situation.

While the 6th Regiment deployed to secure the airport peninsula, the 5th Marines retreated to their Sapper Hill stronghold, which Brigadier General Jofre intended to use as a focal point for the defence of Stanley, but the domination of the British is reflected in an intercepted report:

> British artillery has complete dominance over Argentine artillery. They are hitting targets on the extreme edge of Stanley. About 140 men have been hit by shrapnel. No more men should attempt to go forward because losses will be too great.

First-Lieutenant Jorge Cerezo commanding C Battery, 4th Airborne Artillery Group had placed his five 105mm M56 Pack Howitzers near Moody Brook, however he was not supported by Forward Observation. Fatigue, the cold, the soggy ground and darkness meant every change of direction was laborious. Guns sinking to the axle meant instability. Two guns facing north became unserviceable through equipment failures. Men took cover from counter-battery fire in a water-filled shellholes. As the British attacked Wireless Ridge and the threat against the battery position increased, the gunners ignored the counter-battery fire, nevertheless Cerezo found his position rapidly was becoming indefensible. As the range shortened to 1,800 metres, the gunners fired over open sights and he then formed a defence force and a supply chain from three out of action. He lost two more guns when the firing mechanism of one broke and recoil failure of the fifth led to it falling off its trails. At 9am, the CO ordered Cerezo to cease fire and the battle calmed down, however there was little shelter from the cold and falling snow. About mid-morning, as 2 Para advanced and C Battery opened fire, as Cerezo rammed a shell up the breech of the gun and the block fell out, it was ordered to leave the guns and withdraw into Stanley. At 4pm, Cerezo told his gunners that the Argentines had surrendered.

B Company, 25th Regiment and two 3rd Regiment companies were sent to a defensive position west of Stanley near the war memorial. A senior Argentine naval officer describes Stanley:

> By dawn, 5th Marine Infantry Battalion and 7th Infantry Regiment were falling back toward the naval base around the public jetty, their soldiers a picture of defeat, stumbling, filthy, tired and dragging themselves along. I heard the King Edward VII Memorial Hospital was in front of our lines and that casevac helicopters were ferrying wounded to the *Almirante Irizar* [the Argentine naval icebreaker now flying Red Cross colours]. A lieutenant faking serious injury secured himself passage, not the first instance of desertion in the face of the enemy. A senior officer had, at the height of the battle, gone to the hospital for a blood test for jaundice, which he had contracted months earlier.[7]

During the 12-hour battle of Wireless Ridge, the Argentine casualties totalled about 150, of whom about 15 were 7th Regiment conscripts, four were 3rd Regiment conscripts and five were 10th Armoured Cavalry Reconnaissance Squadron.

CHAPTER 16

Surrender and the Final Battle

'Oh good, the men will be pleased,' said the commander at Pebble Island, upon being told of the Argentine surrender.

As a murky, grey dawn broke on 14 June, the two British brigades in the hills to the east of Stanley had bitten deep into the Argentine defence. The defending 10th Brigade was very close to defeat. Brigadier-General Jofre was warned by Lieutenant-Colonel Comini that hardline elements were planning to use the cover of early morning mist to counter-attack Wireless Ridge. As the remnants of Major Berazay's 3rd Infantry Regiment company were withdrawing through the 4th Airborne Artillery Group positions around Felton Stream, about one and a half miles west of Stanley, three Scout helicopters fired several SS-11 missiles at them, wounding several men. At about 10.15am, M Company, 5th Marines on Sapper Hill watched as three Sea Kings deposited British troops below them and in a brisk but pointless firefight, three 5th Marines were killed, the last to die in the fighting.

Certain defeat fractured the political factions and exposed rivalries with those officers who were politically hostile to President Galtieri expressing discontent at the international humiliation and censure as the Argentine defence collapsed.

Therefore, at about 8am, and after consulting General Jofre on the situation, Brigadier-General Menéndez decided to call Galtieri from the Auxiliary Communications Centre that was in the governor's house so he could have some privacy. General Iglesias, the Secretary of the Presidency, answered his call. Menéndez recalled,

> I described the situation to him; I told him which were the elements that I
> had organised to continue fighting, the places where the English had arrived.
> That at that moment they were already reaching the western edge of the town,
> that really the troops were already physically and emotionally broken, that they
> could not take any more. Essentially, I did not want to see my Army defeated
> and that is why I communicated with the president to propose that Argentina
> accept Resolution 502.[1]

He concluded, 'What I ask of you is that you hurry up, because although
we are fighting, I don't know how much longer we are going to be able
to do it.' An hour later, Brigadier-General Menéndez advised President
Galtieri that although Argentine forces were still fighting, his Army
was near defeat and losing men in a hopeless situation was worse than
surrendering, and suggested accepting Resolution 502. Galtieri replied
that his intelligence staff had assessed that the British were in an equally
precarious position. Menéndez recalls:

> He replied, 'Resolution 502 cannot be accepted after the commitment that
> has been made. I am not the commander, you are and you know what your
> responsibilities and powers are.' I replied that I did know because I had been
> complying with them for more than two months and then I was going to exercise
> them once again.
>   Galtieri replied, 'Look, what happens is that you don't have to get people
> out of the foxholes to go backwards but to go forward!' This was what made
> me decide to reply to him, 'Look, you don't understand me; it seems that you
> don't understand the situation our troops are in here.'[2]

While losses of casualties and men taken prisoner since 1 May numbered
about 1,500, the magazines in Stanley were well stocked and Menéndez
felt he could withstand a siege, even though the British had sea, land
and air superiority, but there was little hope of relief from the mainland.
After Brigadier-General Jofre had already refused an offer of mainland
Skyhawks to napalm Wireless Ridge because he believed the British
response would be catastrophic, Navy Captain Barry Melbourne Hussey,
from Menéndez's governmental staff in Stanley, agreed to contact the
British. When Major-General Moore agreed a cease-fire and the decision
was relayed to Galtieri by Major-General Garcia, Menéndez was ordered
to commit himself to discussing the evacuation of Argentine troops from
the Falklands. Meanwhile, the British advanced as far as the racecourse.

During the afternoon, a small team of British negotiators flew into Stanley and proposed the unconditional surrender of all Argentine forces on the Falkland Islands at 12.15am on 15 June; Menéndez asked for the word 'unconditional' to be crossed out, implying they had agreed specified conditions. Menéndez recalls,

> When I read it and saw the term 'unconditional', I reacted badly. I got very tense and told him: 'General Moore, this is not what we agreed, here it says about unconditional surrender when it is not. Furthermore, this does not honour the way in which the Argentines have fought, as you yourself have just told me.' He asked me what the difference was. I told him that the difference was that I agreed to a surrender with conditions and there it said unconditional, so I would not sign that document. That I did not know what could happen or how we were going to continue the fight, but in those conditions, I repeated, wouldn't sign it. He was thoughtful for a moment, I do not remember if he consulted on the radio or not, and then he said, 'Okay, we crossed it out.' Therefore, he crossed out and initialled his copy and I did the same on mine and then we exchanged copies.[3]

Major-General Moore and General Menéndez had agreed that Argentine units could retain their colours, while commanders and officers could still have the command of their troops and could keep their sidearms to protect themselves from the anger of their men; that Argentine troops should withdraw to the airport area and assemble there; that mixed commissions would be formed to solve the problems that would arise in terms of logistics and personnel injured, casualties, the dead, food; and, fundamentally, that the signing of the surrender document that was drawn up would have to be in a private ceremony, without journalists, and no footage or photos taken.

When the British entered Stanley, they found a largely undamaged town and the litter of a defeated army of ammunition, broken weapons and damaged vehicles, small fires of documents and booby traps. A neutral zone was declared around the cathedral to assemble the Argentines. The defeated Argentines were apprehensive. A naval officer recalls:

> 15 June. I went down to the jetty where a senior naval officer was screaming at conscripts to get off the jetty and accusing them that, because they were no good at fighting, they should clean up the mess that had accumulated in the area. I then heard that senior officers were being taken on board HMS *Fearless*

on orders from the British government and there were some sorrowful goodbyes. That evening Stanley was placed under a curfew.[4]

Meanwhile, in Operation *Keyhole*, Southern Thule, after six years of Argentine presence with the Scientific Station Corbeta Uruguay, was liberated by M Company 42 Commando commanded by Captain Chris Nunn; his brother, a Royal Marine helicopter pilot, had been killed at Goose Green. Conditions were rigorous with whiteout and windchill dropping to -50 degrees. During the night, the BBC again compromised military operations by broadcasting that Southern Thule had been retaken. The next morning, 20 June, the weather improved and nine men from the Navy and the Air Force and one civilian surrendered, and when the naval party landed the next morning, they found the base had been vandalised.

After Admiral Woodward's statements to journalists that the Argentine prisoners were hungry and helpless in the winter weather that hung over the Malvinas ('Starved and abandoned', as was published), in an alleged manoeuvre to obtain a formal surrender from the Military Junta, HQ LFFI decided to repatriate as many prisoners as possible so as to avoid an epidemic. But there were two pressing logistical problems of Stanley addressing the welfare of the Falkland Islanders and repatriating several thousand Argentine prisoners spread across the Falklands. The town was tense. There was no power, most of the prisoners were still armed and in the open and intelligence assessments were suggesting the threat of militant officers rejecting ceasefire. Meanwhile, HQ LFFI and HQ 3 Commando Brigade assembled a small intelligence team of individuals who spoke Spanish, whatever the dialect and ability, and tasked them to collect documents and equipment of intelligence value from Argentine headquarters. Stanley was also without water. About 400 sick and wounded enemy casualties were in Stanley Hospital, at a field hospital in a warehouse and on the *Almirante Irizar*.

16 June dawned cold. During the day, prisoners had been assembled in warehouses in Stanley and were at the airfield. Escorted working parties recovered the wounded, buried the dead and assembled equipment and material. One elderly couple pleaded with a Royal Marine to be gentle

with the prisoners, 'After all, they're so young and confused.' The captured Argentine officer continues:

> I slept on the floor of the Falkland Islands Company offices and it was very cold, without lighting or heating. At about 9am I was told everyone was to go to the airport. We marched against a cold wind and freezing rain. People stumbled along under the weight of packs but soon equipment was jettisoned and the road became a scene of total desolation. I persuaded a truck driver to take our baggage, which made life easier. Arriving at the airport, we found there were no tents or water and people were ripping up corrugated iron to make shelters, while others set vehicles alight to keep warm. I scrounged five tents from 5th Marine Infantry Battalion and after pitching them, we watched those dirty tattered soldiers, about 8,000 of them, swarming all over the place. One managed to kill himself when he accidentally fired the ejection seat of an abandoned Pucara. Ammo, rockets and bombs littered the place. At about mid-afternoon I was told by some Red Cross that we needed tents and water and because there were so many sleeping in the open, there was a danger of some dying from exposure. They told me there was not much they could do because, although General Menéndez had surrendered, the Argentine government had not acknowledged the ceasefire. The Red Cross came across as anti-Argentina.[5]

Two frigates and two landing craft transferred the 8th and 5th Regiments and other units from West Falklands and 150 Argentine Air Force ground crew and Marines were collected from Pebble Island to Ajax Bay. The SAS Sergeant Roy Fonseka, captured by 601 Commando Company near Port Howard, was released after spending four days confined to a 4-foot sheep pen.

After HQ LFFI reached an agreement with the Red Cross and Argentina that Argentine sappers would help clear minefields and defuse booby traps, 34 sappers commanded by a major accepted parole to help 59 Independent Commando and 9 Para Squadrons RE dismantle the minefields and were given white arm bands to denote their status. However, the major proved uncooperative and was transferred to Ajax Bay. A Spanish-speaking Gibraltarian serving with the Royal Engineers who had been attached to intelligence arrived to help interpret. Detailed intelligence searches of Argentine headquarters led to several boxes of documents and equipment being sent to the Ministry of Defence.

Prisoner repatriation would begin that night from Stanley public jetty and prisoners would be transferred to the *Canberra*, due in Port William after dark. The *Uganda* would transfer to the *Bahía Paraíso* the Argentine casualties requiring specialist treatment. Five hundred Special Category prisoners were to be retained as prisoners-of-war until Argentina surrendered unconditionally. Before boarding, prisoners were to jettison everything except the uniforms they were wearing, a spoon and washing kit and would be frisked by the Royal Marines Police and be questioned by a small interrogation team collecting tactical information before being ferried to the ship from the jetty.

Naval Party 2060 on board insisted on the maximum security of the prisoners, however the ship was not ideal for the separation of the prisoners until arrangements were made to confine the officers three to two-person and six to four-person cabins, the other senior ranks in cabins and the remainder were confined to cabins and in five pens on the car deck. This area had no ablution facilities except urinal buckets, which often overflowed as the ship pitched.

At about 8pm, as a biting wind whipped snow horizontally across the single spotlight from a captured Argentine Coastguard cutter moored alongside the jetty, the first column of anxious, cold, wet, weary and battle-stained Argentines stood three-deep facing the jetty, the officers, somewhat embarrassed by their predicament, the NCOs apprehensive and conscripts not entirely unhappy at going home. At the order 'Next!', each prisoner doubled forward and stood in front of the screeners who asked, 'Name? Rank? Occupation?', which was followed by a short interrogation to determine repatriation or remaining at Her Majesty's pleasure. Some officers who had exchanged identities and uniforms with other ranks were mostly betrayed. Heaps of discarded equipment appeared on the square. Some conscripts caught smuggling knives, weapons and equipment were reprimanded. The officer son of a general hurled his two pearl-handled silver Colt .45 automatics into the harbour saying, 'No bloody English are going to have these!' A 601 Commando Company NCO declared, 'It was a boring war'. A young 4th Regiment officer said the Argentine Army had learnt much from the war, in particular that a conscript army cannot defeat a professional army. On board, most prisoners were confined four to a cabin and were overwhelmed by the sheer luxury and kindness of the crew. One steward who had showed four conscripts how to use the shower returned 20 minutes later to find a fully clothed, shivering conscript under a jet of ice-cold water. There had been reports that conscripts were regularly hosed down by their officers for some misdemeanour. Other tales of bullying by officers and NCOs had already emerged.

Shortly after midnight, civilians and soldiers drinking in the Globe Hotel threw smoke grenades and directed a Panhard at a column of prisoners. When Argentines set fire to a store and Stanley Fire Brigade arrived and turned on the tap, there was a cheer as small fountains of water spilled from punctured hoses. Disorder engineered by several officers nearly saw the screening in danger of being overrun until an RAF SNCO examining an automatic pistol accidentally pulled the trigger, followed by silence and then said, 'Sorry about that, chaps!' A 40 Commando troop then arrived complete with fixed bayonets. To counter the determination of some Argentine officers to disrupt the repatriation process, Brigadier-General Jofre was ordered to appoint several English-speaking liaison officers. Spanish-speaking screeners mingled with the prisoners, listening to conversations and countering the disruption.

The next morning, the Special Category prisoners were escorted to the football field outside Government House and flown by Chinook to Ajax Bay. An Argentine Navy officer recalls:

> We were warned to assemble at the football pitch ready to be helicoptered to the *Canberra* but when we arrived, we handed in our weapons, boarded a Chinook and were transferred to Ajax Bay where we were issued with identity cards, escorted into the refrigeration plant, searched and interviewed before being put into a small room. My cellmates included a Canberra pilot, an Air Force SAM-7 observer and a number of Army officers.[6]

Among the prisoners was a qualified German-speaking doctor serving as a medical orderly, an English-speaking university graduate conscript who did not want to return to Argentina and interpreted for the screening team and 181 Military Police Company and their large, well-groomed Alsatians, who gazed blank, brown-eyed stares and cocked their heads when ordered to 'Sit!' in English until it was realised they only understood Spanish. Prisoners complaining of ill-health or with an urgent requirement to return to Argentina were referred to Red Cross officials. When a pistol was found in an Army doctor's medical bag, he was handed over to a Red Cross official who gave him a very public dressing down that he had breached the Red Cross code of conduct.

During the afternoon, 2 Para marched three abreast along the sea front to hold a service in the cathedral. Royal Marines escorting prisoners sat on the grass to let them pass. That night *Norland* arrived in Port William and the screening began again on a night when snowstorms were sweeping down the mountains. As each column arrived, one of Brigadier-General Jofre's liaison officers warned against smuggling being prohibited. Nevertheless, when a 3rd Infantry Regiment conscript was found with a hacksaw tucked into a boot, Brigadier-General Jofre and his two liaison officers were given a traditional sergeant-major's dressing down by a Royal Military Corps captain and warned that if prisoners were caught with prohibited items they would be dealt with severely, as would Brigadier-General Jofre for not co-operating. The conscript was then offered a cup of tea by the Royal Military Police. Soon afterwards, a dumped pistol was found. When the green–bereted 25th Regiment marched into the square under escort, Lieutenant-Colonel Seineldín brushed past Jofre's liaison officers and identified his men to the intelligence team. One soldier surrendered a unit regimental war diary that he had been ordered to smuggle to Argentina.

At midday the next day, *Canberra* reporting that it had reached its limit came as a surprise. About a day later, *Canberra* arrived at Puerto Madryn where the Red Cross supervised the disembarkation of the weary prisoners, who were loaded into lorries and buses and taken to barracks. Meanwhile, when the *Norland* embarked prisoners at San Carlos and Port William, coded signals were detected between several cabins holding officer prisoners planning to hijack the ship. The chain was intercepted and false information fed. The next morning, *Norland* sailed for Puerto Madryn with 2,047 prisoners. The next day, the *Bahia Paraíso* collected several hundred lightly wounded and sick prisoners, mainly ill with dysentery, stomach and painful foot ailments, three soldiers with gastro-enteritis stretcher cases, a conscript with a serious head wound and an unusually large number of pilots, who were quickly sifted out as Special Category.

Meanwhile, a British counter-intelligence operation examining the extent of Argentine espionage and subversion and the extent of stay-behind elements led to interviews of several Falkland Islanders and nine seamen from a Polish fish factory ship pressed into working for the Argentines.

Officers began to generally accept surrendering as inevitable and seemed pleased with the settlement. Most senior officers were adamant that they would be back in the future, some within 20 years, others within five and one within the year. Most agreed they had been defeated by an outnumbered army superior in experience, training and equipment. Many criticised the conscript concept and accepted politics prevented the creation of professional armed forces. The junior officers appeared to have genuine concern for their men and in more than one instance witnessed their units being processed before embarking themselves. One was amazed by the stockpiles in Stanley. Virtually all the NCOs expressed dissatisfaction with the leadership. The conscripts looked upon captivity with stoicism. Their intellect ranged from well-educated graduates to peasants. Very few civilians were captured, although a television war correspondent was selected for Special Category, much to his disgust. Two alleged priests named by some Argentine soldiers as propaganda experts slipped through the net onto the *Canberra* and were lifted.

Meanwhile, about 500 prisoners had been assembled at Ajax Bay. An Argentine naval officer described conditions and his thoughts:

17 June. Although I managed to sleep that night, the room [cabin] was hot and damp. The light remained on although every so often the generator would run out of fuel; we remained very quiet in the darkness until the light came back on in case the guards became frightened and shot us. Breakfast was stew but because only a few us had utensils, most had to use empty drink cans. The toilet was screened off in the corner with one bucket for a urinal and another filled with a liquid that decomposes matter. In the mid-morning we were allowed into the Pig Pen for an hour, a 20×20 metre quagmire, full of rubbish from previous occupants, where we were gazed at by the British and occasionally jeered. When we returned to our cell, we found that it had been cleaned by Argentine other rank prisoners. Water was in a small tub that was replaced infrequently but I later learnt that water was scarce anyway. In the evening we were given supper and then we listened on a smuggled radio that President Galtieri had resigned. About 200 officers arrived that evening from Stanley.

18 June. Another uncomfortable night, but at breakfast, we were advised
by the British to eat because we would be transferring to a ship and nobody
knows when the next meal will be. It had become unbelievably hot in our
cell and we persuaded the guards to let us get some fresh air. I met the same
Red Cross official and he told me that Britain wanted Argentina to accept the
cease-fire and in return would repatriate all the captured forces apart from 400
officers who would be held as hostages to ensure safe passage for the return
of the victors to England. I later learnt that soon after this conversation the
Canberra departed for Puerto Belgrano with 4,500 soldiers. In the afternoon, a
padre held Mass. I sat next door to Lieutenant-Colonel Giménez who was very
angry because he feared court martial for retreating and was worried that he
would be accused of having left the front line. Later, some of the more senior
officers accepted an invitation to attend a mass burial of some Argentines at the
San Carlos cemetery. That evening we listened to the radio and heard Anaya
bidding farewell to President Galtieri.[7]

19 June dawned bright. Stanley was still without water, the Globe Store
was still burning and Argentine work parties were collecting abandoned
equipment, ammunition and debris that littered the roads. 3 Commando
Brigade handed over its positions to 5th Infantry Brigade. 45 Commando
silently plodded along Ross Street in one long snake to an LSL tied up
alongside the jetty. Captain Gardiner later wrote:

As if in answer to a Royal Marine's prayer, the whole thing ended up, unbelievably,
in a pub called the Globe Hotel. Having marched into Stanley to go on board a
ship for a wash, we found ourselves in a smoky, wooden bar-shaped room. 150
Marines, unshaven, dirty, tired, stinking and very lightly boozed – every man a
can of beer in his hands. Just like the end of a map-reading exercise.[8]

During the afternoon, the LFFI prisoner administration team finally
arrived at the jetty; their original task had been to run a prison camp.
An Argentine naval officer recalled:

19 June. We had no breakfast until after we had exercised in the Pig Pen, when
we were given some biscuits and soup but everyone complained about the lack
of food. More prisoners arrived overnight, including some from Stanley. They
reported that all those who went on the *Canberra* had been ordered by the British
to leave everything behind and that it then was all set alight. There were some
harsh words said of the Navy when we learnt the *Canberra* had been escorted
into Puerto Madryn by an Argentine destroyer. One Navy officer came in for
considerable criticism for accepting a dinner invitation with a Royal Navy officer.

> 20 June. The news on the illegal radio from Argentina is very discouraging. Britain had declared she would retain prisoners until Argentina recognised the cease-fire agreement. Argentina would not respond until Britain accepts UN Resolution 509 on the withdrawal of forces, including nuclear submarines, and the lifting of the blockade. It was Father's Day and I was without my children. When we went out to the Pig Pen, it was very cold.[9]

An estimated 10,250 Argentines had been repatriated through Stanley and Ajax Bay leaving 593 Special Category, 35 paroled engineers and about 200 other conscripts. After some initial success in causing disruption, the Argentines were outwitted by a small intelligence team that closed down its operations and handed over to another detachment that landed at Ajax Bay and set up in the bomb-damaged refrigeration plant. One problem faced by all Argentines was that the Argentine Code of Conduct was to give only rank and name. The Geneva Convention demanded that prisoners must also give serial number and date of birth. In total about 90 Special Category prisoners were questioned. Several hardliners did not accept the defeat. The naval officer continues:

> 21 June. By now I was becoming more used to our confinement, although I thought that the lack of vitamins was beginning to take effect. Nevertheless, the strain of living in a small and crowded space was beginning to tell. There was a serious disagreement between the Army prisoners but I suspect it was more a loss of dignity than anything else. When we went to the Pig Pen, it was pouring with rain. On our return I was taken for interrogation. I told them I was only required to give name, surname, number and date of birth and name of father as required by the Geneva Convention. This annoyed the interrogators and I was told that unless I co-operated, repatriation could be delayed. Some officers managed to retain dignity in their dealings with the British, particularly 'Los Anglos'. Our radio was found, which was a great loss.
>
> 22 June. My mood had changed and it was now the Black Hole of Ajax Bay. For exercise the guards took us to the part of the refrigeration plant that had been bombed [on 25 May] and there lodged in the masonry were two unexploded bombs. I was then taken away for more interrogation and played dumb to all their questions. When I returned more officers had arrived and our cell was very crowded.

On 23 June, the Scots Guards took over from the Royal Marines at Ajax Bay. A Red Cross delegation headed by Monsieur Claude Dietrich demanded better conditions, which was quickly actioned. The Argentine naval officer continued:

> 25 June. Two philosophies had developed to fit our lifestyle and both totally opposite to each other. The Los Anglos spoke good English, read English novels and essentially co-operated. Those of Latin descent, mainly Army officers, played dumb and pretended not to understand English and said derogatory things about them. During one argument a Latino said to a Los Anglos naval officer 'That depends on your superiors'. The officer replied 'I do not have any superiors. I have a high-ranking face starting with Anaya' [sic]. Someone then said, 'Watch out because his son is an Army lieutenant and is somewhere around'. When this was realised, the British hauled out the well-groomed, articulate and immaculately dressed prisoner named First-Lieutenant Guillermo Anaya but he refused to confirm his relationship with Admiral Anaya. It later turned out he was his son and was an Iroquois helicopter pilot with 601 Combat Aviation Battalion.
>
> 29 June. In the afternoon we were given a medical inspection in preparation for boarding the ship St Edmund but loading was cancelled until the following day. This sounded like a lie. The problem was still the refusal of Argentina to accept the cease-fire.

Before his diary was found during the search prior to embarkation, the naval officer commented on the value of intelligence and noted that information was lost when Governor Hunt destroyed papers and his secretary was allowed to burn code books (although some code books were found in the Moody Brook Barracks on 2 April). English journalists photographing the surrender in April had harnessed British opinion, and Argentine photographs of 'heroes' were of intelligence interest. The next day, the prisoners were transferred to the Sealink Ro-Ro ferry *St Edmund*. A systematic search unearthed two automatic pistols, parts of an FAL rifle, ammunition and diaries, including that of the senior naval officer.

On 2 July, when the *St Edmund* embarked 25 prisoners, including Brigadier-General Menéndez, a stiffening of resistance was noted. Also transferred on board were the detainees and prisoners captured at Southern Thule and the paroled sappers, one of whom, Corporal Cattay, had lost part of his leg when a mine exploded. A Welsh Guards company held Sunday Mass, organised football matches and deck hockey until all the pucks had been hit over the side. The most popular events were the two meals a day and escaping the cabins to do fatigues on the ship. Daily meetings were held between Major Drewry, commanding the Welsh Guards Guard Force and Camp Commandant on board the ship, and the multi-lingual Monsieur Claude Dietrich, representing the Red Cross and prisoner welfare. Among the prisoners was a son of Admiral Anaya, who commanded the Argentine Navy. The *St Edmund* plied between Stanley and Berkeley Sound until Argentina finally acknowledged the futility of refusing to surrender unconditionally. Without any reply, the British government sent a message transmitted to the Argentines by the Swiss on their behalf on 3 July declaring that there was a 'de facto cessation of hostilities' in the South Atlantic and that the British pilot Jeff Glover, held in the Air Base El Chamical, in La Rioja Province to the north-west of Argentina, should be released.

After the new Argentine Foreign Minister, Juan Antonio Aguirre Lanari, made a statement to the Swiss government that Argentina was already respecting 'the de facto cessation of active hostilities' and the RAF pilot, the only British prisoner, would be released to the Red Cross in Montevideo, the British government decided that the immediate return of the remaining Argentine prisoners-of-war by sea to the Argentine Port of Madryn was the best course of action on the basis of assurances given by the Argentine government.

As the ship set a course to Puerto Madryn, the prisoners cleaned their cabins and quarters and property was returned. The original plan had been to transfer them to Ascension Island and then there was a suggestion of flying the prisoners to the United Kingdom to a prison camp at the Toft Construction Village to RAF Sullom Voe Camp in Shetland. The International Committee of the Red Cross had pointed out that while the conditions on the Falklands were very limited and the British efforts in the treatment of prisoners were acceptable, the Geneva Convention prohibited grouping prisoners on ships.

At 4am on 14 July at the Ajax Bay prison camp, the duty drummer beat reveille and the prisoners were paraded after breakfast by Drill Sergeant Cox. Major Drewry, the camp commandant, was anxious – his headcount was 591 Special Category prisoners, whereas the Argentines were expecting 593, a figure agreed by the Red Cross. The repatriation was low key and after a very seriously wounded corporal was carried to a waiting ambulance, Brigadier-General Menéndez led the prisoners through the checkpoints and down a gangplank and gathered on the quay. Two hours later, Drewry consulted his counting machine and, to his horror, it registered 589 – four missing. When he then consulted the Argentine reception sergeant at the foot of the gangway, he also registered 589. Drewry produced a bottle of whisky and six glasses for the Red Cross delegation and General Garay, in command of the reception, and everyone agreed that 593 prisoners had passed through the checkpoints and blamed a faulty counting machine. It was agreed that the Argentine sergeant at the base of the gangway on the quay had also probably lost count several times. After handover certificates were handed to the Argentine delegation signalling the completion of the repatriation, Captain Stockman signalled to the Ministry of Defence:

> From MV St Edmund. At 10.00 hrs local this morning we completed the release of the last 593 Special Category prisoners under the supervision of the International Committee of the Red Cross at Puerto Madryn, Argentina. In so doing, we have fulfilled the company motto – Sealink sets you free

It was a fitting epitaph to the Malvinas/Falklands War.

CHAPTER 17

The Reckoning

For Argentina, the defeat on Las Malvinas was disastrous from a military and political point of view. It was a national embarrassment and costly in terms of losses and expenditure – and also a saviour.

Strategically, the Junta had failed to acknowledge that Great Britain had, and would, defended allies and territories seeking its support, which included small powers such as Belize, at risk from an equally unstable military power in Central America, Guatemala. Historically, Great Britain considered the Falklands to be a strategically important colony.

The Argentine Armed Forces were known to be inexperienced in conventional war and were undermined by politically dysfunctional generals unable to heal rifts between soft-liners and hard-liners in the national interest. It had some equipment dated from the Second World War as well as modern weapons, such as anti-aircraft artillery and radars and helicopters. The 1960s Plan Europe led to the purchase of French armoured vehicles from the AMX-13 family and Panhards. The change to mechanised infantry doctrine also had its impact. When the Beagle Channel islands crisis with Chile motivated re-equipment with modern armament, the Navy was in transition waiting for modern frigates and submarines under construction in West Germany and two Type 42 destroyers commissioned in 1977 and 1981 from Great Britain. In the same period, the Air Force had bought 24 Mirage V ('Nesher') from Israel. In November 1981, Naval Aviation had received five new Super Etendards and Exocet surface-to-surface missiles. The Humprey-Kennedy amendment to the Foreign Assistance Act improved the purchase and delivery of aircraft spare parts for aircraft, mainly the Skyhawks, Lockheed P-2 Neptune maritime patrol aircraft and helicopters, and for ships. The strategic philosophy of joint service operations was largely undermined by politics and inexperience in international settings, such as NATO and from within the British Commonwealth. In spite of the internal security operations in Northern Ireland, forces had been assembled and despatched 8,000 miles to fight and defeat an army fighting in its own backyard. In comparison, the British Armed Forces had been on constant active service since 1939, except for one year – 1968, the year that Europe came close to war when the Soviet Union invaded Czechoslovakia.

The Consequences of the Argentine Defeat	
11,313	All ranks captured.
1,657	All ranks wounded.
649	All ranks killed.
12	War dogs.
11,000	Variety of small arms, such as rifles, sub-, general and heavy machine-guns captured.
4 million	7.62mm calibre munition rounds.
	ARMOUR
12	Panhard AML 90mm armoured cars.
	ARTILLERY
10	105mm Oto Melara Pack Gun plus 11,000 shells. Also 10,500 rounds at Goose Green.
3	155mm CITEFA L33 Howitzers.
	AIR DEFENCE
15	35mm Twin Oerlikons.
15	20mm Twin Rheinmetalls.
20	30mm Single Hispano Suiza.
1	AN/TPS-43 3D mobile search radar.

Continued.

	The Consequences of the Argentine Defeat *Continued.*
1	AN/TPS-44 3D mobile search radar.
5	Skyguard Fledermaus radar.
	RASIT is a ground-surveillance pulse Doppler radar.
1	Roland surface-to-air missile (SAM).
	Blowpipe shoulder-launched SAM.
	SAM-7 shoulder-launched SAM.
	VEHICLES
100	Mercedes-Benz 1112/13/14 general trucks.
20	Mercedes-Benz Unimog off-road trucks.
50	Mercedes-Benz G-Class 4x4 Jeeps.
	SHIPS
1	Cruiser ARA *Belgrano* sunk.
1	Submarine ARA *Santa Fe* captured.
3	Cargo ships sunk.
1	Spy Trawler *Narwhal* captured.
	ARGENTINE COASTGUARD
1	Patrol boat GC82 *Islas Malvinas* renamed HMS *Tiger Bay*.
	AIRCRAFT
5	Dagger
2	Mirage IIIEA
19	Skyhawk A4B/A4C
3	Skyhawk A4Q
2	Canberra B62
25	Pucara
1	C-130E Hercules
1	Learjet 35A air photographic reconnaissance
5	MB-339 A

Continued.

The Consequences of the Argentine Defeat *Continued.*	
4	T-34C Mentor
	HELICOPTERS
2	Bell 212
1	Alouette III
	SA 330L Puma. This helicopter was returned to the UK and after refurbishment was allocated to 33 Squadron RAF as XZ 449. It was later upgraded to a Puma HC-2 capable of carrying either 20 troops or a 7,055lbs underslung load or six stretcher and six sitting casualties.
	ASSAULT HELICOPTERS
3	109A Hirundo
9	UH-IH Iroquois
6	SA.330L Puma
2	CH-47C Chinook
	COASTGUARD
2	Skyvan
1	SA.330 Puma

The nature of conflict often means that those killed in the fighting or dying from wounds and disease are laid in temporary graves, and are not recovered until the end of hostilities. The Junta rejected the British offer to repatriate Argentine bodies on the grounds that they were already in their homeland. While not a major problem for the British government who are the custodians of casualties through the Commonwealth War Graves Commission on every continent, it was a new issue for Argentina and perhaps inevitably soured by politics, as opposed to reflecting care and sympathy for relatives. In comparison, the British war dead are still members of their service and families, and are commemorated every Remembrance Sunday in November. In early 1983, Geoffrey Cardozo, an Army psychologist, arrived in the Falklands to analyse the service morale and became interested in the disposal of the young Argentine casualties who left home to fight a war. As the Royal Engineers cleared the battlefields and bodies were found, he registered them and visited locations. Many were without identity 'dog-tags' and every effort was made to identify them from, for instance, personal property. Those who could not be identified were given a Christian burial with full military honours, irrespective of rank, and their graves were marked by a white wooden cross with the name of the casualty, or if not, known as *Soldado Argentino Solo Conocido Por Dios* (Argentine Soldier Known Only by God). Locations were lodged with the Commonwealth War Graves Commission.

Brooke Hardcastle, the Goose Green farm manager, then donated land at Darwin for an Argentine cemetery. Darwin Cemetery (*Cementerio de Darwin*) is at Teal Creek, near Darwin. Initially, families of Argentine veterans were not informed of the existence of the cemetery. Today, the Argentine cemetery is visited by families of those who died during the war. Initially, it listed the remains of 236 Argentines who were killed or died of wounds on the Falklands. After the remodelling in 2004 by the Commission of Parents and Relatives of the Fallen in the South Atlantic War, the names of 649 Argentine soldiers, sailors and airmen who lost their lives are inscribed on glass plaques, with no indication of military rank or service, as requested by their families. The cemetery is protected by a walled enclosure with a cenotaph including an image of Argentina's patron saint, the Virgin del Lujan. There is a replica of the cemetery at Pilar, in Buenos Aires Province, but with 649 crosses bearing the names of the each of the fallen.

Details of Argentine casualties in direct support of the ground forces has been calculated from public sources, in particular from *Lista de Bajas de Combatientes del Conflicto del Atlantico Sur que incluye: Oficiales, Suboficiales y Soldados del Ejercito Argentino* and the *Marine Corps Desembarco No 145*. Non-battle casualties were not available. Not listed are one Argentine Navy, two Coastguard, 14 non-aircrew Argentine Air Force and several merchant seamen killed supporting the Argentine ground forces. Of the Argentine Army killed, a reservist of the 1954 induction died as did two each from 1959 and 1960 and 101 from those who entered the Army in 1981. Of the serving conscripts inducted in February 1982, 33 were killed, most were with 12th Infantry Regiment at Goose Green. 7th Regiment Infantry suffered the heaviest casualties losing 38 killed and 164 wounded on Longdon and Wireless Ridge. The most senior rank killed was Colonel Clodoveo Arevalo, who was on the staff of HQ 5th Army Corps and was Director of the General Roca Military Institute in Comodoro Rivadavia, who died when his UH-1H helicopter crashed in the sea in fog responding to a report of British commandos landing in the area of Caleta Olivia, Santa Cruz Province, during the night of 29/30 April.

By the first half of the twentieth century Argentina had developed into a proud nation supported by stable politics, a thriving economy, the Riviera of South America and the home of the tango that emerged in the 1880s along the Río de la Plata, the natural border between Argentina and Uruguay. Then in 1946, General Juan Perón, who had been military attaché in Italy during Benito Mussolini's rule, won the presidential election on a policy of spending the gold reserves accumulated in the central bank, his politics of 'buy now, pay later' saw the once glamorous country slip into debt, inflation, unemployment and coup d'états managed by Juntas of military officers with little or no experience in international diplomacy and tact, let alone domestic politics.

Argentina's principal regional allies in 1982 were Panama, Brazil, Venezuela, Peru and on occasion Cuba, and while they sympathised with Argentina and recognised the existing dispute, they did not accept the use of force to resolve it. While the United States was regarded as supportive under the Inter-American Treaty of Reciprocal Assistance, the White House had a strong relationship with Great Britain going back to the First World War that was strategically more important than military dictatorships combating Communist insurgency in South America and threatening Central America. Successive attempts by Juntas to resolve left-wing revolution, subversion and communist guerrillas in Argentina led to the War against Terrorism (commonly named 'Dirty War'– 1975–83) and although the internal security operations had been deployed under the civil government of Isabel, Perón's widow and favourite of the people, the economy was in dire straits. This led to military dictatorships by officers with very little experience of constitutional government. The precarious national economy and democratic instability had stagnated the country and a diversion was needed to demonstrate that Argentina was a powerful nation with a predominant strategic role in the South Atlantic. Argentina badly needed a success.

But the Argentine Navy could not compete with the highly experienced Royal Navy and its nuclear submarine force and was largely confined to the safety of 12 nautical miles territorial limit from the mainland coast. The sinking of the Second World War ARA *General Belgrano*, mechanical failures of the aircraft carrier ARA *25 de Mayo* in early May and limited time over target by aircraft left the land forces isolated and exposed.

Within three days of the surrender on 14 June, President Galtieri, who had led Argentina into defeat, resigned and Argentina was deluged by recriminations and the desire for a credible democratic government was accelerated. On 1 July 1982, the retired General Reynaldo Bignone was appointed president, a virtual unknown to the public and yet another general selected by the Junta. His immediate problems were to manage the embarrassment of defeat, manage increasing evidence of offences committed during the Dirty War and repair the regional reputation of Argentina as South and Central American countries reminded him, 'I told you so'. Allegations of field punishments within the Army in particular were mentioned by prisoners-of-war. As with most defeats, a profound crisis of self-confidence and bitterness emerged with the younger front-line officers, angry that they should bear the burden of the surrender.

Bignone needed to restore credible general elections and avoid the undermining of military rule without promoting the disintegration of the military institution. But the armed forces were stained by questionable activities committed during the Dirty War, including Bignone, and a political space opened for ambitious Peronists. But they were slow to fill the political void and in stepped Raúl Alfonsín, of the Radical Civic Union, elected president in October 1983 and who took office on 10 December. A lawyer by profession, he had defended victims of the military regime.

As Argentina tottered towards the memories of constitutional government, Alfonsín, by decree Number 158/83, announced the prosecution of members of the Junta including former presidents Videla, Viola and Galtieri, but the enactment of the 1986 'Full Stop' Law (*Ley de Punto Final*) paralysed proceedings against those accused of having committed the crime of forced disappearance of persons during the dictatorship. Several months later, the law was supplemented by the Due Obedience Law (*Ley de Obediencia Debida*), also issued by Alfonsín in 1987, which established a presumption that crimes committed by members of the armed forces were not punishable, although this was repealed by the National Congress in 1998 and by the Supreme Court of Justice in 2005.

Meanwhile, the failure of the Malvinas Recovery was being investigated. President Galtieri had ordered Brigadier-General Edgardo Calvi to report on the performance of the Argentine Army and consequences of the war in order to inform, identify lessons learnt and develop a single historical document as commemoration to those who did not return home. Calvi had commanded Remounts and Veterinary Command in 1977, the 1st Armoured Cavalry Division in 1979, had been Deputy Chief of the General Staff in 1981 to 1982 and was commanding the Buenos Aires Military Zone. He had also commanded the Military Institutes in 1982 and was responsible for training and the curriculum in military colleges and schools.

The final Calvi Report included examination of military operations, the conduct of the Military Government and observations that arose from the conflict. The commission did not sanction or instruct proceedings and grant distinctions, but limited itself to forwarding the information found. On this basis, in July 1982 the Commission for Updating and Improvement of the Army and the Special Advisory Commission for the Awarding of Decorations were formed to conduct investigations. Calvi sent a formal report to the Commander-in-Chief of the Army, Division-General Cristino Nicolaides on 16 November, however 99 per cent was classified, which led to suspicions that the report was an embarrassing and frank report of a defeat. Later, the Drafting Commission of the Official Report of the Argentine Army on the Conflict in the South Atlantic was formed and given access to all the necessary information. It reported on 7 July 1983, intending to publish the report in two volumes based on accounts of events and conclusions and circulate within the Army and also make it publicly available. The commission stated,

> That it is convenient to make known to the Institution and public opinion, the facts developed by the Argentine Army in Malvinas, through an objective description and in such a way that it constitutes a true basis for the analysis of the events. That the various actions carried out are a valuable source of experiences for the different areas of leadership, the use of which will contribute to the improvement of the Institution.
>
> That the events, reconstructed and recounted in a single document, represent an important contribution to the historical heritage of the Army and a tribute to its members, who fought with nobility and with stoicism endured the vicissitudes and hardships of combat.

The report noted that Operation *Rosario* was so secret that the Chiefs-of-Staff were isolated from all operational and logistic planning. Operationally, the armed forces were structured and trained to fight a South American adversary and had little chance against experienced and battle-hardened forces. Galtieri had not consulted the General Staff in decision-making and three generals had demanded that Menéndez be replaced. Galtieri had told Menéndez that the Malvinas issue was purely diplomatic and would be resolved by Foreign Minister Nicanor Costa Mendez at the UN. While the US was cited as providing the United Kingdom with key tactical advantages, fundamental mistakes included faulty intelligence and a lack of common sense. Crucially, senior officers were sent to the Falklands to exploit their administrative and technical capability and knowledge of English rather than their ability to command, organise, equip, administer and train an army and prepare to face an adversary capable of conducting world class operations.

> The invasion of the Falklands surprised many top officers... The secrecy surrounding the initial operations kept the Chiefs-of-Staff isolated from logistic and operational planning... We want to arrive at the truth but without sensationalism and without out-of-context conclusions, because isolated facts cannot give us a real idea of the suffering and the struggle that the people who represented us in the South Atlantic went through.

In conclusion, the Argentine Armed Forces were inexperienced and ill-equipped, used some equipment that dated from the Second World

War, had joint service formats that had not been developed and senior commanders competing with each other who were unable to form alliances in order to undermine a power that could call upon significant operational support from the Commonwealth and NATO. The report concluded that the defeat should not blight the long list of triumphs and the defeat should be considered as the inevitable consequence of power relations between two forces. Calvi concluded that no further military attempts should be made to capture the Falklands.

It was perhaps no surprise that General Daher was highly critical of the report and blamed the defeat on a lack of co-ordination between the Army, Navy and Air Force. He criticised the notion that the Malvinas threat was prominently an air-naval theatre of war and that Army commanders were too quick to surrender. When he accused the Air Force of losing a few aircraft and 'then there was no more Air Force', his comments provoked the anger of the Air Force.

In addition, at the same time as Calvi was investigating, on 2 December 1982, the Junta appointed the Committee for Analysis and Evaluation to investigate 'the significance of the experience in the South Atlantic and analyse the political and military strategic management'. It was chaired by Lieutenant-General Benjamín Rattenbach and a commission of two officers each from the Army, Navy and Air Force to examine the performance of the Argentine Armed Force, the history of the Anglo–Argentine dispute from 1833 to 1982 and to review political, military and strategic planning. The working group appointed by the Military Junta to analyse the report suggested that, due to its content, not only in regard to the conduct of individuals but also to the plans then in force, 'it should continue with a high degree of reserve, in safeguarding the interests of the Nation, of the Institutions and of the Negotiations in International Politics', recommending its classification as 'Political Secret' and 'Military Secret', and that in terms of the duration of said classification, 'Because of its intimate relationship with the facts and attitudes that concern the conflict, it lasts until the Argentine Republic recovers its rights over all the South Atlantic Islands'.

Specifically, the mission of the commission was to submit a report to the Military Junta, which would contain its well-founded opinion on:

1. The performance in the exercise of the functions and the emerging responsibilities regarding the political and strategic military leadership of the conflict; and 2. The responsibilities of any person, be they of a disciplinary and/or honourable nature that arises from the proceedings that, in their opinion, should be investigated and judged by the respective common or military jurisdiction, in the manner that corresponds legally and by regulation. The final report concluded that strategic and operational planning was ill-conceived and poorly developed and defeat had been invited almost from the minute that President Reagan told President Galtieri that the US would 'necessarily' side with an ally, Great Britain.

The Navy was heavily criticised for its absence, while the Air Force and the majority of Army units were judged to have performed well. Field and air defence artillery, cavalry, helicopter and commando companies were assessed to have displayed a high degree of professionalism. The A4Q Skyhawks and Super Etendards pilots inflicting damage on the Royal Navy was out of proportion to their previous experience. The 5th Marines were credited with 'outstanding performance'. The report is critical of the quality of the Army leadership at all levels regarding the conscripts as cannon fodder and for failing to supply winter clothing, adequate food in a hostile environment and resorting to field punishments for the inexperienced – as opposed to demonstrating leadership. Nevertheless, Rattenbach concluded there had been 'numerous acts of extraordinary courage… we should be proud of the nobility with which the arms of our Fatherland… Our armed forces can be satisfied with their performance.' His report was scathing of the political and strategic decision to invade. He concluded that junior officers and other ranks had been the victims of logistical failures, such as the restriction of meals to one a day, weak leadership that induced the general breakdown of discipline, undermining of morale and operational failures. Some chapters were particularly damning of the Junta.

At the same time as Calvi presented his Official Army Report in early December 1983, politics again interfered when extracts from the Rattenbach Report were leaked to the press and overshadowed sensational news about the application of severe sanctions to those responsible for military leadership. A copy of the Rattenbach Report had been leaked to the Argentine press in an anonymous envelope found in the toilet of a bar in Retiro in Buenos Aires, and the conclusions and sentences requested by the commission for the accused were widely publicised in the country. Although an investigation was carried out to determine responsibilities, it was never clarified how the report had been leaked to the press. A few days later, after a new government was formed, the Official Army Report, now commonly known as the 'Calvi Report', was quietly shelved and would go unnoticed by public opinion. In February 2012, President Cristina Fernández de Kirchner issued decree Number 200 ordering that the complete Rattanbach Report and Annexes be released into the public domain.

For years, members of the Argentine Armed Forces had complained of the abuse of soldiers and junior officers by senior officers and other ranks. Allegations of corporal punishment were mentioned by Argentine soldiers to British soldiers during the repatriation phase after the surrender, mainly for theft of food, looting in settlements and falling asleep on duty, and were reported to Argentine liaison officers during the prisoner repatriation. The matter resurfaced during the presidency of Cristina Fernández de Kirchner through the Centro Ex Combatientes Islas Malvinas (CECIM) ('Malvinas Islands ex-Combatants Centre') to promote the excesses of the Dirty War as equal to Malvinas veterans being equated as victims of the military process. Several officers and non-commissioned officers were sanctioned behind closed doors without the issue being made public in order to avoid increasing the general upset against the Argentine Armed Forces still ruling the country.

The well-known book *Chicos de la Guerra (Kids of the War)* by Daniel Kon, a freelance writer, first published in August 1982, barely two months after the war ended, explains that many conscripts had no idea why they were going to war. The logistical organisation was so bad that soldiers stole food from supply depots. Although these events existed, other fantastic stories referred to Gurkha soldiers being killed walking on minefields under the influence of drugs and cutting throats with their kukris, particularly on Mount Longdon. The author relied on interviews with soldiers after their return from the islands using fictitious names to protect their identity. In the prologue, he warns about the scope of the work:

I think I know what will be the objection that can be made to this work. A handful of war stories is not the story of the whole war. Good, this is not intended to be the history of war; Yes, the testimony of these young people and their war, the one they lived through. A group of boys, it could be said, does not constitute a whole generation; what these young people think cannot be taken as the thought of all the conscripts who fought in the Malvinas Islands.

In November 1983, exposures in the Rattenbach Report and the Military Junta led to 16 Army, Navy and Air Force officers being accused of negligence for their performance during the war and now facing courts martial before the Supreme Council of the Armed Forces. The defendants, which included Galtieri, Anaya and Lami Dozo, were collectively accused of 'not being prepared for a confrontation of such characteristics' and 'failing to take advantage of diplomatic opportunities for an honourable and feasible solution'. Defendants also included those with Strategic Level responsibilities, such as Vice-Admiral Juan José Lombardo, and those with direct command in Malvinas, including Generals Menéndez, Jofre and Parada. The prosecution sought 12 years imprisonment. Galtieri was cleared in December 1985 of human rights violations during the Dirty War; however, he could not deny the Malvinas defeat and when he, Anaya and Lami Dozo were found guilty of incompetence and imprisoned, they appealed to the Federal Criminal Chamber of Appeals, a civil court, but were still found guilty. The prosecution appealed for heavier offences and in 1989, they were sentenced to 12 years and stripped of their ranks. The rest of the defendants were acquitted of the charges, including General Menéndez. President Carlos Menem pardoned Galtieri, Anaya and Lami Dozo in 1991, but they then faced further human rights accusations in 2002. Galtieri died six months later in January 2003, Anaya in January 2008 and Lami Dozo in February 2017.

Meanwhile, in the 1986 World Cup, Argentina regained some self-respect at the expense of England. The footballer Diego Maradona was the captain of Argentina, a country badly needing a success. The country was drawn in the quarter-final against England in the Aztec Stadium in Mexico City. Maradona scored twice. His first has often been referred to as the 'Hand of God' goal because he knowingly tapped the ball into the net with his hand but failed to admit the offence, and the Tunisian referee failed to question the foul. England was somewhat demoralised about the decision as Maradona scored his second goal four minutes later as he dribbled the ball past the English defence with 11 consecutive touches. It was later voted by FIFA as the goal of the century.

The 1956 Suez Crisis, the British attitude to the independence in Rhodesia and the tepid response to the installation of the Research Station in the South Sandwich Islands was seen by some in Argentina to be 'an Empire in retreat'. There was the belief that in a 'colonial conflict' in its back yard, the United States of America would remain neutral. Further, while the British maintained commitments to NATO and other international alliances and its Operation *Banner* in Northern Ireland, its experience in expeditionary operations saw the Conservative Government of Prime Minister Thatcher assembled a task force that was far more experienced than its enemy, and humbled an arrogant Junta. The US Foreign Relations Department's conclusion in 1983 is succinct − 'Argentina selected the wrong enemy.'

Endnotes

Chapter 2

1. Quoted in Alejandro Luis Corbacho, *74 days under the Argentine flag: The experiences of occupation during the Falklands/Malvinas War*, Serie Documentos de Trabajo, No. 682 (Universidad del Centro de Estudios Macroeconómicos de Argentina, 2018), p. 2.
2. Middlebrook, *The Argentine Fight for the Falklands* (Leo Cooper, Barnsley, 2003), p. 3637.
3. Guillermo Sanchez-Sabarots, as quoted in Middlebrook, *The Argentine Fight for the Falklands*, p. 3637.
4. As quoted in Graham Bound, *Falklands Islanders at War* (Pen and Sword, Barnsley, 2002), p. 2523.
5. Hugo Santillán as quoted in Middlebrook, *The Argentine Fight for the Falklands*, p. 3637. For an account by Santillan in the original, see 'Foro de la Ciudad – Operación Rosario por Hugo Jorge Santillan', *Gazeta del Progreso* (2018).
6. Quoted in Pinkerton, '"Strangers in the Night": The Falklands Conflict as a Radio War', *Twentieth Century British History* (Volume 19, Issue 3, 2008), pp. 344–375.
7. Nick van der Bijl, *Victory in the Falklands* (Pen & Sword, Barnsley, 2007), p. 23.
8. Rex Hunt, *My Falkland Days* (David & Charles, Exeter, 1992), p. 234.
9. Michael Bilton, Peter Kosminsky, *Speaking Out: Untold Stories From The Falklands War* (Andre Deutsch, London, 1989), p. 233.

Chapter 4

1. Speranza and Cittadini, *Partes de Guerra. Malvinas 1982* (Grupo Editorial Norma, 1997), p. 43.

Chapter 5

1. Pablo Vicente Córdoba, *Malvinas. Relatos de guerra de los Ava Ñaró (indios bravos)* (Gráfica Gutemberg SRL, Monte Caseros, 2007).

Chapter 7

1. Colonel (R) VGM Oscar Minorini Lima, *Malvinas: Honor y Recuerdos Imborrables* (Editorial Dunken, Buenos Aires, 2012), p. 49.
2. James Lockhart, New Revelations from Argentina's Falklands Campaign; September 2015; www/warontherocks.com/a-tortured-war-on-the-south-atlantic-rocks-new-revelations-from-argentinas-falklands-campaign/
3. 'Argentine Prosecution orders the arrest of 26 officers for alleged torture against conscripts in the Falklands', Merco Press, South Atlantic News Agency, 5 February 2023.
4. *El Combate de Goose Green* (Editorial Planeta, Buenos Aires, 1994), p.70.
5. Nick van der Bijl, 'Battle of Port San Carlos, May 1982', *Britain At War* (Key Military, May 2017).
6. *Borbón: Equipo de Combate Marega – Equipo de Combate H/BIM 3'* Desembarco Separata N° 20 (Buenos Ares, 1997), p.37.

Chapter 9

1. General (VGM) Omar Edgardo Parada, *Malvinas: Llagas de una Guerra* (1884 Editorial; Buenos Aires, 2012), pp.324–325.
2. Alejandro L. Corbacho, 'Reassessing the Fighting Performance of Conscript Soldiers during the Malvinas/Falklands War (1982)', *CEMA Working Papers: Serie Documentos de Trabajo* (271) (2004).
3. Piaggi quoted in Boyce, D. George Boyce, *The Falklands War* (Hampshire: Macmillan, 2005), p. 131.
4. Eric Goss to author.

Chapter 10

1. John Smith, *74 Days: An Islander's Diary of the Falklands Occupation* (Century, 1984), p. 219.
2. Hugh McManners, *The Scars of War* (HarperCollins, London, 1993), p. 238.
3. Captain Andrés Ferrero, 602 Commando Company, *5th Infantry Brigade in the Falklands* (Leo Cooper, Barnsley, 2003).
4. EL RI 4 EN MALVINAS, Diego Alejandro Soria, http://www.aveguema.org.ar/.

Chapter 11

1. Isidoro Ruiz Moreno, *Comandos en Acción – El Ejército en Malvinas* (Editorial Claridad, Buenos Aires, 2011), p. 376.
2. John Witheroe, *The Winter War: Falklands Conflict* (Quartet Books, 1982).
3. Kim Sabido, *The Falklands War: The Full Story* (The Sunday Times Insight Team, Sphere Books, 1982).

4. Sergeant-Major George Meachin, Yankee Company.
5. Captain Jorge R. Farinella (VGM), ¡*Volveremos!* (Editorial Rosario, Rosario, 1985).
6. John Cartledge, 'Returns to Battlefield', *Merco Press*, SA News (15 April 2002).

Chapter 12

1. Vincent Bramley, *Two Sides of Hell* (Bloomsbury Publishing, 1994), p. 9.
2. Ibid.
3. Jon Cooksey, *Mount Longdon: The Bloodiest Battle* (Leo Cooper, Barnsley, 2004), pp. 35–6.
4. *Relato de Colemil, un aborígen infante de Marina*, El Grupo Nottingham.
5. Héctor Rubén Simeoni, *Malvinas Contrahistoria* (Editorial Argentinidad, Buenos Aires, 2019, second edition). p. 167.
6. Carrizo-Salvadores, 'Malvinas: Relatos de Soldados', *Círculo Militar* (Vol.722; Buenos Aires, 1985).
7. Julian Thompson, *No Picnic*, Guild Publishing, 1985, London.

Chapter 13

1. Captain Carlos Alfredo López Patterson, in Héctor Rubén Simeoni, *Malvinas Contrahistoria* (Editorial Argentinidad, Buenos Aires, 2019, second edition) pp. 109–110.
2. Andrew Tubb, 45 Marine Commando Recce Troop.
3. Captain Gardiner quoted in Max Arthur, *Above All, Courage: The Falklands Front Line: First-Hand Accounts* (Sidwick & Jackson, 1985), pp. 389–390.

Chapter 14

1. Nick van der Bijl; *5th Infantry Brigade in the Falklands* (Leo Cooper, Barnsley, 2003).
2. Carlos H. Robacio and Jorge Hernández, *Desde el Frente: Batallón de Infantería de Marina Nº5* (Instituto de Publicaciones Navales; Buenos Aires, 2004, Fourth Edition), p. 267.
3. Ibid, p. 298.
4. Brigada-General Oscar L. Jofre and Coronel Félix R. Aguiar, 'Malvinas: La Defensa de Puerto Argentino', Círculo Militar (editor), (Buenos Aires, 1990), p. 258.
5. Second Lieutenant Augusto La Madrid, quoted in Martin Middlebrook, The *Fight for the Malvinas*, pp. 260–262.
6. Ibid.
7. Robacio to Peter Kosminsky, television interview, 1987.
8. Jorge Sánchez, 'El Batallón de Infantería de Marina Nº5 Ec – Gesta Malvinas 1982', Desembarco Separata 2; Cuerpo de Infantería de Marina (Nbr.158, Buenos Aires, October 1996).

9. Major Jaimet, quoted by Colonel Alberto Gonzalez.
10. Nick van der Bijl, *5th Infantry Brigade in the Falklands* (Leo Cooper, Barnsley, 2003).
11. Robacio: *El Batallón de Infantería de Marina N°5 Ec – Gesta Malvinas 1982*, Desembarco Separata 2, Cuerpo de Infantería de Marina (Nbr.158, Buenos Aires, October 1996).
12. Jofre quoted in Hugh Bicheno, *Razor's Edge: The Unofficial History of the Falklands War* (Orion, 2007).
13. Jofre, quoted in an article in *Gente* magazine.

Chapter 15

1. Private Felix Barreto quoted by John Browne, 'The Falklands War – Wireless Ridge, The Argentinian Story', *Submariners World* (14 June 2012).
2. Private Jorge Abdul, quoted in Daniel Kon, *Los Chicos de la Guerra* (New English Library, 1983), pp. 102–103.
3. Martin Middlebrook, *The Falklands War 1982*, p. 371.
4. Private Patricio Perez, as quoted by John Browne, 'The Falklands War – Wireless Ridge, The Argentinian Story', *Submariners World* (14 June 2012).
5. Santiago Gauto, as quoted by John Browne, 'The Falklands War – Wireless Ridge, The Argentinian Story', *Submariners World* (14 June 2012).
6. Miguel Savage, 'I never get over that I have double problem that I was also fighting against British who were also a good family,' *The Scotsman* (30 March 2002).
7. Frigate Captain Adolfo A. Gaffoglio, quoted in Nick van der Bijl, *Nine Battles to Stanley* (Leo Cooper, Barnsley, 1999). Gaffoglio was Commander, Naval Post Malvinas in Stanley. His captured diary is held at the Military Intelligence Museum.

Chapter 16

1. General Mario Benjamin Menéndez in Carlos M. Túrolo (h), *Malvinas, Testimonio de su Gobernador* (Editorial Sudamericana, Buenos Aires, 1983).
2. Ibid.
3. Ibid.
4. Frigate Captain Adolfo A. Gaffoglio, quoted in Nick van der Bijl, *Nine Battles to Stanley*, Leo Cooper, Barnsley, 1999.
5. Ibid.
6. Ibid.
7. Ibid.
8. Nick van der Bijl, *Nine Battles to Stanley* (Leo Cooper, Barnsley, 1999).
9. Frigate Captain Adolfo A. Gaffoglio, quoted in Nick van der Bijl, *Nine Battles to Stanley* (Leo Cooper, Barnsley, 1999).

Index